CONSCIOUSNESS

THE BOOK

What Goes Around, Comes Around—
with a Difference

Image of Uroborus, from Greek *oura* (tail) and *boros* (biting) meaning "he who bites his tail," an ancient symbol for cycles of renewal in nature. I use it here to illustrate my loop of engagement (*see* Chapter 7), which sets up an ongoing comparison between motor and sensory signals in my brain. Any resulting disparity gives rise to attention and awareness (analogous to binocular vision giving rise to depth perception). Consciousness itself is prompted by my need to make a fitting response to the "bite" of novel or surprising stimulation.

CONSCIOUSNESS

THE BOOK

Steve Perrin

Lulu.com

O

Earthling Press

BY STEVE PERRIN

CONSCIOUSNESS: The BOOK (2011)

CONSCIOUSNESS: The inside story (Blog)
www.onmymynd.wordpress.com (from 2008)

Acadia's Trails and Terrain (2002)

Acadia's Native Flowers, Fruits, and Wildlife (2001)

The Shore Path, Bar Harbor, Maine (2000)

ACADIA: The Soul of a National Park (1998)

MYTH TO MYTHOLOGY: Experience as a Resonant Synthesis of Meaning and Being (Dissertation, 1982)

Lulu.com O Earthling Press, Bar Harbor, Maine
Consciousness: The Book, Copyright © 2011 by Stephen G. Perrin
All rights reserved. Published 2011
Printed in the United States of America
ISBN 978-0-9651058-8-0

Front Cover: Rodin's "The Thinker," block print by the author.
René Descartes, "Mind and Body," Wikimedia.
Back Cover Diagram: Introspective map of the author's conscious mind. This entire book serves as the caption for the diagram. Consciousness is represented by the large circle, located between two hidden substrates, 1) the physical world, and 2) the author's brain. Introspection provides access to neither substrate. Planning for action is represented on the left, sensory processing on the right. Understanding is based on three tiers of mental processing: 1) sensory stimulation rendered as concrete phenomena, 2) sorting of phenomena into conceptual categories, and 3) connection of categorized phenomena into fields of understanding. Reflexes bypass consciousness altogether; habits and routines develop through repetition or rehearsal; ideology stems from rote memorization; and consciousness harmonizes its several dimensions to create a sense of situated awareness. The author's unique self invests values and feelings in these processes, and he works through judgments, goals, and projects to make himself happen in particular situations via his ongoing loop of engagement within his physical environment.
Back Cover Photo: The author in 2010.

I saw Fair Haven Pond with its island, and meadow between the island and the shore, and a strip of perfectly still and smooth water in the lee of the island, and two hawks, fish hawks perhaps, sailing over it. I did not see how it could be improved. Yet I do not see what these things can be. I begin to see such an object when I cease to *understand* it and see that I did not realize or appreciate it before, but I get no further than this. How adapted these forms and colors to my eye! A meadow and an island! What are these things? Yet the hawks and the ducks keep so aloof! and Nature is so reserved! I am made to love the pond and the meadow, as the wind is made to ripple the water.

Thoreau, *Journal,* Nov. 21, 1850.

What are these rivers and hills, these hieroglyphics which my eyes behold?

Thoreau, *Journal,* Aug. 23, 1852.

Consciousness, then, does not appear to itself chopped up in bits. Such words as 'chain' or 'train' do not describe it fitly as it presents itself in the first instance. It is nothing jointed; it flows. A 'river' or a 'stream' are the metaphors by which it is most naturally described. *In talking of it hereafter, let us call it the stream of thought, of consciousness, or of subjective life.*

Wm. James, *The Principles of Psychology,* 1890

CONSCIOUSNESS: THE BOOK

CONTENTS

To
Occupy Wall Street
and
the 99 percent

PREFACE

From my perspective—which is but one seven-billionth of collective human consciousness—it is only natural for me to believe that my view of things is the way the world really is when, in fact, it is simply the way I see the world from my personal point of view. How I see the world is just that, how I *see* the world, not how the world *is*. All awareness is partial, selective, and largely shaped by the observer's situation and point of view. Attribution of reality is subject to the complex mental state of each particular observer in whatever situation she believes herself to be in at the time. That fact demolishes any claim I might make to being an authority on events in anyone's mind but my own, much less any so-called "real" world as may lie beyond that. Which is precisely the point I am setting out to make in this book. Reality is the fable I tell myself in trying to fit into my worldly circumstances and survive safe and sound.

How did I come by this view? To start with birth order, I am a middle child, the second of three boys born a year-and-a-half apart. Reconstructing those early days, I have my father approving of my elder brother's every act; my mother doting on my younger brother until he gets too unruly. I see myself as turned loose in the world, and by default, quickly coming to rely on my own inclinations.

Not looking to either parent for overt guidance or affirmation, I adopted a code of independence. At an early age, I became a maverick roaming the hills on my own to see what discoveries I could make and fun I could have. In my wanderings, I always had adventures I'd never had before, and that became a way of life that has stuck with me to this day. Start to finish, I'm my own man. What I lack in team spirit I make up for in self-direction and dedicated concentration on various projects. It doesn't surprise me that in examining my personal brand of consciousness, projects stand out as basic units of mental processing and organization.

Early on, I showed signs of being visually keen. At age four, I sent away for my first camera for a box top and a quarter, and have worked in photography ever since. In school, I was interested in science, astronomy, biology—what things were and how they worked. In college, I tried physics at MIT, then the humanities at Columbia, ever seeking to balance my mental portfolio. I have always been more of a generalist seeking the big picture than a specialist confined to a particular discipline. All I want to know is how life got started in the universe, plays out on this Earth, and what the point is.

Following my natural bent, I became a Signal Corps photographer in the Army, a fashion photographer's assistant when I got out, then a photographer for the Information Service at Iowa State University, ending up as head of a fourteen-room darkroom suite as a photographer at the Harvard College and Smithsonian Astrophysical Observatories in Cambridge. Eventually I got restless providing photographic services to others, so applied for and got a fellowship to teach creative photography at Phillips-Andover Academy, which led me into teaching the humanities, poetry, English, and art at Abbott Academy and Walnut Hill School. Then I set out to see what I could write on my own. I moved to Maine in 1986 and lived on a thirty-acre island for two-and-a-half years, shutting my mouth, opening my eyes. I evolved a sense that the best education was to be had by going somewhere and seeing with fresh eyes what was happening there (pretty much a replay of my childhood). That was not my first foray into place-based learning, but by far the most dramatic, myself being the student, coastal Hancock County, Maine, the locale. After twenty-five years, I'm still here and still at it, putting my mind and body where my values are in a kind of looping engagement that enhances my experience of a particular place, while giving me the chance to refine how I understand and react to it. That is basically the method I have come up with for understanding myself and my world at the same time—by making myself happen in apt response to my immediate surroundings.

Before moving to Maine, I took a graduate course in personality theory to find out how people develop styles of interpretation opening onto such a wide diversity of discordant world views having little to do with one another. The rule of life appeared to emphasize conflict and enmity, not harmony and cooperation. Why should that be, and what made it so? Finding I could weather graduate-level classes, I pursued master's and doctoral degrees at Boston University School of Education, culminating in a dissertation meant to detail the landscape of human experience as I understood it some thirty years ago. I'm still working away at that program on my own, devoting every day to independent study of the workings of the only mind I have any chance of knowing, trying to understand why the world appears to me as it does, why I interpret sensory phenomena as I do.

Recently I posted 201 reflections on consciousness to my blog on that topic, using each post as a scratch pad for jotting down ideas to collect into a book. I learned two lessons from that exercise: first, that my mind reveals itself to me if I don't confound it with the crude notion of an external reality, and second, that although intro-spection is made possible by the workings of my brain, my brain is no more evident to me than the engine of a car is evident to a driver who merely steer its travels to purposes of his own.

The best way to learn about mental life is still introspection by the one person having access to a particular stream of conscious-ness, and there is no better way to know yourself on the inside of your mind than by a program of concentrated self-reflection. I don't know how, but consciousness lets me stand above myself and look down on the workings of my own mind *as if* they were laid out in front of me as a kind of map of the landscape inside my head. This trick, I believe, is made possible by the very nature of attention itself, which seems to operate by reciprocally mapping different areas of neural activity onto one another, so that I not only "see" parts and wholes in relationship, but have a sense of myself attend-ing to now one, then the other. Not that there is a little homunculus in the control room of my mind watching me watching. My entire mind is the control room from which my personal awareness cannot be separated. I am that center; it is who I am. Mind and awareness are one and the same, not opposite poles of a duality.

Scientists aren't taken with introspection because it is inexact and specific to one unique person so results cannot be generalized to all humanity through statistical procedures. But the real world is not the product of statistical manipulation, and to understand human experience, we have to sample minds inside-out to discover what is happening on a truly human level. Life is lived one life at a time, each different from all others. Our individuality is our hallmark, every mind bearing the stamp of singular awareness. Note that dis-coveries take place in individual minds and are not self-evident to the population at large. There is only one Copernicus, one Galileo, one Newton, one Einstein, one Emily Dickinson, one Mozart, one Picasso, one Eleanor Roosevelt.

That is why knowing oneself through introspection is so impor-tant in today's world as an antidote to the pandemic of mind control sweeping the globe as countless subgroups from corporate executives to tyrants to terrorists try to take over the minds of those they picture as put on Earth as lesser beings for them to take advantage of, keep under control, or abuse in some way. There's a lot of that going around these days, feeling superior toward those who are different in some regard from the standard model set by the powerful who are armed (with weapons, clever lawyers, or bank accounts) and ready to subdue all who oppose them. I say, divided we stand, united we fall, for, in the end, we all suffer the one terminal fate. It's what we do on our own as *individuals* that tells who we are and what we stand for. If not for the dignity of our unique and distinctive personhood, how are we to contribute to the well-being of people and life forms that appear wholly strange to us?

Every life and every mind is precious because there is no other like it. We are precious on our own merits, not because we belong to one group or another. Our uniqueness renders us precious, not our commonality. If we were all the same, we'd have nothing to talk about or learn from one another. Life would be homogenized, a uniform standard product of human orthodoxy. Beware dogma and right thinking. Think on these things—and you already know why I am writing this book. Urged to surrender mind and body for the sake of conformity, we sell our individuality, creativity, independence, and personal freedom at our peril.

The remedy, I suggest, is not to take on the powerful at their own game (because they make the rules and hire the umpires). Rather, to develop the resources latent in independent minds so that we become immune to the influence of higher powers by guiding our lives on the basis of skilled use of the most powerful asset we have—a mind truly our own. A mind that doubts, questions, weighs, judges, prioritizes, and then decides to act effectively in answer to whatever situation challenges us at the time. Such a mind cuts the unknowable world down to a manageable scale in terms of projects and relationships we can conduct through motivated, personal action, not as servants of a powerful elite defining who we are by our usefulness in their schemes.

It helps to remember these four things: 1) we have only a very short time to learn everything we will ever know; 2) none of us lives in the so-called real world; 3) we're still the same little kid who developed a cartoon of a world as a child, and much of that cartoon persists to this day; and 4) the way we see the world is the way we see the world, not the way the world is. Our opportunity, then, is to learn what kind of person our bodies and the forces acting on them—including natural, cultural, and biological forces—have made of our flesh and bone. To be effective, we must know ourselves inside-out. In truth, we can't know anyone else nearly as well as we can know ourselves. All knowledge is truly self-knowledge.

We are not here to live up to others' expectations, but more to fulfill the destiny we forge for ourselves through dedication, concentration, and years of hard work. In choosing our companions, we are wise to trust those who support our efforts to work things out for ourselves, while we grant reciprocal respect to their mental integrity.

It has taken me a lifetime of seventy-nine years to get to this point. A great many people have helped me get here. My parents gave me gifts they didn't realize they were giving. Through his own independent actions, my father gave me trust in my inner capabilities; my mother, a painter, gave me not only a visual approach to life, but the coast of Maine where she was born and raised, including Taunton Bay, the place on Earth that—through mutual interaction—has largely made me who I am today.

Inadvertently, by means of the books gathered on his shelves, my father introduced me to the writings of Thoreau, though I put off actually reading *Walden* until I flew to my father's funeral in Seattle when I was almost thirty. Of all men, Thoreau has exerted the greatest influence on my mind. Followed at a distance by psychologist William James (*The Principles of Psychology*), French phenomenologist Maurice Merleau-Ponty (*Phenomenology of Perception*), Michael Polanyi (*Personal Knowledge*), I. A. Richards (*The Philosophy of Rhetoric*), Joseph Campbell (*The Masks of God*), and E. O. James (*Seasonal Feasts and Festivals, The Ancient Gods, From Cave to Cathedral*).

Where do words come from, that they can be so affecting from afar? I don't even know where my own words come from when I open my mouth to speak, or sit at a computer as I am doing now, writing this very sentence. They flow from my mind, that I know, and within it from the dynamic forces making up the situation I believe myself to be in at the time.

At Columbia, my creative writing teacher, Kevin Sullivan, read my papers to the class almost every week—either because they had some merit or—more likely—were absurd. I owe him a debt for alerting me to the slim line between the two. In ed school at Boston University, which I attended when just shy of fifty, David Kestenbaum, Paul Nash, and Sigmund Koch exposed me to ways of observing and talking about the mind, as well as the behaviors it generates. This was in the sunset days of behaviorism when consciousness was still regarded as unworthy of study.

This past winter I read eight books by Gerald M. Edelman, 1972 Nobelist for his work on the immune system, who for over thirty years has directed his attention through neuroscience to developing a theory of how individual brains achieve consciousness. Edelman comes closer to describing consciousness as I find it in myself than any other neuroscientist. His account is challenging to read because so grounded in unfamiliar processes as if the brain were a planet unto itself. Yet if I were to make a fresh start at understanding my own mind, today I would follow a close reading of William James with a provocative dose of Edelman.

I view the rush of modern American life as the enemy of introspection and knowing my own mind, which takes time to get the hang of and to savor. So much to do, so little time. What a sad story, as if we are born to scurry around doing errands and not conduct our own lives. As if the bidding of others were commands to do as we're told. Whose life are we expected to live, anyway? Not our own, certainly. Thoreau liked a broad margin around his inner life, and today such leeway is hard to find because social pressures leave little room for musing and self-direction as altenatives to rushing to work, to school, to shopping at the mall. See ya, gotta go. No time to wait around, to figure things out, to stay in touch with oneself. The clock ticks, ticks, ticks.

What to do? For myself, I plan to devote what time I have left to acquainting my own mind, the chief instrument I have for discovering the nature of my personal universe, and for making myself happen as a citizen worthy of its teachings. O

CHAPTER EXCERPTS

CHAPTER 1. A MIND AT WORK: Through an introspective adventure lasting thirty years, I have found that my brain does not fully account for my personal consciousness because another substrate shares that burden as well—the environmental substrate provided by my situation in the world. My mind intercedes or mediates between those two substrates, between my embodied brain and its environmental situation. Consciousness, that is, emerges precisely from its privileged position between a specific rock and a particular hard place, between its brain and the situation it engages in interacting with its worldly surroundings. Introspection reveals the details of that lifelong engagement as we make ourselves happen in the world (p. 3f.).

CHAPTER 2. SENSORY PHENOMENA: What is it about the workings of my mind that leads me to mistake a trash bag for a crow, a TV antenna for an airplane, a windblown cedar for a man scraping paint? How can I *not* see flowers that are right in front of me? How can I visualize a cat that does not exist? How can I hum a tune one night while washing dishes and forget it the next while performing the same chore in the same place? How can I watch a procession of familiar images pass in the night sky while I know I am watching a light show generated by high-energy solar radiations interacting with Earth's magnetic field? Yet these and many more incidents are examples from the actual history of my sensory experience. I don't think I am crazy, yet how can I account for such seeming craziness in a world that we generally take to be real in-and-of itself? (p. 24).

CHAPTER 3. INTERPRETATION: Our lives are not destined in advance. We make them happen to suit our yearnings, proclivities, appetites, and motivating circumstances. Categorization is our tool for getting what we want. This and not that. We make choices in a few milliseconds, changing everything that follows—forever. The future is contained in this instant, and then this, and then this. We make ourselves happen through a succession of micro decisions we don't realize we are making, even though they change every other decision after that. I still remember seeing that trash bag as a crow, that cedar as a paint-scraping human, those auroral lights as a meaningful procession of familiar creatures. In my own way, I bring the landscape to life, looking for things I am afraid of, uncomfortable with, angry at, hungry for, or in love with, and so on. At the same time, I kill off alternative versions of that same landscape by shunning what I don't want to entertain as a phenomenon in consciousness. It is my move, now and forever. I am the decider, the director of my attention, to this, this, and this—but not that (p. 49).

CHAPTER 4. UNDERSTANDING: The world as we understand it is not the world as it is in-and-of itself. Rather, it is a world of our own making or taking, concoction, categorization, interpretation, understanding, and so on. The world we so deeply believe in is, in fact, the world we were taught by others to see as the one-and-only real world, but *seeing as* is not seeing things in themselves. It can be more a wolf dressed in sheep's clothing to make a favorable impression on gullible minds. For proof I offer Santa Clause, Humpty Dumpty, Mickey Mouse, the Tooth Fairy, the Angelic Host, Zeus and other gods, and the Easter Bunny as evidence that the world we understand in our heads is but a rough approximation of the world that bodily supports us during our life-long journey spiraling around our neighborhood star as it carries us along on a journey of its own (p. 59f.).

CHAPTER 5. BUILDING A WORLD INSIDE-OUT: Children go through a brief stage, before they develop effective categorizations, of breaking free from their immediate concrete perspectives by relying on random cues within their environments to direct them toward appropriately outrageous predicates in calling people names. "You're a" (with much looking around the room) " ... a lamp shade, a ... dirty dish, a ... a car in the driveway!" All followed by riotous laughter at the spontaneous creation of such adult-sounding humor (he's a turkey, pig, weasel, skunk, rat, commie pinko, fairy; she's a sweetie, honeybun, doll, chickadee, bat, witch, shrew, etc.). Playing with categorizations leads to mastery in labeling sensory patterns as we choose to depict them by mapping meanings onto existential figures in awareness. (p. 82).

CHAPTER 6. FEELING AND EMOTION: I am a self-made empiricist dwelling wholly within the confines of personal experience. The idea of empiricism is suggested by the Greek word *empeiros* meaning to skillfully press ahead in a situation of some peril, that is, to experiment through trial and error. Which accurately sums up the method I am using to compose these chapters based on self-reflection, and then to gather them into a book—a risky venture, indeed. First I compiled a blog of 201 posts as a kind of scratchpad for random reflections about my personal consciousness; then I teased out fifteen major topics covering what was on my mind; I put the topics in sequence, and, devoting a chapter to each topic, set up a basic narrative on introspection as a means of describing what I discovered. So here I am, staking my mental life—not on what I have been taught by others—but on subjective experience. How risky is that? Yet I know no other way to make sense of myself, my acts, and the unknowable world but by keeping close watch on the one mind in which events accord with my personal awareness. How else am I to know myself except inside-out? To me, introspection is the essence of empiricism. To know myself as an instrument of awareness is a prerequisite for knowing anything at all. I have no choice but to continue pressing ahead into the perilous unknown (p. 92).

CHAPTER 7. LOOP OF ENGAGEMENT: I find evidence for my looping engagement with the ambient world of energy and matter (which stirs sensory figures within me) in the many disconcerting occasions when my personal loop breaks down, leaving me stymied and at a loss to know what to say or do next. Whether thwarted by a car that won't start, jar lid stuck in place, password I can't recall, or some other obstacle to my earnest intentions, the sensory feedback I get tells me my expectancy is no match for the occasion and I'd do best to make a fresh start. Which I do, once I figure out an alternative route for getting my plans back on track. Or not, in which case circumstances force me to give up. Words that come to mind for describing such occasions: balked, bothered, frustrated, interrupted, spooked, failed, disappointed, dashed, stymied, thwarted—in a word, defeated. I have lost the game, opening me to a host of strategies for doing better next time. Which I vow to adopt, or at least consider in healing my wounded pride. Indeed, the more I am invested in a particular engagement, the more I stand to lose if it fails. Loops of engagement entail peril, which, I propose, is why we all have them—to keep us abreast of our standing in a given situation we can view only subjectively, inside-out. If things go our way —the car starts, the lid comes off, the password comes to mind— then our vocabulary shifts and we speak of our achievement in glowing terms: success, victory, triumph, breakthrough, progress, recovery, winning, overcoming, moving on, getting ahead. Things fall into place and we can move on to the next round of the loop—graduation, advancement, the championships. Or at least get dinner on the table after picking the chicken off the floor and rinsing away the grit. The play's the thing. The loop will go on (p. 121).

CHAPTER 8. SITUATIONS: Loops of engagement extend the influence of individual consciousness into the earthly milieu serving as its current situation. Within that province of localized activity, each such loop contributes to the flow of ongoing events. That flow, in turn, alters that situation itself in various ways as told by energies falling on participants' senses, causing sensory figures to re-form. These revised figures lead to revised interpretations and comparisons within that situation and, in turn, to revised feelings, understandings, modified plans, and programs of action. That is, situations evolve, enabling ongoing participation in individual and communal lives among the inhabitants of a particular scene or place on Earth. In this way, through participation in situations, individual consciousness contributes to its surroundings, and those surroundings shape sensory phenomena at the core of consciousness in return. This is our contract with the universe, that those of us who participate in a given situation will mutually interact with—and change—one another in fundamental ways. We are citizens of earthly situations. Existence is what we, together, are able to make of it (p. 134).

CHAPTER 9. SPEECH: I will make the claim that speech acts occur in situations, and the meanings they "convey" are precisely those situations as construed in the minds respectively entertaining them. That is, participants are basically speaking within a situation as they interpret it for themselves, so the meaning of any exchange is more elicited or evoked than "conveyed." This simple yet profound example suggests that speech might be more subjectively created on the spot than is assumed in the conventional model of a message being sent and received. What if there is no message, but only two minds on more-or-less the same track concerning a particular situation? What if the situation itself is the message as construed by those minds respectively? Marshall McCluhan had it almost right: it isn't the medium that counts; the *situation* is the message (p. 153).

CHAPTER 10. VALUES: Are there essential human values that lead us to direct our personal energies in ways common to all people? Clearly there are: obtaining food and drink, finding protection from the elements, expressing ourselves erotically or sexually, having and raising children, meeting our basic energy needs by controlling one territory or another, sharing life within a tribe or community of people we identify with, staying healthy and productive within that community, living in harmony and integrity with our neighbors, feeling safe, and dying a good death. Without having such values biologically built into our individual selves (as Edelman asserts), we are at the mercy of those around us, who might well use us for *their* purposes, not ours. (p. 175).

CHAPTER 11: GOALS: In my own mind, I use goals to translate my personal understandings, feelings, and values into strategies that will bring about situations in which I am likely to thrive. I don't just endure events as they happen to me, but (when I can) take an active role in making myself happen in such a way to bring about just those situations that I imagine will promote my survival—that is, the survival of those values that make me who I am or want to become (p. 186).

CHAPTER 12. PROJECTS: Projects are tactical campaigns to translate our inner selves into effective participants in a world we share in common with others. A world we refer to as the *real* world, but is actually far less "real" to each of us than the inner world of sensory figures as meaningfully interpreted by our minds, which is the only world we have immediate access to because it is couched in the neural language of our brains. For each of us the outside world is a second-order derivative of phenomena as we interpret them. In using projects to address the outside world, we translate our inner experiences into outward acts intended to achieve a certain effect. That effect is then translated back into the language of our nervous system by our senses as guided by our expectancy at the moment, to be processed in a neural network that sharpens its features so we are able to compare patterns we hoped to bring about against the patterns that actually appear. Comparison is at the heart not only of consciousness but of the loop of engagement connecting our inner and outer worlds in terms of the situation we picture ourselves being engaged in then and there. If both the expected and actual versions fall within a range of congruity we can accept, we move on to the next stage of the project; if not, we refine our attention and motor control, and try again (p. 204f.).

CHAPTER 13. REALITY: Consciousness, then, depends on a working mind finding itself in a stimulating, energy-rich surrounding situation, both self and situation engaging in an ongoing exchange that can endure for one human lifetime. That exchange itself constitutes the reality of the two taken together as what we call consciousness. Reality resides neither in the person nor in her surroundings, but in the bioenergetic interaction between the two operating in tandem through the looping engagement they establish with each other. That, in essence, is the upshot of my introspective research. Reality comes down to our forming a secure relationship with our surrounding milieu—our niche in the universe—whether it is composed of significant others, work opportunities, energy sources, or situations in which we can make ourselves happen in the face of difficulty or opposition. Essentially ecological, reality is our term for the dynamic exchange of energy between inner and outer substrates that keeps us undead (p. 219f.).

CHAPTER 14. CONFLICT: So here we are, single-mindedly leading our lives while rubbing shoulders with seven billion others doing exactly the same, all doing our best to engage the situations we respectively face, all hating to be thwarted in reaching goals we set for ourselves within those situations. Both cooperation and conflict are potentially built into every human interaction and relationship. Conflict (from Latin *conflictus,* collision, from *confligere,* to come to blows) should be taken as the norm, not the exception. Which sounds like the view of a hardened pessimist, but taken as a word to the wise, I mean it more as precautionary advice to be on the lookout for probable sources of strife rather than wishing such sources would go away or not exist. Before lashing out, we must credit our opponents with strengths and convictions of their own in order to learn what they have to teach us. That is, it is better to look for icebergs in the North Atlantic than trust the steel hull of our vessel to get us through dangerous waters, no matter what. In an enlightened era, we would respect the uniqueness of everyone we meet, including spouses, children, relatives, friends, co-workers, students, public servants, criminals, and the public at large (p. 240).

CHAPTER 15. POWER: True power comes from keeping myself on track to becoming the person I am determined to be, which I realize by working on the projects I have set myself for achieving that end. Such power is not the power of contentment but the power to engage my situation as I am able. Not ten years from now, but in the coming minute, then the minute after that. Grand plans for the future are hard to realize, so effort has to go toward taking next steps. This is done by engaging the world *where* I am, *when* I am there, so my actions are concrete and specific, not diffuse and abstract. True power is now, right here, not sometime later, somewhere else. That's what I mean by putting my body where my values are in making myself happen as I do (p. 265f.). O

INTRODUCTION

I do not hold with theories of normal or abnormal psychology because, since each person is demonstrably unique, "normal" is a fiction of convenience in the mind of one particular person or another.

As those familiar with my books about Acadia National Park already know, I am a big believer in place-based learning. It turns out, however, that after an extensive course of introspection, the place I have visited the most and know most about is the inside of my mind, for that, indeed, is where I live.

It is common to assume that when we open our eyes we look out upon the so-called real world. But I ask myself which is more likely, that I am privileged to look upon such a world, or that I experience an insider's view of a subjective version of that world as tailored uniquely for me from such dimensions of my personal consciousness as sensory figures, memories, expectations, attention, feelings, values, and sense of occasion?

After thirty years of facing into that question, I have to say I know much more about my subjective version of the world than any "objective," conceptual version I piece together from scraps I pick up almost at random, and mercilessly edit to suit my personal convenience and liking. Quite simply, I do not see the landscape in front of me so much as the inner landscape rendered from my personal point of view at the time, with all its distortions, omissions, embellishments, fabrications, and illusions. In truth, I spend much of my time trying to compensate for the errors built into my everyday view of the world. In this I think I am no exception.

My life experience has taught me that the world most readily accessible to me is the one on the inner side of my sensory receptors, backed by my mind's several subjective raw materials such as expectancy, attention, sensory impressions, interpretations, limited understandings, autobiographical memories, feelings, and motivations. These are the mental bricks and mortar I use to construct a world I take to be real, but only if I keep checking to make sure I stay on the level as I shift from one life situation to another.

Thirty years of personal introspection tell me I interpret figures in my sensory world of phenomena in order to act more-or-less effectively in a situation as I construe it, even though I can't directly confront that situation apart from how I construct it in personal consciousness. I build that situation in terms of phenomena, interpretations, and understandings of what I take those figures to *be* and to *mean* as influenced by the values, emotions, and expectancies steering my attention at the moment.

In planning and acting on the basis of that felt understanding of my situation, personal consciousness sets up a looping engagement with a world I can only know sketchily in itself, enabling me as an independent actor to trade overt physical gestures for ambiguous sensory input, followed by a series of adjusted interpretations and gestures, mediated by personal judgment, values, goals, and prior experience.

Round and round go the pulses coursing through my nervous system, *from* action, *through* the gap of the world, *to* interpreted sensory patterns, reconsideration of those patterns, refinement, adjustment, and further action. All of which can take place on several levels of discernment at different rates of mental processing.

For example, the *reflex level* of processing is the fastest, so when someone throws a fistful of sand in my face, I shut my eyes, turn away, and duck down—all in one swift motion without having to think. The *rote* or *habitual level* of mental processing is almost as fast, so I can automatically recite the alphabet or say "Hi, how are you?" without thinking, with perhaps only a split-second pause to consider my options. Acting on the *level of assumptions and ideology,* nervous processing allows for action both fast and bold. Most such hastily planned actions take place below conscious awareness.

This repertory of unconscious responses wonderfully clears my mind for decisive action across a wide range of situations, which for practical purposes becomes reduced to a single situation calling for a predetermined course of action readily available for very little effort.

Full consciousness, on the other hand, allows for consideration of myriad details, values, feelings, situations, interpretations, understandings, and perspectives, so is cumbersome in comparison to reflex, habitual, rote, and ideological courses of engagement. Full consciousness tailors actions to specific complexes of awareness at high levels of discernment, ultimately allowing decisive action after careful consideration of often subtle, ambiguous, or contradictory evidence. On the *level of full conscious discernment,* action may be delayed for days or even years while I decide what to do.

Two routes through the mind, two ways of making myself happen in the world—that represents one of the chief findings of my thirty-year course of introspection in facing up to the presence of each alternative available to me at every moment of self-awareness. I seem to be two sorts of person combined in one nature. Which to me suggests that we all have both paths open to us at every juncture, and the one we choose tells who we are in that particular situation. Such, I hazard, is the human condition.

Am I a right-answer person with a ready response for every occasion? Or am I an explorer who fits his actions to a succession of different situations, trying to behave appropriately in each one so that he becomes a larger, more capable person as a result? It makes all the difference in how I make myself happen in the courtroom, boardroom, halls of Congress, voting booth, schoolroom, bedroom, and beyond. How I act tells who I am under the particular circumstances I am aware of at the moment.

If consciousness is characterized by a loop of engagement in one situation or another, what is the nature of such engagements in sparking consciousness itself?

It strikes me that the ancient Greek image of the *Uroborus*—the looping serpent grasping its own tail—is very much the image of what I call the loop of engagement. To me, Uroborus symbolizes the loop by which I connect my actions to a world unknowable in itself. Energy radiating from that world impinges on my senses, completing the endless circuit that sparks consciousness in my mind from the disparity between my purposive actions and the sensory figures informing me of the effects of those actions. If everything goes as planned, I have no need to be conscious. But an error signal alerting me to a disparity between my intentions and the results I achieve kindles my attention and rouses my mind.

The ancients recognized Uroborus in connecting the path of the setting to that of the rising sun, the circling of stars and planets about the poles, the seasonal round of the zodiac, and the eternal renewal of natural cycles in successive iterations (as in the ongoing regeneration of plant and animal life), as well as in metaphors of virgin birth and reincarnation. The upshot in each case is an instance of insightful intelligence created by the disparity between an action and its subsequent effect on the sensory side of the same system that proposed and created it.

To bring Uroborus closer to home as a more concrete image, I will mention activities in which I find my own loop of engagement very much alive, as in witnessing the duel between baseball pitcher and batter where each strives to outdo the other in an atmosphere binding them together not only in their respective minds, but in the minds of their fans who are captured by the drama of territorial defense and aggression. The same tension arises during a chess game between matched players, or a tennis game between players of equal skill, or even a game of solitaire pitting one's prowess against the random shuffle of a deck of cards.

Games are exercises in engagement at which we sharpen our turn-taking, our venturing within rules, our understanding of novel situations in rapidly changing circumstances. In games we find excitement by keeping to the leading edge of our awareness, always doing our best on move after move. Playing games, we are alert, attentive, alive. Even watching films, videos, or TV, we can become engaged, eyes fixed on the screen, the action primarily aimed at us, the few overt moves we can make reduced to searching the screen for telling details, scooting for the popcorn stand, the fridge, the bathroom. Mass media are done unto us much as experiments are done unto rats in a maze, but under the circumstances we don't feel manipulated, as we don't in our dreams, because hooked on the drama of the illusory situations we are drawn into.

Reading a book can be an adventure in engagement, word by word, sentence by sentence, paragraph by paragraph, chapter by chapter—we are hooked on finding out whodunit, how the story turns out. Jazz, folk, or symphony performances can stir our loops of engagement (as they do the performers'), as can reading or writing poetry, knitting sweaters, cooking dinners, teaching, learning, working, watching waves on the shore or clouds in the sky—anything allowing comparison between what we do and perceive at the same time. Our loops of engagement make us human.

This is particularly evident in the valence of our strongly held opinions by which we declare ourselves opposed to or in favor of so many issues as subject to feelings of yes or no, good or bad, joy or sorrow, desire or avoidance. Such affective polarities reveal the disparity between our personal values and those of our neighbors, that is, between how we would act and how we observe others acting, bringing conflict and strife to our attention, arousing us, jolting us to consciousness.

Even watching other people make themselves happen—Bernie Madoff, say, Osama bin Laden, Rupert Murdoch, or the brothers Koch—we can witness their loops of engagement repeating themselves in characteristic patterns of action and attention, creating their personal styles, making their lives turn out as they do. People-watching is a kind of performance art by which we compare our lives with others', how we manage our loops with how they manage theirs. Keeping up with the stars requires adopting their lifestyles of engagement, or at least imitating the portions we envy or admire. Our fascination with heroes and celebrities stems from their living in full public view so that we intuit the styles that make them who they are in our eyes. Including them in our personal loops, we incorporate their ways into ours. There always being a huge disparity between how *they* live and how *we* do only gives us a powerful motive to change our ways by imitating them as closely as we can. Or, if they are infamous, we recognize their villainy and preserve our personal virtue by steering clear of them and their cohort.

Balancing our physical actions and gestures against the impressions those actions have on our senses, we come alive through the disparity between our intentions and sensory stimulation, pulling ourselves ahead through our own efforts, making ourselves happen more or less as we intend to, checking the results as we glance at our reflections in store windows as we pass by, patting our hair, tugging at skirts, tucking in shirttails. Telling jokes we heard at the office or what happened at school, we keep those loops going round, feeling like our striving or accomplished selves, doing the best we can to make sense of a life and a world not known for their inherent meaning, logic, beauty, or purpose.

Everything we strive for and do is achieved through exercise of our respective loops of engagement. Through pointed activity coordinated with attentive perception, we monitor the progress of our efforts, projects, and relationships in mapping out our pathways in life, striving to actually do what we want to do and become the persons we hope to be.

In the first chapter, A Mind at Work, I present the stories of eighteen incidents from my life that I find salient, memorable, and yet mysterious. The rest of the book develops themes arising from my grappling to make sense of these and other everyday incidents to find out what they can tell me about the workings of my mind. O

CONSCIOUSNESS

THE BOOK

CHAPTER 1

A MIND AT WORK

The following eighteen stories from my everyday life all bear an emotional charge even in recall. I remember them because they apparently have something to teach me. Which is that awareness requires personal effort and skill, and can easily go wrong. I am made to remember such stories because at every millisecond of life my survival may be at issue. If I don't pay attention, who will? Isn't that precisely the mission I undertook in being born as a self-conscious person? I have to train my mind to interpret sensory phenomena as accurately as it can. That is, since I can't tell the difference between myself and my mind, I must earn my own trust.

The way I seem to build that trust is through trial and error, or successive approximation, which is how I learn almost everything. The learning is *my* learning because it is *my* mind that does all the work, and is changed as a result. This book is about that subjective process of learning, using my own mind as an object of study simply because it is the only mind I have access to in sufficient detail.

Neuroscience is much concerned with the structures and processes in the brain that make consciousness possible. Introspection, on the other hand, is concerned with the subjective experience of consciousness itself. As an emergent property enabled but not fully accounted for by the workings of the brain, consciousness must first be met head-on across the full range of its living details if we are to develop an appreciation for its nature and idiosyncrasies. Through an introspective adventure lasting thirty years, I have found that my brain does not fully account for my personal consciousness because another substrate shares that burden as well—the environmental substrate provided by my situation in the world. My mind intercedes or mediates between those two substrates, between my embodied brain and its environmental situation. Consciousness, that is, emerges precisely from its privileged position between a specific rock and a particular hard place, between its brain and the situation it engages in interacting with its worldly surroundings. Introspection reveals the details of that lifelong engagement as we make ourselves happen in the world.

And to add an evolutionary note, through introspection I discover that natural selection is not an impersonal process done unto me, but one I participate in as skillfully as I can. We are creatures of both our genetic heritage and our environmental interactions. We all have the option and ability to put ourselves forward as candidates for survival by doing our self-reflective homework to improve our grasp of life as an engagement between our minds and the surroundings we find ourselves in. Darwin was right about evolution being an issue on the individual level. And since that is where I personally live—on that level—it is my job to learn how to gauge my current situation accurately by accounting for the telling details of my sensory experience. I wasn't taught that in school, but it is at the core of every life lesson I ever learned.

To begin, I tell eighteen stories about my mind being stuck between a rock and a hard place, trying to make sense of myself in my current surroundings in order to make an appropriate response—that is, a response that will improve my chances for survival in my present situation. My argument is that it is under such pressing circumstances that we can best appreciate our minds as they strive to understand what is happening so to adopt a course of action likely to be both suitable and effective.

To the stories, then.

INCIDENT 1. CROSSING BRATTLE STREET: I am heading for a bookstore on the other side of Brattle Street in Harvard Square. The street is one-way coming out of the square, so I look left and see a delivery truck rounding the corner, coming my way. It hasn't picked up much speed, so I can easily make it across. Except I can't. I step into the street and am felled by a cyclist coming from the right, heading the wrong way against traffic. I jumped right into his path. Stunned, looking up from the roadway where I fell, I see the truck bearing down on me. The driver jams on the brakes and comes to a stop just inches from my shoulder. I wave him a weak apology, then rise on wobbly legs. The biker says he's sorry. Blaming him for my stupidity, I shout back, "I hope you rot in hell!" The truck driver waits, which I take as an invitation to cross, so I do, this time looking both ways. Not looking is not seeing, leading to not remembering why I was heading for the bookstore in the first place. My objective was to beat the one-way traffic; it never occurred to me

4

that a vehicle might be coming the other way. That oversight created a blind spot in my awareness that almost did me in.

INCIDENT 2. COWS ON THE BAR HARBOR ROAD: Driving home a little after sunset, I am reluctant to turn on the wipers when it starts to rain. Peering through the drops gathering on the windshield, I see what looks like two cows by the side of the road ahead. Cows on the road to Bar Harbor? I doubt my own eyes. What else could be black and white, and that big? One of them flicks its tail: definitely two cows. Seconds later, as I pass by, the cows turn into two motor-cyclists stopped by the side of the road to don black rain gear striped with white, and I realize the tail flick I saw was really the flicking motion of an arm as the nearer rider shrugged on her black and white rain jacket. Not seeing the motorcycle between them, some-thing about the spacing between the animated black-and-white forms was more appropriate to cows than to people. Make that two bikers on the road to Bar Harbor.

INCIDENT 3. DYING CROW: I am driving along a country road and see a dead crow ahead. No, not dead, a *dying* crow—its wing still feebly flapping the air. A shadow on the edge of the shoulder show-ing signs of life—worst-case scenario. I can't just drive by and leave it to suffer. Dread wells within me. I don't want to stop and wring its neck, but what can I do? I'd rather keep going. Then, as I ap-proach the dying form, I see it differently—an empty trash bag blowing in the wind. Yes, definitely, a black plastic bag agitated by the wash from passing cars. Relieved, I drive on.

What I first saw was a dying crow. That was my lived reality. The size was right, the color, the lift of the wing. I had the whole scenario worked out in my head, a low-flying bird colliding with an onrushing car. I had seen it many times before with crows, gulls, pheasants, owls. But that was only a first approximation. As my approach filled in additional details, the crow morphed into a trash bag of similar size and complexion displaying the same flapping motion. My mind had tricked me. I had tricked myself. Unconscious fears and expectations led me astray.

INCIDENT 4. PLANE CRASH: I am on the sidewalk heading down-town. Glancing left, I see sunlight glinting off a giant plane just over the rooftops, angled downward where there is no airport. I look ahead to get my balance, then look back. This time I see not a plane but a TV antenna on the ridgeline of a house with, yes, sunlight glinting from its many swept-back elements.

My mind appears to place a series of bets about the nature of its current situation. Through successive approximations, it gets a better hold on circumstances and offers a clearer sense of the situation as a basis for judgment and appropriate action. I didn't have to call 911 after all.

INCIDENT 5. FRED ON FIFTH AVENUE: I am walking along a bustling New York sidewalk in late fall. Jostling crowds are moving both directions. Through a brief gap, I see a familiar figure swinging along ahead of me. I know immediately who it is, an old friend from Seattle I haven't seen in years. The gait is right; the overcoat is right; the hat is right. Yes, even scarf and shoes. Fred! The jolt of recognition gives me a burst of speed as I stride to catch up with him. I weave through the crowd, which has abruptly become an obstacle course. Fred keeps on and I follow behind, making slow progress. It takes me over a minute to get directly behind him. Should I call out? Grab him by the shoulder? Race by and present myself? I stride next to him and raise my arm above his shoulder to give it a clap . . . and quickly drop it to my side. Wrong nose, wrong mouth, wrong chin. I've been chasing a stranger. A wave of disappointment stops me in my tracks. Now, where was I going?

When he briefly taught at Harvard, E. E. Cummings sometimes wrote the comment on student papers, "Good but poor." Winded on Fifth Avenue, I found myself *Right but wrong.* From the back, the figure ahead looked like Fred and moved like Fred. I would have sworn it *was* Fred. From the side I saw additional details that were not Fred-like at all. An innocent mistake. But under stress of battlefield conditions such suppositions could lead to death from a burst of friendly fire.

My consciousness appears to blend two sorts of signals, one perceptual, the other conceptual. The perceptual stream suggests something exists in the world; the conceptual stream categorizes or interprets that phenomenon in light of my current situation. Chasing after Fred, I didn't realize these two signals were mismatched until my perception was clear enough to show how wrong I was. Leaving my anticipation collapsed in a heap on the sidewalk.

INCIDENT 6. MUSTARD JAR: Where's the mustard? I open the refrigerator and scan the shelves. I know just what I'm looking for: a small, squat, thick-waisted jar of clear glass half-full of my favorite, dark-yellow condiment. I don't see it at first. Probably behind the milk; no. I know we have some, I used it yesterday. Check again. Move things around to peer behind them. Pickles, yes. Mayo, yes. Relish, yes. Broccoli, carrots, leftovers wrapped in foil; yes. Mustard, no. Misplaced in the freezer? No. On the counter? No. The table? No. Aliens must have taken it. I go through the search routine again; then in reverse order. No mustard anywhere. Major frustration. Man-child has taken it to his room? He never does that. Slowly fuming, I open the refrigerator door one last time. Aha! I spy the round, bright red lid. The jar was right in front of me all the while, lying on its side next to the milk. I was looking for its profile while it was presenting its top. Wrong gestalt. Blindsided again.

Such is consciousness. Full of pitfalls and surprises. I generally find what I look for, except when I don't. If perceptual phenomena don't match my expectations, I tend to disregard them as if they didn't exist. They don't measure up to my search criteria. Like the 2008 mortgage crisis. Who saw it coming? Yet it was in view all the time; we just weren't looking for it. Some saw the parts they were interested in creeping up, but very few saw the big picture. It just didn't jibe with the conventional mythology of open markets and laissez faire capitalism, which were alleged to heal themselves.

I have read lots of explanations of *what* happened. And *how* it could happen. But the picture shifts every day as we hear from different perspectives. The crisis is viewed variously as a financial collapse, a failure of government regulation, an investment-market-insurance-banking catastrophe. Pundits review their notes on the Golden Age, the Great Depression, the oil embargo, the savings-and-loan fiasco, the dot.com collapse, the Enron-auditing game. And now the mortgage meltdown based on worthless paper selling at inflated prices so all concerned could get their piece of the action. First from over-stressed homeowners, then through Big Brother bailouts. Like me and the little mustard jar, the experts are looking for what they want to find, not what is actually looking right back at them.

INCIDENT 7. SUNFLOWERS: My partner lives in an apartment above her pottery studio. Bed and computer on one end, counter, stove and refrigerator on the other; a one-room apartment with no secrets because you can see the whole space and everything in it from wherever you happen to be. I went up to get my camera case and came back down so we could go for a walk. "Do you like the sunflowers?" she asked. "What sunflowers?" "In the vase on the counter." I'd walked within six inches of them and never saw them. Not once but twice.

The likes of dying crows and crashing airplanes, consciousness frequently presents me with figments. Too, like mustard jars and sunflowers, it sometimes hides objects in clear view. These effects are often transitory, dependent on storylines offered as snap judgments. Or on expectations, my level of attention, or what else in on my mind at the time. It's as if my mind is a prankster and loves to play tricks on me just for fun. But of course there's no difference between me and my mind. I am really playing tricks on myself. Consciousness *is* what I can know of my mind. There's no tiny projection room in my head where I screen my latest takes on reality.

I've learned not to take even my own consciousness at face value. It frequently deserves periodic checking and verification. In fact, experience has taught me to doubt every phenomenon that rises in my mind. Impostors and rip-offs—like hackers and conmen—are everywhere, even within consciousness. Or as I say now, *especially* within consciousness because that's where the trouble often starts. Autobiographical memory, for instance, that trustworthy standard, is always suspect. I was shocked to hear my younger brother claim that *he* was the one who liked Brussels sprouts when we were kids, not me. Did the good old days play as we remember them? Probably not. There's no warranty on childhood memories. I have a vivid recollection from when I was eighteen months old of playing with a dog under the dining room table, of climbing on a chair, then onto the table, and being held up to look into a white bassinette to see my baby brother just home from the hospital. Did that really happen? If so, it would be my earliest memory. I tell the story, but have no way of knowing if it is true.

INCIDENT 8. HOUSE SCRAPER: I am walking home on icy streets, the north wind pushing me up Holland Avenue. Glancing ahead, I see the back of a man scraping paint from the clapboard house at the end of the street, his body pressing some tool against the wood, swaying side-to-side. Looking down at my feet, I warily plod ahead, half walking, half sliding. At the T where Holland runs into Mt. Desert Street, I look up—and see a windblown cedar tree where the paint scraper had been, resembling him somewhat in form and motion, but clearly a cedar, not a man. Who would scrape paint in winter anyway?

INCIDENT 9. CLIP-ART CAT: It is evening. I am in the kitchen putting away dishes. The drainer is to the left of the sink, the cupboard to the right and above. The cupboard door is hinged on the left, so when I open it, it blocks my way as I move back and forth. I move out and around the cupboard door, out and around. Suddenly a loud shriek—I have stepped on the cat. Leaping up reflexively, I do some fancy footwork to release its tail from underfoot. In my mind, I picture a strange cat looking up at me—mildly I would say, unblinking—blue-gray face surrounded by an aura of soft fur. Trouble is, there is no cat. I have not had a cat in my apartment for twenty-five years.

I figure that moving back from cupboard to dish drainer, I caught the open cupboard door with my shoulder, swinging it open wider than usual. The shriek was the bottom hinge complaining under stress. I don't remember it squeaking before, but when I tested it, there it was, that exact cry. My immediate response had been to import a cat into consciousness, as if an imaginary animal would explain the whole scene. I responded quickly and appropriately to the cat that wasn't there, and quite inappropriately to the hinge that was and always had been there. Now, where did that cat come from—that specific cat I saw looking back at me? I'd lived with several cats in the past, but never one like that. It looked like your basic tabby, a stock cat ready to leap out of the wings on cue when the occasion demanded. Not like a real cat which would take its time and probably head the other way, this one was right there in my mind when consciousness called for it, blue-gray with a ruff, looking up at me without blinking. The meaning of that shriek was right there, a cat, not a dry hinge. By way of proof, a clip-art figment to embody the shriek in my ears.

It was if my consciousness demanded an explanation, immediately, at all costs. But since feeling is first, as the poet says, maybe it was feeling—a sudden surge of alarm—and not meaning, that made me jump without thinking. That might explain the whole scene, even if I had to conjure up a cat to stand in for the true explanation. That shriek really startled me. Upset me. It came just as I was stepping back to avoid the cupboard door, so my body assumed it was the step that caused the sudden noise—and reaching in to its bag of tricks from bygone days, came up with a cat, which obligingly howled. I, feeling responsible, immediately leapt up and, mid-air, "saw" poor tabby, a ready stand-in for the unsuspected source of the squeak. All in a fraction of a second, without rehearsal. Rube Goldberg could not have done better.

The great mystery is how expectancy could back up its claim by pulling a stock photo out of thin air. I kept seeing the same image all evening. Even after I had gone to bed, there was that damned cat, the most innocent face ever put on an ambiguous squeaky phenomenon.

INCIDENT 10. CLOUDS UP AHEAD: Clouds, nothing but clouds. I am looking for a first sight of the Rocky Mountains, but all I see through the windshield is clouds. Flanked by my brothers and two dogs, I am in the back seat of the car. My parents are in front. I am leaning forward, looking down the road toward the western horizon. Which is hidden by clouds. The family is moving to Seattle. We've driven from central New York to eastern Colorado, which is flat, offering long views ahead. Of clouds. I keep looking. Ten minutes. Fifteen. Half an hour. Nothing but clouds. I am about to burst with disappointment when, suddenly, the white clouds, those same ones I've been peering at all the while—turn into snow-capped mountains. The Rockies! I see them! Nobody says a word. They've seen them all along.

Strange business. Again, looking but not seeing. Or seeing the wrong thing. Then in a blink, seeing rightly. The pattern doesn't change, but the interpretation is suddenly different, turning white clouds to snow, concept of clouds to concept of snow. Unwittingly, it's seer's choice.

INCIDENT 11. BURIED REMAINS: Fresh out of high school, I'm in Nespelum, Washington, on the banks of the Columbia River. This time there are clouds, too, but I'm not looking at them, or at the river. I'm too busy digging a hole in the ground. Looking for Indian artifacts on the Nespelum Reservation. The Chief Joseph Dam is under construction, and this ground will be flooded. I'm a volunteer with a team of archaeologists from the University of Washington. Three feet down, I think I've found something. Hard, white. I switch from trowel to whisk broom and toothbrush. Whisk, whisk; brush, brush. There's a suture. Looks like a skull. Brush, brush; blow, blow. See, it's rounded, like a dome. Gotta be a skull. We haven't found any human remains on this dig. I'm gonna be first! Brush,

brush. The dome has a funny edge. A ridge, like Neanderthals had. This has gotta be really old. After what felt like hours of brushing away a few grains of sand at a time, I have much of the dome exposed, ridge and all. A real archaeologist comes by to see how I'm doing. "Whatchagot there, Steve? Looks like some kind of turtle."

The more I learn about the workings of my mind, the further "reality" drifts into the fog of awareness. Sadder but wiser, I am left with the view from my personal perspective, eager, naïve, and sure of itself. Cats belong underfoot in kitchens, descending jets are appropriate at rooftop level, crows belong by the side of the road. Where else would Neanderthals be if not underground? Embarrassingly, I interpret visual patterns not from the leading edge of human understanding, but on the basis of limited experience and false assumptions based on my personal perspective and sense of the situation I am engaged in at the time. To keep things simple, my mind supplies the boldest and speediest account of what's going on. It doesn't wait to figure things out. Faster than a speeding bullet, a possible (if not probable) explanation is on call at all times through emotionally-tinged expectancy.

Like shockwaves preceding that bullet, expectations seem to radiate from the leading edge of my experience. Expectations that may be, 1) fulfilled, 2) partially fulfilled, or 3) denied. In each of the four cases—cat, jet, crow, turtle shell—there is a partial resemblance to the sensory phenomenon that caught my attention as I initially interpreted it. The hinge did cry out like a cat. The TV antenna was swept back like the wings of a jet; both were metallic and gleamed in the sun. The wafting trash bag fluttered as a dying crow might lift its wing. And the sutured dome resembled a skull of sorts. In each case, the setting of the sensory pattern was appropriate, my first interpretation apt. Apt, perhaps, but a stab in the dark.

My own expectations prepare me to act quicker than I can think when I need to. They are at the forefront of my loop of engagement with the current situation, full consciousness following behind to mop up when the situation I anticipate turns out other than I first thought. This doesn't happen only occasionally. Every time the phone rings, I hazard a guess who it is. When someone raps at the door, I come up with a quick list of possible rappers. I am full of dire predictions of what might go wrong. Raising children, I was

11

always on the outlook for danger, even in the most innocent situations.

Events in my life always unfold in a context of expectancy. In comparable situations, I rely on past experience in looking ahead. Current and future situations are anchored to my earlier life. That's how I propose expectations in venturing into the unknown. Not consciously, but I do it just the same. My life unfolds through a series of successive approximations. The broader and deeper my experience, the better forecaster and prophet I become. Until a singularity occurs, an event rare or unique in my experience—a car suddenly cutting me off, an abrupt change in the wind, an earthquake such as I experienced in Seattle in 1947, Pearl Harbor, 9/11, a financial crisis. Then expectation pleads, "Who could have known?"

What I make of such events is that I engage phenomena *as if* they represent goings-on in the real world. Until I catch them faking it on their own. On *my* own, for these phenomena-as-interpreted are my doing. I am the faker and none other, caught in the grip of personal experience, which can work like a trap. One of my most basic illusions is that the phenomena I entertain fairly represent the situation I am in. Except, as it often turns out, they are a simple cartoon of a far more complex situation than I realize. Reality, I see now, is generally more constructed than given.

INCIDENT 12. VOICE IN THE NIGHT: I'm living in Cambridge some years ago. I wake up one night to hear someone in the street calling "Fa" in a hoarse voice. Looking for his dog, I figure. Or his father. "Fa," "Fa," he goes on. And on. Little Johnny One Note. "Fa." "Fa." I hear the sound, but it holds no meaning for me. I doze off. Then it strikes me—he isn't crying "Fa," he's yelling "Fire" at the top of his wheezy old lungs. I look out the window. Flames are shooting from the roof of the house across the street. I call the fire department.

Another auditory illusion of my own making. Not a squeaky hinge this time, but a familiar word in my native language. Which I did not recognize, even though I know native New Englanders often drop their final r's. Reminding me once again that meaning does not reside in words themselves but in the ears (or semantic memories) of those who speak, hear, or read them.

INCIDENT 13. SINK SONG: Another sink story. In my married days, I am washing dishes after dinner. The kitchen is a small nook off the dining area, with a window over the sink. It is dark outside, so I keep my eyes on what I am doing. Enclosed in that space, I feel snug in performing such a comfortable chore. The radio on the shelf plays an old tune I haven't heard in years. Not remembering the words, I hum along as I wash. The tune sticks with me as I clean the counter. The next night, I go through the same routine, this time with the radio off. That same tune springs to mind out of nowhere, and I hum the melody I heard yesterday, this time from memory. The same tune over and over till I'm done. The night after that, I can't remember the name of the song, the singer, or the melody itself. It was briefly rekindled, but now it's gone, and I have no idea what it was. I remember wanting to remember, and not being able to, that has stuck with me. That is the pattern I remember—emptiness when I wanted fulfillment. The yearning to have what I lost. Those three nights out of a life are still with me as a pattern I cannot bring back, much less interpret.

Sounds like a surrogate for a marriage gone down the tubes. Except that isn't how it felt at the time—it felt reassuring to hear an old song I had once known but had forgotten. And reassuring to recall it the next night on my own. And sad to have forgotten it the night after—all mapped onto the image of washing dishes. It is the layering of those maps that intrigues me now. I am a visual person; it is just like me to forget something I hear clearly at one moment and can't bring back at the next. I do that with names all the time. If I don't write them down, I won't retain them. But the reciprocal connections in my brain persist, from song on the radio to kitchen sink, and back again from sink to song.

It is by such looping connections in the brain—Edelman refers to them as nerve paths forming "reentrant" loops—that categorization and interpretation are made possible. I now believe that such links or reciprocal mappings make it possible for sensory patterns to kindle conceptual meanings, and concepts to fulfill themselves in sensory images. The looping engagement between phenomena and interpretations endures as long as the nerve connections between them remain in active use. Forgetting is due to *not* activating the circuit for a long enough period so that the links fade, or even die, key synapses becoming inoperative. This is conjecture, but it represents what I think may have happened in the case of the forgotten sink melody. In a physiological sense, the song literally died away.

INCIDENT 14. MEMORY STICK: I'm in the middle of transferring JPG files from my desktop to my laptop. I've got them in my memory stick. I am hurrying so to be ready to meet Diane who's going to drive me to the ophthalmologist in Ellsworth. . . . *Rinnggg* goes the phone. Diane wants to know can we meet fifteen minutes earlier than we said? Sure, I tell her. Click. Now where was I? Transferring files. Memory stick. Which is . . . where? I go to my desktop. Not there. I go to my laptop in the other room. Not there. Recheck the desktop. Nope. Recheck the laptop. Nope. Near the phone? Nope. Dining room table? Nope. Scour my apartment. Nope. Almost time to go. I'm getting frazzled. I sit and think, picturing the memory stick. Small, black, with a neck strap, also black. My wall-to-wall carpet is midnight blue. That must be it. I look on the floor beneath my desk—Eureka! The memory stick isn't in the USB port, so I figure I'd already copied the files. I paste them onto my laptop and I'm out the door.

That phone call and change in concentration cleared what I was doing from working memory (that segment of the loop of engagement which holds onto details just long enough to get the job done). The thread broken, I couldn't remember what I was doing or where I was when the phone rang. Whatever it might have been was on the verge of consciousness, but I couldn't bring it back, so had to reconstruct it. Both computers were on so I must have been using them to . . . Ah! Transfer those pesky JPGs. I probably put the memory stick on my lap to do something else, and when I jumped for the phone, it fell on the rug.

My memory is fragile unless I really concentrate. And even then there's no guarantee I can resuscitate it once it's gone. How many hours have I spent looking for my glasses? Which is why I wear them on a cord around my neck. People tell me they keep losing their cordless phones and remotes. I've finally learned to outsmart such forgetfulness by keeping a car key on my belt. Actually, two keys just to make sure one of them works. I still remember that hollow feeling when I'd leave the B.U. library at 11:00 p.m.—and find my keys in the ignition of a locked car in a cold parking garage. I've misplaced so many gloves that I've often worn a mixed pair. As a photographer, I've spent weeks looking for misplaced or misfiled negatives. I'd print them, and then they'd float off to negative heaven, never to be seen again.

I'd been a still photographer in the US Army Signal Corps in the 1950s. In those days we used 4x5″ film in Speed Graphics. You know, with black bellows, a sheet of ground glass in the focal plane, wire viewfinders, and shutters that had to be cocked before every shot. And flashbulbs, because the lenses were so slow. I often had to work fast at the leading edge of my concentration. I'd get poised to make an exposure. Have I cocked the shutter? Turned the film holder? (it held two sheets of film, one on each side). Pulled the slide? Put in a new flashbulb? I'd done it all a thousand times, but I couldn't be sure I'd done it this time unless I checked at the last instant. I'd trained myself to perform the full routine automatically as soon as I'd made an exposure. But I did it all unconsciously, so never remembered I had.

INCIDENT 15. QUARRY PHOTOS: I have long planned to write up the history of granite quarrying in Sullivan and Franklin, Maine. My grandfather was a stoneworker, and died of silicosis from all the stone dust he breathed. At fifty-five, he died nine years before I was born, but a cousin told me I am a lot like him. I've been sitting on my notes for twenty years, waiting for the right time to do something with them. That time is now. I've discovered PowerPoint presentations in the meantime, and am making one covering the years 1806 (when the Commonwealth of Massachusetts granted the entire Township of Sullivan to Bowdoin and Williams Colleges) up till 2010 when most quarries are inactive, yet a few local men still work the stone. I'm almost finished, and want to round things off with a sequence showing a modern crane hoisting blocks of granite from the last local quarry still in operation.

Checking now and then with Conrad, operator of Sullivan Granite Company, to see what's going on, today I find him getting ready to cut granite with a diesel-fuel torch on the end of a ten-foot pipe connected to an air compressor. That's exactly the shot I want to begin with, so spend the next two hours taking pictures of Conrad, torch in hand, cutting around the edge of a huge block of granite on the bottom of his quarry. He literally burns the stone away along one side of the block, turning solid stone into dust, which shoots out of the opposite end of the cut. Lighting the torch is the most dramatic stage of the process, and I get two shots of four-foot flames driven by compressed air from the mouth of the torch. I shoot from every conceivable angle, the most dramatic being looking over Conrad's shoulder at white-hot grains of granite plunging like meteors into the black cut.

Then it's home to download the several hundred images I've made onto my computer's hard drive so I can size and finish them in Photoshop Elements, getting them ready to add to my PowerPoint.

I've used my Panasonic Lumix camera for six years, so have gone through this routine hundreds of times. I connect the camera to my laptop with a cable, transfer the images to the program that lets me copy them to the photo files on my hard drive. When I first view the images stacked up ready for copying, I am stunned by the ones showing flames shooting from the torch. Taking a closer look, I get caught up in the sequence, checking to make sure I didn't miss anything. I go through them all, and am happy I captured the cutting process at every stage from every angle. After five minutes of scanning the entire sequence, I close the program (when asked if I want to delete all the photos, I click "Yes"), disconnect my camera, double-click delete all images once, then again, and put the camera battery in the charger to get ready for my next photo session.

Abruptly, I feel blood rushing to my face. The one thing I didn't do was copy the photos onto my hard drive. They're gone from my camera . . . and my computer. I scramble to see if by some chance they're in the trash, which they aren't. I just deleted them without copying them, not once but twice. Deliberately—something I'd never done. How could this happen? I realize that scrutinizing the pictures before I copied them led me to feel I'd already copied them because that's how I always do it, copy first, then look. Seeing the two frames showing flames streaming from the torch had caught my attention, breaking the rhythm that leads me through the process of downloading pictures. Leaving me empty, discouraged, feeling stupid. In a word, thwarted. What could I do? I charged the camera battery, got in the car, drove the thirty miles to Sullivan, and redid the shoot. This time the torch was already lit so I didn't get any pictures of those four-foot flames.

All of which goes to show what a creature of habit I am—and how vulnerable to anything that distracts me from my standard routine. Interrupting the process breaks my habitual train of thought, disorienting me, voiding what I am trying to do. It was getting caught up in the images themselves at the wrong time that did me in. Distracted, I forgot where I was in time and space, causing me to leave out the most crucial stage of what I was doing—getting those images from camera onto hard drive. I couldn't blame this one on a ringing phone. *I* provided the distraction. The time to congratulate myself on a great shot is after I truly own it, not before.

INCIDENT 16. AUDIENCE OF ONE: I am in the second row at a talk on sex education. The female speaker, an invited expert, keeps looking

at me and no one else in the audience. I feel uncomfortably conspic-
uous the whole time because I find her always returning my gaze.
Afterwards, I ask her why she singled me out, and she said I looked
just like her son. She was talking to him, not to me; I was a dummy
sitting in a chair. In certain circles, that is called transference, but at
root it is miscategorization—or metaphor—treating a plum as if it
were an eggplant because there is a certain resemblance.

The US invasion of Iraq in 2003 as a misguided show of manly
vengeance for the leveling of the Twin Towers by disgruntled Saudi
terrorists fits much the same pattern, transferring not our fondness
but our hurt and anger onto an innocent nation we didn't particularly
like, even though we had used it in the 1980s as a pawn on our side
in the Cold War. The invasion is a good example of national leaders
portraying one thing as another because, in their minds, they mix up
two different things, as the sex education speaker confounded me
and her son. *Seeing as,* it turns out, is a quality of mind shared by
many of the incidents I introduce in this chapter, suggesting that my
mind—and perhaps others as well—operates metaphorically more
often than I realize.

INCIDENT 17. CARTWHEEL AURORA: The center of the spectacle is at
the zenith overhead, apparently directly above my island camp in
Franklin, Maine. It is midnight. On my way back from the latrine, I
look up—to see streamers shimmering from around the horizon
toward that celestial vortex where, wavering, flowing, they whirl
together in a pulsing gyre of living forms that spreads and contracts
and shifts its shape as I watch. Glowing spiders turn into snakes into
eyes into butterflies. The air is clear, sky dark. Each star is a vivid
mote of light. The air fairly hums. Beneath the stars, the cartwheel
rings its changes without repetition as if two eyes aren't enough to
take in the spectacle and I need ears as well. I am having a whole-
body experience. Candle flames turn into running wolves into great
whales into chickens, rays shooting above the trees all the while,
feeding the starved gyre, spinning it round and round and into itself.
Roses turn to sparklers turn to ants turn to luminous lizards. The
spectacle goes on for hours, each second consuming my entire attention. What if I blinked and missed a crucial transition? Continuity
is of the essence. But eventually, cold, stiff, tired, I not only blink
but go to bed, my head swimming with the best auroral display I've
ever seen—and am likely to see in my lifetime.

INCIDENT 18. DIAGNOSIS: In the mid-1960s, I was in the hospital undergoing a week of diagnostic tests. It was a teaching hospital maintained by a distinguished university. Every day my doctor led students like so many white-clad ducklings to the door of my room, where they ogled me in my bed, and murmured faint quacking sounds out in the hall where I couldn't hear what they said. I remember my insides being insulted in the most intimate fashion as if I wasn't conscious or even there. But I was there and remember the week as painful, harrowing, and humiliating. It's hard being reduced to an experimental subject on a par with a guinea pig or rat. Barium enema, upper and lower GI series, Sigmoidoscopy—I remember them to this day.

Worst of all was the consultation at the end of my stay. I reported as instructed to the Great Doctor's office, a huge, bare room with an ornate desk in the center facing the door. The room was dark, the only light coming from a green-shaded lamp on the desk, reflecting from my medical folder onto the heavy mass of my benefactor's jowls from below. "I thought you had cystic fibrosis," he said, "but you don't." Long pause. "What *do* I have?" "I don't know, I have done everything I can for you." I saw immediately it was my fault. I had made him seem unknowing and foolish in front of his ducklings. That was the end of that diagnostic foray.

Thirty-five years later I found out I had celiac disease, and had had it my entire life. That's what the Great Doctor might have found if it hadn't been masked by presumed symptom of cystic fibrosis. It was all out in the open; he just didn't see it. As I didn't see the mustard jar when it was right in front of me on the refrigerator shelf. Instead of mapping my symptoms onto his superior understanding, he had forced a map of his suppositions onto my innards as a classic category error. They didn't jibe, his theory and my gut, so the case was closed. Except it wasn't a case, it was my life, and instead of being closed, I went desperately onward as I had been going up till then, no wiser than before.

Our minds give us a chance to put our tentative judgments out there as fixtures in the world. And even more importantly, to evaluate how effective our actions are in accomplishing what we set out to do. The looping continuum of action and response is the medium in which our judgment improves, our actions become more appropriate to our circumstances as we come to understand them in ever finer detail. Or our looping engagement can lead to that if we let it by taking full responsibility for our awareness as a fallible guess or estimation. Which sometimes, as the Great Doctor illustrates, we are reluctant to do.

As I am fond of saying, we find what we expect to find. And if we don't, then we can take that as an opportunity for redefining our search criteria. Our minds provide a rough estimation that can grow sharper through trial and error. In my case, that's the only way I have learned anything in my life. I mean truly learned through dealing with the many dimensions of my lived experience. By falling on my face, picking myself up, and wondering where I went wrong, I gradually learn to avoid similar missteps in the future.

Here I have tried to show that fitting phenomena to concepts while on the run in particular situations is tricky business requiring skills and experience not generally employed in everyday life. Highly trained professionals and specialists make mistakes as often as laypersons do. No one has immunity against category errors, illusions, or misinterpretations. Or inattention for that matter. These are simply facts for the wise to guard against, not universal human failings. Living with our mistakes on a daily basis gives us a chance to do better.

In Chapter 2, I will take a closer look at sensory phenomena, the high price we pay to see them clearly, and the violence we are likely to do to alternative patterns and interpretations. O

SENSORY PHENOMENA

I can usually tell the difference between a crow and a trash bag, yet under certain conditions I readily confuse the two. The same is true of cedar trees and house scrapers, squeaky hinges and yowling cats. In such cases I commit category errors, confounding one thing with another. This reminds me of the illusory "chair" constructed in the mid-1930s by Adelbert Ames from rods and pieces of wood strung on wires to look like a chair from one particular angle, but from every other angle like rods and pieces of wood strung on wires. It's not that objects aren't what they seem, but that the human mind interprets sensory phenomena (figures that appear in awareness) the best it can under circumstances that are often confusing or ambiguous.

My mind interprets sensory figures by sorting them into conceptual groupings it is already familiar with (e.g., chairs, boats, birds). I store concepts and their identifying labels in memory, but the sensory figure at issue is a recent arrival. It's not that I see a crow but I see a pattern resembling what I *call* a crow. To do so rapidly—in a fraction of a second—my mind strives to recognize a patterned structure within the phenomenon at issue. Particularly, a structure that will have a look of familiarity in being similar to figures I have met before. My repertoire of conceptual categories is ever on the lookout for new members, and vice versa, a new figure in awareness is a ready candidate for adoption into one preexisting category or another.

Pattern recognition is a two way street on which particular phenomena and categories are united by the mental situation that joins them together. As a result, the pattern takes on a certain emotional coloring and relevance within the mind hosting that situation as entertained in awareness. Put that way, it sounds cumbersome, but when my mind does it in a fraction of a second, it seems as though the identity of a particular figure inheres in the figure itself and is not mapped upon it by a concept having meager sensory content.

Categorization or—as I prefer to call the process, "interpretation," to emphasize my personal role in the matter—is important to consciousness in its being aware *of* any meaningful figure beyond a purely sensible scene (figure, phenomenon, or pattern). Such mental processing happens so fast it is largely unconscious, and I become aware of it only when I catch my own mind making a category error or omission, as in many of the incidents I cite in Chapter 1. The aim of my introspective method is not to theorize about perception and cognition, but more to study instances when the process runs a bit rough, indicating there is more going on in that instant than I know. Instead of dismissing it, I pay attention to the roughness to see what it can tell me.

I find that I reach for sensory figures by paying attention, and learn a good deal about the expectations I cast upon the world in order to be able to perceive anything at all. Which leads me to believe that perception is a two-stage process involving both a reaching *for* and a taking *in,* the first being a somewhat vague and indistinct questioning of my surroundings, the second a more concrete and detailed response in terms of energy impinging on my sensory transducers (eyes, ears, nose, etc.), which translate that external energy into a flow of ions and chemicals in my brain. My mind answers the question by recognizing a sensory figure that is more or less relevant to that chemical flow. We all know the insect net is not the butterfly, and so it is with concepts and percepts, the one being used to capture the other, yet both are necessary to a perceptual process in which they play complementary roles.

It is difficult to talk about sensory figures without considering the mental workings that bring them into being in the first place. That is, the interpretation or the category must already be in mind in order for the figure to be *recognized* when it appears. If that weren't so, we'd spend much of our time like William James' infant in a world of "booming, buzzing confusion." To avoid such an unsatisfying state, we learn to interpret situations, and to discover the names things are called in our circle of language users. The name is not in the thing itself, but in our minds as we search for a sensory figure whose qualities we more-or-less anticipate. When a particular figure alerts us that, indeed, we have found such a phenomenon, the category and the label are already on the scene because we ourselves brought them with us as part of our search criteria. Learning a language is a matter of learning what to expect to find in a particular situation, and then to recognize the sounds people make when phenomena appear as anticipated. Looking up in daytime, we expect to see clouds in the sky, and at least a hint of the sun. In nighttime, we are not surprised to find the moon in one phase or another, and at least a few stars, with perhaps a bright planet here or there. Oh, look, a meteor; I was hoping we'd see one.

I intend the eighteen incidents in Chapter 1 to serve as evidence that phenomena exist as sensory figures apart from the identity we bestow upon them. How we sort them into categories is our doing, not the phenomenon's, not the world's. In the "blind walk" (an exercise in sensory exploration), if a blindfolded student exploring her environment utters the word "stone" upon touching an object, that verbal gesture is provided as the name of a concept by the blindfolded explorer, not by the stone itself. Stones don't deal in concepts, people do. And what the explorer bases that interpretation on is a quick assessment of an object she touches as rendered by her brain into a phenomenon featuring certain qualities such as roughness, hardness, size, heft, surface continuity, and so on. Where has she encountered such a group of qualities before? In the characteristics of the many "stones" she has handled over the course of her life, summarized in the concept bearing the label *stone* in semantic memory. So when she meets those qualities in the wild, instead of enjoying their phenomenal properties, she calls out "stone" to make sure she receives credit for giving the right answer, which she supposes is the point of the exercise because that is the sort of thing she has been trained to do in elementary school.

For indeed, as children we learn to organize our sensory impressions by mimicking the responses our peers and elder make to phenomena in *their* minds, which we take to be identical to those we witness in *ours* at the same time. We learn how to reach for sensory figures as others do, and to make responses similar to theirs. That is, to make the same gestures and noises, in the same way, on the same occasions they do. Gradually through our formative years, we refine our grasp of such occasions, gestures, and noises, calibrating our sensibility in harmony with our significant others', noticing the particular sets of sensory features that elicit a familiar response. Those sets of features enter our repertory of significant sensory events, together with the gestures and sounds made in our formative community by those who, by example, teach us to be properly human. That way, in the different sensory modalities, we pick up habits of seeing (hearing, touching, tasting, smelling, moving, hurting, etc.) to form the repertory of sensory engagements on which our lives will be based. That repertory is a learned response, not to events in the world, but to sensory figures in our minds representing the combination of energies ambient in our childhoods, together with the molecules we ingest in our food and the air we breathe.

Taken together, that set of concrete sensory figures retained from childhood sensitizes our brains by training our networks of sensory and motor neurons to respond selectively to the recurrence of such figures, and to variations upon them, so that we come to see (hear, touch, etc.) the world a certain way from a hard-won personal perspective. Looking upon such figures as salient features of our sensory worlds, we now seek (or perhaps avoid) similar figures as reminders of our primal identity in being who we are. Salient sensory figures have histories—and consequences—with profound implications for our making ourselves happen in the world we grow into.

Interpretation allows us to match what we know with what we encounter in awareness, underwriting a sensory figure with a concept having a name, so that all three elements converge in a single experience *as if* they all came from some outside reality instead of being conjoined in the mind of a particular observer. But in fact the *sensory figure, name,* and *concept* are different facets of one mind, not an external reality, which is a convenient fiction built after-the-fact, not before the experience is had. Reality, then, results from a string of habitual assumptions about its nature, assumptions based on the bioenergetic processes by which each mind grapples with its world of experience. Such assumptions are stored uniquely in the memories of each person on Earth. For convenience, individuals with somewhat similar outlooks group themselves by the ways they suppose the world to be, forming cultures based on common assumptions about the nature of reality.

In these pages I am proposing a culture based on a single person's experience and the conclusions he draws by reflecting on his findings as a thirty-years' experiment. Which sounds egotistical, as if I were the judge of the world. But, no, I am not proposing I have a privileged view onto the world as it is. Rather, my purpose is to shed light on the workings of one man's mind—namely, my own, because that is the only mind on Earth I have more-or-less direct access to. That way I preserve the integrity of my day-to-day experience, not that of the world or so-called reality itself. The eighteen incidents I present in the first chapter are meant as raw data provided by my own mental processes. I offer them as incidents drawn from my struggle for personal truth, opposed to any notion of physical or universal truth.

If I were pursuing world or universal truth, I would not be anywhere near revealing it via a study of one unique mind. That would take collaboration between a great many different minds through centuries of study such as have been devoted to ongoing discussions of reality since groups of people began comparing notes about such things in Paleolithic times, or perhaps even earlier. My question in this chapter is what those eighteen incidents can tell me about the sensory phenomena they feature as revealed to my introspective gaze. My purpose is to suggest that such an effort is not a sign of vanity but might be something others besides myself could take on in regard to their own sensory experience—sure to be very different from my own—so they could form their own conclusions about the nature of their brand of mental activity. That is, I want to share my experiential method, not any conclusions I might draw in which I can only speak for myself. But at least in the end I will be able to speak about *something,* and if you carry out a similar exercise, we can compare our respective somethings to see whether or not we are on the same track, or even parallel or divergent tracks. Then we'll be able to engage in a meaningful discussion based on personal exploration rather than make random, conjectural jabs in the direction of reality as we might if we got together today.

What is it about the workings of my mind that leads me to mistake a trash bag for a crow, a TV antenna for an airplane, a windblown cedar for a man scraping paint? How can I *not* see flowers that are right in front of me? How can I visualize a cat that does not exist? How can I hum a tune one night while washing dishes and forget it the next while performing the same chore in the same place? How can I watch a procession of familiar images pass in the night sky while I know I am watching a light show generated by high-energy solar radiations interacting with Earth's magnetic field? Yet these and many more incidents are examples from the actual history of my sensory experience. I don't think I am crazy, yet how can I account for such seeming craziness in a world that we generally take to be real in-and-of itself?

Consider the case of the snowcapped Rockies looking to my thirteen-year-old mind like a line of low-hanging clouds. Living in upstate New York, I had seen plenty of both clouds and snow in my life. How did I get them confused for over half an hour? Both reflect light and appear white. Both are variant forms of water vapor. Both float in or fall from the sky. Yet I was certain I was looking at clouds and not snow. What made me so sure of myself? Especially when I was anxious to see the Rockies. Which may be similar to my deep conviction in Nespelum, Washington, that I was unearthing a human skull, a scenario so attractive that it blocked me from recognizing a turtle shell when I uncovered one. Or, again, when I went to my partner's apartment to retrieve my camera case, I was so determined to find it that I couldn't see a vase with four bright-yellow Mexican sunflowers within inches of my eyes. And then there was the case of the great doctor being so eager to see signs of cystic fibrosis he failed to recognize symptoms of celiac disease.

Are we condemned to see only what we want to see, or are in the habit of seeing? Are we set in advance to take the world in as phenomena which accord with expectancies we are not even aware of? Phenomena which, while we reach out to the world, are shaped by ideas and concepts seated deep in our memories and our minds?

Questions, nothing but questions. No wonder we avoid introspection. It reduces us to a state of doubt and uncertainty when our lives depend on taking decisive courses of action in the so-called real world. It is far easier to believe that the world as we view it is real than that we are such bumblers and fools. Who will publically admit to not knowing or trusting her own mind?

In my case, I don't generally think of myself as a fool, but I must allow that I can be fooled. I can be naïve, ignorant, misguided, mistaken, and plain wrong. In fact, those are the routes by which I have learned to be sure of anything at all. First comes error, then doubt, then questioning, then correction. I can't seem to avoid that sequence. And beyond correction, likely a series of further corrections after that.

When I worked as an engineering aide at Boeing's Renton plant in the mid-1950s, I reviewed data recordings from earlier flights of prototype B-52s to see if the engines on one wing were burning more fuel than those on the other, causing the plane consistently to yaw or veer to one side. The issue was making safer landings at night and in bad weather by sending a beam of energy upward along a runway so the autopilot of an incoming plane could engage that beam and come in for a landing without human intervention (or error). In such a ground-controlled approach, the trick would be for a plane crossing that beam to acquire it and accurately turn along it, and so glide at an appropriate angle down onto the runway—without drifting off course. Allowance was made for the plane to cross the beam one more time at an angle, giving it one more chance to adjust its course according to the desired angles of approach, so ensuring a safe landing, avoiding a series of successive approximations that would eat up both time and distance before the proper corrections could be made. The engineers involved in designing that system wanted to avoid the all-too-common human error of pilots flying blind, believing they knew what they were doing on a hunch, committing the plane to what they thought was the best course—only to crash into a mountain next to the runway in its narrow valley.

That is, Boeing engineers wanted to build an autopilot that would improve on fallible human judgment when based on poor information, enabling them to design a control system that avoided such mistakes as pilots would be likely to make under stress. To design such a system, engineers had to accept that even highly-trained pilots would make errors under certain conditions. Pilots are human, and all humans make mistakes.

Which all of us, as pilots of our own actions and affairs, do well to remember, but frequently overlook due to stubbornness, stress, hurry, social pressure, poor preparation, or even arrogance. In my case I often find myself plunging into the deep end of the pool when more properly I belong paddling around in the shallows. There are no degrees or certificates that guarantee error-free judgments. Particularly regarding the interpretation of sensory phenomena based on patterns of energy we acquire one way or another without being sure which category they best represent.

Recall the sex educator who addressed me as if I were her son—chiefly because that son and I were both bearded, thin, and of comparable age. She clearly did it unwittingly, not because it made sense. For practical purposes (addressing an audience of strangers), she made the strange situation somewhat familiar in order to put herself at ease. There was method in her fixing her gaze upon me—sensible if irrational method. Anyone who knows himself well will recognize such unreasonable instances in himself as the best approximations he is capable of making under difficult circumstances. Since no familiar face was in the audience, the speaker simply imported one as an approximate fit to a strange face that *was* there. An exact fit not being possible, she—like others of us on similar occasions—settled for an inexact match to the child of her womb that was close enough for her limited purposes.

Is this best-fit strategy actually perceptual, or is it more conceptual in nature? Where is the perceptual looseness, the compromise? As I have claimed, unconscious expectations often play a role in such situations, as long as the match is close enough not to notice it isn't perfect. A man scraping paint isn't a good match for a cedar, but if the cedar is blowing back and forth in the wind, and it narrows to a kind of neck above a shoulder of longer branches, then if the glance is necessarily brief, a man scraping paint is good enough for some purposes. In the cold, when footing is treacherous, a cedar tree posing as a man is an acceptable approximation. The main quality they share in common is their side-to-side motion, backed up by being roughly similar in size and shape. But the factual tree isn't posing as a man, it's my interpretive faculty that nominates the switch as a plausible match to the structure of the phenomenon. I'm not dealing with real men and real trees, I'm dealing with phenomenal qualities of size, shape, and motion as suggestions calling forth the best fit from my repertoire of plausible categories to apply to that image, rough as it may be, as a first approximation.

But I have to ask—as in the case of the clip-art cat in which I jumped up at hearing a hinge yowl like a feline, where did that cat— where did that man in the guise of a paint scraper come from? Surely a tree would have been more likely to spring to mind than a man scraping paint in mid-winter. I can't give a definitive answer, but my hunch is that it was the particular combination of the three prominent clues—size, shape, and motion—that together made the category "house scraper" a more likely bet than "wind-blown tree." The wind was strong enough that I had never seen a tree bend side-to-side in that way. I believe the unusual combination of sensory qualities in my mind called for an unusual category to best interpret it. The size was right, the shape, the motion. Somewhere in my brain is a loop of nerve cells once activated upon sight of a man scraping paint—and that same loop was activated this time by a cedar of a certain size and shape blowing in a similar manner. There's a subjective kind of logic there, but not any trace of more formal logic such as you might study in school.

Which suggests that each of us applies an experiential kind of logic in interpreting sensory phenomena in cases where we are on our own and haven't any better standard to fall back on. I remember as a fifth and sixth grader interpreting almost anything that was said in school as a dirty joke. Sexual innuendos were rife in school because they were rife in my tender mind.

Child soldiers with real guns are so dangerous because they make very loose connections in interpreting the situations they are in and what is happening around them. The rape of women and girls in Eastern Congo by young soldiers suggests to me that the men responsible are not really men but boys playing at being grown up without knowing how to go about it in a constructive manner. Perhaps their superiors tell them that rape is how real men prove their manhood. Pondering their brutal behavior, that's the interpretation I lay upon their actions. Certainly one of the most prevalent problems in the adult world is men projecting all sorts of fantasies on any female body within view, and as far as I know, the same is true if the viewer is female and the body male—or perhaps female. The logic applied in categorizing bodies of either sex depends on particular loops in individual brains, and the relative maturity, judgment, and experience of the minds entertaining those loops. If cultures fail to shape inexperienced minds in empathic ways—by prohibiting any display of sexual identity in public, for example—then roving bands of repressed youths with guns might well impose their collective sexual ignorance and fantasies on that culture for lack of any better introduction to the ways of the adult world based on caring and respect.

If I am capable of turning two motorcyclists on the road to Bar Harbor into cows (admittedly under conditions of poor visibility), I have good reason for making sure my first impressions are backed by the best information I can get before I act, not after. Acting out of fear or anger, or under the influence of drugs or alcohol, often defies that precautionary principle in interpreting sensory phenomena. A cow is a cow is a cow—except when it's really two motorcyclists viewed through drops on a windshield at dusk—or by someone whose judgment is clouded by powerful emotion, drugs, booze, or inexperience.

The most extended example of self-delusion I have provided is the case of the cartwheel aurora that went on for several hours. I wasn't on drugs or alcohol, but what I saw was a parade of illusions nonetheless. When I woke up next morning and looked up at the sky, I wondered where they could have come from, those precise figures I had mapped onto shimmering streamers of light during the night. Then I remembered Leonardo finding faces in aging stucco walls, and myself looking at inkblots or linoleum floors and seeing not spilled ink, linoleum, or floors, but gorillas, angels, old men, and all manner of distorted beings I could never have imagined on my own. The streamers giving rise to my nighttime illusions were mapped in my mind *as if* they were animals in a circus of bizarre or fetching curiosities. In the aurora, the different forms followed in such quick succession, I don't believe I could have anticipated any one of them. My interpretation was keyed solely to the flow of phenomena, which in itself contained nothing of the rapid-fire categorizations I provided in the instant. I seem to have a file of available categories or interpretations in my head, a clip-art file ready to project on the world. I am equal to any pattern or shape I may stumble across. That way, I see something, at least, not simply an emptiness or a blur. But it's a bit scary, thinking of the possible repertory of categorizations we might draw from in making sense of our everyday experience.

What are the sensory qualities that are likely to elicit so fast a response? In the human visual system, there are over forty maps of such qualities in different parts of the brain. These include individual neural maps as well as maps interacting with one another regarding visual qualities such as motion, color, pattern, texture, direction, edges, size, contrast, coherence, surface, shape, similarity, sequence, shading, gradation, and so on. We are not aware of these mappings, but they tease out the salient features of a phenomenon likely to be worthy of attention. In following the flow of auroral lights overhead, I—the mind that I am—focused on kinetic qualities I associate with living beings, and took from them shapes I could interpret in terms of concepts forming more-or-less good matches to those pulsing waves of light.

I give faces and face-like patterns high priority in my visual mappings, along with animate (self-moving opposed to lifeless) beings. If I can turn a decorative cedar into a house scraper, I am certainly able to turn a celestial lightshow into a parade of creatures including whales, spiders, and dinosaurs. It's largely in the motion, shape, and coherence of episodes in that unending stream of light that I discovered the familiar forms I projected onto the phenomena in my head, interpreting patterns of flowing light as beings I could recognize as having seen before. What I *saw* was the creatures passing in parade; what passed before me was flowing energy streaming upward toward the zenith, then whirling as a gyre in a pool at the top of the celestial dome.

Such is my inner awareness, always doing its best to make sense of the passing scene, always mischievous, always seizing on minimal clues to interpret the present situation as accurately as my personal survival deserves. I can only know the world I live in as my mind reaches for it and presents it to me. Which sometimes I (the mind that I am) get right, sometimes wrong. Often, my own consciousness prefers a reality of its own making to what is more probably a true picture of my current situation. The incident of the cartwheel aurora is a good example of that proclivity in action. Which suggests to me that concocted realities may not be all that rare or unusual. It all depends on the details my mind seizes upon in formulating the patterns it presents as phenomena for me to identify and interpret.

French phenomenologist Maurice Merleau-Ponty traces perception to its roots in *styles* of reaching for awareness. I believe he was exactly right because that idea explains or accounts for a good part of my own conscious life. As a visually-oriented, tree-hugging, free-thinking, New England male nature lover, I reach out for experience in a characteristic way that bears the signature of a personal style I have evolved over the years to give me the kind of world I need to sustain me as I know myself to be. Much else is shoved aside as irrelevant or distracting. My personal style finds it easy to discover animals in the night sky, mistake trash bags for dying crows, and visualize motorcyclists as cows by the side of the road to Bar Harbor.

Actually, I have a repertory of styles, depending on the situation I believe myself to be in. I switch from one style to another as I think is appropriate. Alone with my computer, I swear under my breath when an incomprehensible error message appears, or little balloons pop up making comments or telling me things I don't care to know. In Quaker meeting, I wrestle with spiritual decay in the human world, by which I mean the lack of compassion and respect for strangers and other creatures that share the only inhabited planet we know of in the universe. Monitoring conditions in Taunton Bay, I do the best I can to interpret what's happening as an indicator of the bay's ecological state. With my sons, I reach out with love for them both and concern for their respective well-being. As a maker of PowerPoints, I am on the lookout for the strongest way to get my meaning across. In extreme cases, I may even display multiple personalities. But in my heart of hearts, I am always my one self with a single set of values. It's how that one self responds to different situations that skews my perception one way or another.

I am often aware of how other people's perceptual styles differ from mine. I sometimes credit such people with deviant views, but it may not be their views so much as their habitual styles of consciousness. That is, how they reach for personal experience. Or what they need in order to feel like themselves in a strange situation. Some become clowns, others withdraw or get moody. We cite these as personality traits—as if we each had but one way of being ourselves—but I think they may be more the result of grasping for something familiar in a rapidly changing world. Which affects the style of our reaching out in order to get what we need to feel familiar to ourselves. Once we are no longer children, we still yearn for the comforts we had when others took good (or bad) care of us and we didn't have to fashion reality on our own. It's hard being a responsible adult because what we are responsible *for* is nothing less than managing our view of the world and its affairs. Not managing the world itself as it *is,* but our *view* of such a world. That is, our personal consciousness *of* whatever it is we are concerned with at the time. Taking that world at face value makes it easy to blame others for its sorry condition when, in fact, we are hugely responsible for both the sensory phenomena we entertain in consciousness, and how we interpret them in a meaningful way.

If we follow the dictum "know thyself" as deeply as we can, that realization is where we are apt to end up. Which, besides being based on a sample of one, may be why introspection gets such a bad press. It heads us toward places we are reluctant to go because once there, we have little choice but to take charge of our own mental lives and the worlds we create for ourselves in depicting the situations we believe ourselves to be in.

But in my view, artists do that all the time. They externalize their sensory, phenomenal worlds in order to share them with the rest of us. This is what it's like being me, they say, not once, but again and again to make sure we pay attention and hear what they are trying to make clear. It's the same with politicians, athletes, actors and actresses, talk-show hosts, and other celebrities who take great pains to remain in public view so the world won't turn its back on them and leave them alone. This is for your own good, they say, but it's really for theirs so they know who they are.

As a result, I have smatterings of Mozart, who died 220 years ago, in my brain as if he were alive today, along with aspects of Picasso, Rube Goldberg, Eleanor Roosevelt, Julia Child, Emily Dickinson, and hundreds of other painters, musicians, dancers, poets, writers, and celebrities in my personal pantheon. Edward Weston and Ansel Adams shape a good part of my visual mind, with help from August Sander, youthful Henri Lartigue, Harry Callihan, Edvard Munch, Johannes Vermeer, Franz Kline, and William Turner. These people have shared their consciousness with a great many people, including me. I am grateful for their generosity, no matter how self-serving it might have been. It has made my experience far larger than I could have made it from scratch on my own.

Which is why I seek out the phenomenal consciousness of others as expressed in their works, and welcome their prints, paintings, music, poetry, writings, dances, films, sculptures, and other songs of the heart into my soul. I don't use the word soul very much, but I think of it as the part of me within reach of those working alongside me toward similar goals. When so touched, I have a sense we are speaking the same nonverbal language which is phenomenal in nature. We don't have to bother making meaning through theories and concepts; the sensory patterns are sufficient for building a bond between us—often a one-way, instructional bond from one generation to the next.

Such experiences convince me that sensory phenomena are the heart of conscious life. What they might mean or signify in reference to concepts is largely irrelevant. Beauty of sensory rhythms and relationships is truth enough. Which is why I think of sensory phenomena in terms of aesthetics and patterns, not meaning, reason, logic, or understanding, all referring to larger, more encompassing theories or frameworks beyond themselves. Conceptual matters and mental constructs cannot stand alone without support from such frameworks. Sensory phenomena, on the other hand, are sufficient unto themselves because it is their internal dynamics and relationships that make them coherent, not their external dependencies.

One essential ingredient of beauty is simplicity, by which I mean the ability to detect internal sensory relationships through a lack of intervening complexity. Clarity of those rhythmic and structural relationships is another essential. When different parts or maps in the brain dance to the same music, we feel that vibrant connection as a unifying force making a cohesive whole of those different parts. In chaotic situations, that sense of dynamic integrity is not possible, and we exhaust ourselves seeking order where it is masked or does not exist. Different parts of the brain harmonizing with, reinforcing, or complementing one another lead to a sense of sensory integration that is so rare as to draw attention to itself by providing a pleasing alternative to the experience of all-pervasive confusion and disruption. Our aesthetic sense is a gauge of clarity and harmony present on the phenomenal level of consciousness—the level of immediate sight, sound, taste, touch, and coordinated motion, all of which are as noticeable as they are exciting because so exceptionally rare in everyday experience. Museums, concerts, and scenic landscapes are refuges of phenomenal sanity, places where we remind ourselves what we are capable of producing or enjoying when not caught up in the commotions and agitations of daily life.

Through their respective works, artists do for their audiences what our minds do for each of us individually in shaping and presenting our phenomenal worlds as clearly and emphatically as they can under current conditions. Clarity and appropriate emphasis are keywords of consciousness. My attention is ever on the outlook for what is of concern or interest to me at the time, as well as what is out there that I should know about in order to make an appropriate response. This is why there are two sorts of salience, one determined by my personal concerns, the other by noteworthy events taking place in my present situation, both enabling me to make the best use of my skills and energy in being who I am, where I am. Which are also some of the chief uses of art, and why we selectively engage with it as we do. Whether music, painting, sculpture, dance, opera, ballet, or any other, art goes to the heart of attention and phenomenal awareness; it is by no means an optional frill. Think of how Paleolithic cave paintings have sharpened the sensibilities of all who have seen them, whether in their era or ours. Think of people everywhere making music through fine control of their breathing and hand gestures—giving life to auditory phenomena in their own and their listeners' ears. Speech is based on sharing the uttering and hearing of auditory phenomena. Imagine a culture without dance, how impoverished it would be. The sharing of personal sensory phenomena is the essence of every culture on Earth. Phenomena are the medium by which we are alert one to another. Without them we would not be ourselves or, further, even human.

In my case, my attention brings phenomena to life as a kind of personal question seeking to restore balance to my relation with my world. What do I want to do now? What is there to do? Sometimes beamed toward the inner me, sometimes toward the outer world, but always seeking to improve the relationship between that world and myself. In my childhood, the phrase, "What's for dinner?" was directed at the one who decided what I was to eat. When I used to eat out, "What looks good?" was directed at myself in the process of choosing from a menu. Both are based on my sense of being hungry and wanting to eat. Attention is motivated by wanting to explore my options because the time has come to take next steps toward one goal or another. What do I want? What are my options? . . .

Suddenly a <*loud crash*> comes from outside. "What was that?" Meaning, How does that affect me? What do I do now? Was it thunder, or did some poor soul crash into a light pole? Do I get my raincoat, or call 911? I'm going to check, be right back. Exit. . . . Return. Not to worry. Just a dump truck banging its tailgate. Carry on as before.

Sensory phenomena are given us to help us decide what to do now and how to act to achieve goals in the future. Which is one of the chief uses of consciousness in helping us make ourselves happen in a manner appropriate to situations we may not fully understand. Which is also why we have art—to help us engage the world in a meaningful way. That is, art gives us a world from another's point of view, and our job is to make some kind of response to that view consistent with our values and history of experience. When we go to an art exhibit, a concert, an opera, a ballet—or a sporting event for that matter—we want to be fully ourselves in responding to the phenomena such events are likely to kindle in our minds. The internal, aesthetic structure of sensory figures reveals our basic approach to experience—the kind of order we are looking for. Questions give us a way to sharpen the interrelated details of the phenomena we actually encounter. What's happening now? Who's got the ball? What's the score? Who's on first? What next?

Inquiry is another name for attention. We want to know something that is likely to affect us. We want to see something more clearly, in greater detail, to know what to do and how to act. Which is also what we seek from art in incorporating it into our lives so we

34

can live more effectively in the future. Art is another's answer to our question, "What's exciting to you?" "How do you live?" "What can't you live without?" "What's the most important thing you can do with your time?" In short, "What's the meaning of your life?" Your particular life, here and now. Art shows us what is phenomenally (i.e., aesthetically) possible; what we do with it is for each of us to decide.

Incident 1 in the preceding chapter shows how dangerous it can be to take phenomena for granted. Crossing Brattle Square, I got hit by a bicyclist going the wrong way against traffic, which put me sprawled in the path of a delivery truck. My *not* looking for phenomena precluded my entertaining them in consciousness, leaving me vulnerable to a mishap I could not predict or even conceive. That might have been the end of this book, right there as a bloody splotch in Brattle Square.

A good portion of my concern with sensory phenomena is about detecting change in my environment (trucks moving in my direction, for instance), as well as changing phenomena resulting from movements I make while walking or turning my head. These two sorts of changes have different signatures in consciousness because in observing one I hold myself still (as in a seat at school or in a theater) and in the other I must subtract effects due to my own movement from the resulting sensory patterns in order to navigate through the world and be clear about what I see. I think of these two kinds of phenomenal changes as *it*-changes and *self*-changes. An it-change, for instance, would be the apparent round of the sun through the sky from east to west in about twenty-four hours. A self-change would be my walking through woods while avoiding branches and roots. Calibrating it-changes in seconds, minutes, hours, days, and years, they become measureable against a standard of *time*. Calibrating self-changes in inches, feet, yards, and miles, they become measurable against a standard of *space*. To go further, our concept of time is based on it-changes set as standard measures of duration; our concept of space is based on self-changes set as standard measures of our range of motions (it is no accident that our English system of measurement is based on dimensions of monarchal body parts). The import being that our two most fundamental systems of measurement are based on calibrated (that is, finely categorized) phenomenal changes in human consciousness. Time and space do not exist in the universe apart from human consciousness. They are our mental schemes projected outward for the purpose of calibrating the universe in terms meaningful to humans, and humans alone. Categorizing it-changes in convenient yet fictional terms, we project our minds outward, interpreting our planet and its surroundings in terms of the sun's apparent motion through the heavens as a reflection of Earth's daily rotation about its fictional axis, taming the universe to our phenomenal point of view. Doing the same for self-changes, we calibrate the universe in terms of the length of a long-dead king's foot, or the standard meter measured as the distance light travels in a vacuum in $1/299,792,458^{th}$ of a second. When humans become extinct, space and time will disappear from the universe, leaving uncalibrated change, which will continue as it always has, untouched by our anthropomorphic systems of measurement. Change will continue without end, but not relative change, measured change, calibrated change. There will be no phenomenal sense of time and distance. No more mapping of concepts onto sensory patterns.

One thing phenomena are *not* is sensations relayed by our senses from the external environment. Highly crafted by our neural apparatus, phenomena are largely our doing through selection from among the myriad signals impinging on us at any one time, many others being inhibited entirely, those remaining being heightened in contrast, clarity, and emphasis, all largely accomplished without our realizing we are doing any such thing. Beyond all awareness, we humans adjust our personal consciousness to suit ourselves, each according to his or her inclinations concerning how best to achieve phenomena which measure up to personal expectations. When we talk with one another, each speaks from a different universe of experience that cannot be translated with exactness into any other mind. We use the same words to mean different things, and different words to mean similar things. Roughly, we speak a common language on comparable occasions, while just beneath the surface of consciousness we inhabit unique mental worlds. Which is why every single one of us is worth knowing as a distinct individual in a universe of individuals, while lumping us together in great generalities (nations, tribes, corporations) does an injustice to every member of the group.

We idly go on believing we live in the real world, a world we can smell, feel, see, hear, taste. We're kidding ourselves. The whole of existence is in our personal experience, not any outer world. Life is an inside job, beginning with attention and sensory phenomena. Coming out of a movie, we often have a sense of seeing the world for the first time. Everything is new, fresh, clear, and really strange. Those bricks! That car driving past—look at those receding tail-lights! That line of parking meters! Movie vision—necessary to making sense of transitory images on a screen—takes over our seeing for a time, but quickly wears off. Our conventional outlook reasserts itself and everything returns to "normal." But conventions are conventions, not reality. Reality begins with phenomena—the sharper, the more seemingly real.

To end this brief discussion of phenomena, I recognize that I still may not have made myself clear, so will mention another way we deal with them on a cultural level. The many field guides we use to aid us in identifying birds, butterflies, seashells, minerals, trees, and so forth serve as a readily accessible index to some of the common species we are apt to entertain in the course of our experience. As I see them, these are more indices of phenomena in consciousness than of species in the field. It is our individual awareness that is being calibrated through study of such guides, not the species themselves. The guides show us what to look for in distinguishing one type from another so we can learn to recognize them on sight (or sound in the case of bird calls).

If you have a shelf of such guides in your home or office, I congratulate you for taking pains to recognize the subtle differences in phenomena that are important to you. Encouraging students to make such distinctions is one of the chief goals of an education that will serve and expand throughout life. The job of actually using these guides falls to each student because the book itself is unable to import the distinguishing marks it illustrates directly into a human mind. That you must do for yourself through practice, trial, error, and repeated trips into the field. I have spent much of my adult life leafing through field guides in order to become more discerning in recognizing and learning the habits of species I encounter in daily life because they share my native haunts and I am apt to meet them in making my daily rounds. Here is a description I wrote of one such encounter:

> Picture the hulking naturalist on an Acadian mountain ridge, hunkered down, peering back and forth through bifocals between wildflower guide and puzzling bloom on its midget stem, unable to describe what he thinks he sees in terms the

guide will accept, guide holding back the sought-after name until the description is more precise, blackflies looking on at first, then mobbing, then going in for the kill, the naturalist hitting back between swings of attention between book and bloom, bloom and book, blackflies persisting, book resisting, bloom bobbing in the wind, naturalist sticking it out for twenty minutes, then, no wiser than before, fleeing for his life (*ACA-DIA: The Soul of a National Park,* p. 241).

This example depicts my effort to couple a given phenomenal specimen to the category in which it properly belongs so I can recognize it by name in future, connect it to similar blooms in the same genus or family, and distinguish it from those that are different. In this chapter I have largely dealt with sensory phenomena on their own. In the next chapter I will shift my attention to the process of interpreting phenomena in terms of the specific characteristics they exhibit in order to group them with similar phenomena as inhabitants of a mental category having a name and a conceptual identity over and above exhibiting a particular sensory appearance. O

CHAPTER 3

INTERPRETATION

The incidents I relate in Chapter 1 unfold under the influence of a sensory misunderstanding or misapprehension of one sort or another. The plotline runs from initial error to eventual correction, replaying one of the basic dramas of human existence. In Chapter 2, I look at the sensory underpinnings of those incidents, indicating that the misjudgment in each case is clearly my own. In this chapter I deal with the fundamental process by which I map categories (classes of abstract concepts) onto sensory phenomena, allowing me to interpret them (rightly or wrongly) from a particular point of view.

I know this is an important issue because English has so many heavyweight words to use in describing and discussing it: categorization, recognition, identification, interpretation, abstraction, construal, intentionality, among others. Where Germans cite the proverb, "A well-loved child has many names," in this case I say, "There are many well-traveled paths to the heart of awareness." No facet of mind is more worthy of study than how people map what they know onto what they perceive, and vice versa. We seldom witness ourselves engaged in that reciprocal process, and it all happens so fast—in milliseconds—that we're done before we know we're doing it. I try to open the process to personal view through the introspective approach I rely on in narrating those eighteen incidents in which I catch myself in the act of making a perceptual error.

I think Ludwig Wittgenstein got it right when he identified "the echo of a thought in sight" when dealing with the interpretation of visual illusions. Sometimes more a resounding boom than an echo. Thinking and seeing (hearing, etc.) are different but interconnected forms of mental activity. This is where mapping comes in, referring signals in one mental domain to those in another, and back again in an ongoing exchange determining the content of consciousness. I am not directly aware of the mapping process itself; what I (like Wittgenstein) discover through introspection is the interaction between thinking or knowing and the phenomenal appearance of whatever it is I am consciously paying attention to.

Which makes me ask, what do I mean by "thinking"? I do not mean muttering to myself in formal language. When I lived alone on an island in Maine, I frequently talked to myself—and found whatever I sought to vocalize was already over and done with before I parted my lips. I recognized kernels of preverbal thought that I understood without having to translate into speech. I wondered if those kernels were language-free, so that in learning a language, what we learn is to turn such thought kernels or preconscious nuggets into sounds according to the local recipe for transforming situations into words. No, thinking is something other, even though I find myself rehearsing the process of translation into language, the kernels or nuggets of thought are independent of syntax as well as fine motor control of tongue, lips, and jaw, backed by coordinated releases of breath. Thinking precedes all that. Thinking, I think, is preverbal.

When I speak of intuition, I think *that* is the level my meaningful mental nuggets are on. They are preconscious in the sense of being forerunners of awareness. I *feel* them more than hear or say them, as I *feel* conceptual echoes in concrete sensory patterns. The nuggets are independent of any particular medium of expression. I can't go any deeper than that without developing hypotheses concerning how thoughts are generated in the brain, which is far beyond my introspective capabilities. But I will tentatively update Wittgenstein by proposing that facets of consciousness communicate with one another by trading signals back and forth between them in establishing a situation within which linguistic thought, formal speech, and other acts can arise through subsequent motor effort. I would say there is an echo of that neural traffic in sight and other sensory phenomena, however it may originate. That may not stand to reason, but it stands to my personal intuition and feeling.

I think, too, that aesthetics and coherence are qualities originating at that deeper level than I can reach through introspection. I can sense they are there, but I can't experience them clearly. It is on that level of consciousness, I suggest, that categorization arises, and misidentifications take place. When I feel I am onto something important, the feeling arises at that same level—as a kind of inkling of encouragement foreshadowing increasing clarity ahead if I only keep going. Do I know what I am talking about? Clearly not. Do I feel what I am talking about? Yes, clearly. Just as Michael Faraday could "see" lines of magnetic force passing through the air, I visualize a strong connective field in my mind between sensory phenomena and the repertory of concepts or interpretations eager to trade with them in coming to agreement on what sorts of categories best represent a particular set of sensory qualities.

If I didn't visualize such shadowy connections, I wouldn't be writing this book. The question is, esteemed reader, do you find and recognize them in yourself? When you say, "that reminds me of something," do you have a feeling for how having one thing in mind can suggest another thing you were not thinking of before? When you hear "San Francisco," does that direct your attention to things that were not said? When asked to associate with "dog," "pizza," or "Baghdad," what comes to mind? Do you appreciate the connections by which they did, in fact, appear? And so on. I am trying to encourage you to undertake an informal program of introspection as we go through these pages together. I want you to get to know yourself on the inside as well as you do by looking in the mirror in order to form an internal image of your appearance. People on the street glance in store windows all the time to review their reflections as they pass by, perhaps straightening a skirt or patting their hair as a result. I think we should perform similar acts of grooming as we stroll through our minds—to make our thoughts presentable to ourselves, so we have a better sense of the shades and echoes they convey and where they might come from. Knowing ourselves better in this way could make us more presentable to ourselves and to others, which would be a public service provided by personal introspection.

The issue is, how do concepts in memory become available to sensory phenomena, and the other way around, how are sensory phenomena suggested by concepts as discrete aspects of memory? How, for example, do streaming trails of pale green light in a midnight cartwheel display of aurora borealis (the streamers serving as metaphorical spokes in a great wheel centered on the zenith) suggest a parade of animated forms as resounding echoes courtesy of my prior experience? I think it was the relative luminosity and flowing motion of those streamers of light that elicited a rapid stream of signals from memory into my ongoing awareness. That much I am pretty sure of, though I don't know how it could actually happen.

In the incident of motorcyclists being seen as cows, that conceptual interpretation was prompted by the black-and-white coloration of their raingear, as well as the hurried flicking motion of one of their arms in donning the jacket that I subjectively recognized as the flicking of a tail. In both incidents (bikers and aurora) motion and shading were qualities common to both the sensory and interpretive aspects of each experience as I witnessed it. The same is true of my mistaking a stranger for my friend Fred. He looked (from the back) like Fred, and he moved as I remember Fred moving. And the same is true of the black trash bag I cast as a dying crow. Blackness is common to both, and the wind-driven fluttering of the bag looked to me like a wing rising and falling. In not seeing the snowcapped Rockies when they were in full view, again, it was whiteness and (lack of) motion that confused me. And it was in the swaying "hip" motion of the cedar that I thought I recognized a man scraping paint. My confounding a turtle shell for a human skull was sponsored by their both being domed with prominent sutures where different bones joined together. I had never thought of a turtle shell being buried in earth, whereas my lifelong fascination with archaeology brought the possibility of unearthing a skull to the fore. In deleting the quarry photos before I saved them, it was my going through them shot by shot *before* I saved them—something I had never done in six years—that led me unconsciously to think I had already saved them out of habit when (this one time) I hadn't that threw me off. The echo of a procedural habit in sight. In the incident of the visiting sex educator keeping her eyes fixed on me, yes, as I later learned, her son and I matched in being thin and bearded, so I must have prompted a visual echo of her son in her eyes, but I didn't know that at the time. And in triggering the clip-art cat, the squeaking hinge served as the echo of a great many cats I had heard yowling in my days as a cat owner.

Many echoes, indeed. But the most telling instance of all is one I haven't mentioned since introducing it—the tale of the song at the sink. The first night, while washing dishes, the song played on the radio as an auditory phenomenon. The second night, with the radio off, the song played in my head (memory) in the same setting. The third night, again the same setting, I knew there had been a song, but I couldn't remember what it was. I had lost both the memory and the sensory melody. I think now it was the setting at the kitchen sink and the routine of washing dishes—the situation itself—that had cued the song from memory as an echo so clear I could hum along with it. And even now many years later, I feel a yearning for that lost song, even though I retain no idea what it was. Yet the yearning persists. These undercurrents of feeling and fading echoes are like thought kernels which engender speech. The essence is in the kernel itself; the speech act (when I am talking to myself) comes invariably as an anticlimax. I feel hollow putting those words out there to hang in the air when I knew what I was going to say before opening my mouth.

Thought kernels, inner shades and echoes, undercurrents, yearnings: these are the stuff from which category errors are made. This is the shimmering substratum where I live my life—inside, not in any mysterious "outside" world. Categorization, recognition, identification, and interpretation are inside jobs. The entire auroral display, for as long as I witnessed it, was a ringing of changes in my head, not in the sky where I was free to attend it or not. I was paying attention, close attention, so the whole sequence was playing in my mind, like an echo, like a song. I gave myself to the event for over two hours, dedicating my bodily energy and attention to following its changes. To living those changes. I was totally immersed and engaged. That event was what was playing in my head at the time, activating a specific set of nerve signals, inhibiting others. Which I engaged as one of the most compelling experiences of my life.

Aristotle and Immanuel Kant are two of the great minds who have shaped the discussion of categorization over the millennia. Aristotle pictured categories as depicting real differences in the world; Kant saw those differences as residing in the mind itself prior to perceptual experience. I side with Kant in viewing perceived similarities and differences as judgments on phenomena as they exist in individual minds, whereas Aristotle saw (yes, categorized) them as universal assertions of fundamental modes of being in the world. Both Aristotle and Kant were interested in categorization as a universal process, so paid slight attention to the vagaries of individual minds—which is precisely what intrigues me about how we each interpret phenomena for ourselves in the heat of making sense of phenomena as we live them under the particular conditions which pertain at that moment. I believe reaching for and grasping sensory experience is not subject to universal laws or principles, but is a process each of us finesses in her own way according to her personal repertory of styles for making meaning of events as she sees them. Instead of laws of perception, I find myself (through introspection) doing the best I can to make sense of phenomena as they emerge in awareness. It is that *emergent awareness* I am interested in because that is the forefront of consciousness where I personally invent the world I live in, not where such a world is handed to me by some external agent apart from my own neural apparatus. The world I live in is *my* doing, not the world's, not some mediating agent's.

Which is why, much as a dog worries its bone, I worry such incidents as I provide in Chapter 1. I have gotten to a point in my worrying of events as I interpret them that allows me to feel some of the underlying pressures driving me to interpret or categorize a phenomenon one way or another. It feels like intuition, I say, which means it is a function of my preconscious mind harking to the echoes resounding through it in a particular situation as I am able to construe or construct it. Construction is a very active process. It is what I am able *to make of* a sensory pattern in the situation governing my attention at the time. Interpretation is largely a matter of immersing myself in a situation and seeing what comes from—what I make of—that experience of immersing and seeing and making. Is that pattern best seen as a crow or a trash bag? Is this a human skull or possibly a turtle? When turtle is suggested to me, I immediately know it is right, though it never occurred to me on my own. I am my own worst categorizer when I "know" beforehand I am right. Rather, interpretations are possibilities or probabilities, not certainties, for they can always be taken differently—depending on what I make of the situation, which is always subject to change. Absolutes? Universals? True beliefs? Ultimate truths? Higher laws? They may appear as such, but as Italian playwright Luigi Pierendello reminds us, "It is true if you think so." Meaning that truth is in the mind of the observer as an operational truth under the influence of a specific situation as construed at the moment by one particular individual with a background of more-or-less relevant experience.

How unnerving is that—to live in an ambiguous or meaninless world until we characterize it one way or another for ourselves? Instead, we stick to our polarized views, certain we are right, just, true, with all virtue on our side. Today (the day I am writing these words) happens to be midterm Election Day, November 2, 2010, the day the people authorized so many Tea Party candidates to head for Congress. Opinions are flying like brickbats around my head, each narrower and more preposterous than the other. The governor-to-be of Maine wants to open classrooms to creationism, so-called. I've had voices barking at me out of the phone for a week now, telling me how I should vote, who's a scumbag, who is the true savior of the world. The recorded voice of Bill Clinton called this morning, followed by a governor from out-of-state. How nice of them to take an interest in how I vote. Except that isn't how my mind works. If I don't grapple with the forces acting inside me and, instead, let such voices do my work for me, what is the point of my being conscious? Why bother? If I don't take the trouble to make my own judgments and interpretations, I might as well not exist. What is the point of consciousness? Of having a mind of my own? Of living my own life? No, I say individuality is the greatest gift on Earth, the gift of being myself and no other. If I am not conscious for myself, who, then, am I being conscious *for?* I become a zombie, a pawn of someone else's will. No thank you, where's the challenge and adventure in that?

Categorization is the stuff of mental life. The responsibility of deciding what kind of world I live in is mine alone, as is the choice of how I want to conduct myself as one seeker among seven billion others, accompanied by trillions of fellow nonhuman creatures, each on a meaningful track of its own. I wouldn't have it any other way. As unique individuals, each of us has value to all others. As clones, we are worthless. Worse than worthless—like so many disposable diapers, we trash the landscape when we could be contributing to the mutually constructive engagement of all peoples on Earth. Or at least take care how we interpret events in order to make the best of them through personal actions as unique contributions to the ongoing situation that is daily life as we know it and live it.

I get like this on Election Day when I see the future of the world hanging in the balance within people's minds. So much rides on today's vote—nothing less than getting the best candidates into office to govern on our common behalf. If I let others decide for me, I am voting for *them,* not myself. If I am not my own man, whose man am I? That's a very scary question because it goes to the heart of individual consciousness. Do I belong to my culture, my family group, my political party, my social class, my education class, my occupation class? How do I categorize myself and my personal actions? What if I let myself be influenced by the wrong sort of people, people I don't even know so I can't be sure who they are or whether they're being genuine or not? Maybe they're using me for their own purposes and not telling me. Then I am committing my life to serving *their* agenda. What's in that for me? Their approval, their money, their gratitude? Talk about selling your soul!

The point is, categorization matters. Interpretation of any life situation matters. Being true to my own experience, doubt, and intuition matters. Making good decisions on my own, then living with the consequences until I die—these really matter. That's who I am, the guy who lives that way, and dies that way. The guy who knows no other way but to learn from personal experience. Let my gravestone declare, "He lived as he was, his own man." If that's not the case, who then, or what exactly, will be buried under my stone? A bone from some powerful wizard in place of my zombie body? Some sacred relic from one of the corporate or entrepreneurial elite? In a free-enterprise system, we live surrounded by others eager to commandeer our minds. Countering any claim they might make to my personal consciousness, I do believe I will go it alone, my mind, such as it is, staunchly intact.

Dealing with categorization in this chapter, I do not mean to be a chameleon, switching between terms, categorization to interpretation to identification to recognition. A more suitable image would be a juggler trying to keep all his Indian clubs whirling at once, fearing that dropping one would lead to dropping them all. I do think there is one underlying process that goes by many names. If you page through your dictionary from one to the others, you will frequently find the same key terms and phrases shared among them.

CATEGORIZATION: Sorting into categories; classification.
IDENTIFICATION: Recognizing features defining a category.
INTERPRETATION: Explaining the meaning of; construing.
RECOGNITION: Identifying as having been perceived before.

All share in common the intending of a mental object from a particular point of view, or the grasping of one mental facet by another. It is seldom made clear that the two mental aspects involved are of different orders of specificity or generality, concreteness or abstraction, more commonly met with in matters involving induction (from concrete instance to abstract concept or principle) or deduction (from abstract principle to concrete instance). Normally, discourse is kept pure by confining it to "finite provinces of meaning" or "fortresses of belief." When members of different domains of orthodox mental habits and beliefs confer across the distance between them, they run the risk of cross-pollination, resulting in hybrid or poorly defined terms and concepts. Philosophy, psychology, and neuroscience frequently consider aspects of mental life from different perspectives, sometimes leading to confusion between terms based on quite different sets of assumptions.

When a discussion has continued for over two thousand years from Aristotle's day to ours, terms tend to persist because of their history of acceptance by being written down in the great collective work dealing with human thought and ideas through the ages. Specific assumptions are more apt to keep abreast of modern research as new generations of investigators are educated, leaving some key terms stranded in antiquity without adequate support in modern terminology. Which I believe to be true in the case of *perceptual categorization.* Categorization persists as a basic element in discussions of key mental processes. Gerald M. Edelman, for instance, now visualizes categorization in terms of *pattern recognition,* a means of "carving up" sensory input into objects of significance to a species (*Second Nature,* 2006, p. 20). My interest in the process of categorization has been heightened by Edelman's many references to the topic, but I think it goes beyond pattern recognition in that I see the process as not only entering the scene *after* patterns are established, but also playing a role in shaping those patterns to suit the specific species and individual member concerned. As I see it, categorization assists consciousness in plucking recognizable phenomena from thin air by seeking patterns already familiar from prior experience, the "carving up" representing a stylistic predilection for patterns recognizable as having been not only seen before, but found meaningful or useful in some way.

By skewing or shaping the formation of sensory phenomena through expectancy cast onto the world of potential sensory patterns, categorization becomes a cooperative project between an individual and his environment. Candidates for survival become ever more fit as they become increasingly competent in shaping their perceptual and behavioral worlds through conscious activity. Fitness, that is, is not strictly a matter of passively being acted upon, for, indeed, the canniness of individuals reflected in their skills and actions affects the outcome of their efforts. I vote for including learning through experience as an aspect of survivability and heightened reproductive success. Survival is not something done to us through selection, but part of a process in which we engage as active participants because we have a stake in the results.

When I was in Cub Scouts, I wanted to enter one of my chickens in a contest to determine who in my den had the most unusual pet.

Before the event, I was wrestling with my big brother. At one point he perched on top of me and banged my head against the floor, knocking me out. When I came to, looking down at my shirtfront and neckerchief, I asked, "What am I doing in this uniform?" Stunned, I did not make a very good candidate for survival. Slowly, I came to. I returned to my senses, or they to me, and I began to grasp my "predicament," which stems from Latin *praedicamentum,* translation of Greek *kategoria,* meaning to assert or predicate—that is, to categorize. The moral of my story being that when not fully conscious, we are unable to categorize such familiar phenomena as our own appearance, so are unlikely to survive. Accurate categorization is essential to mental life; without it we are not long for this world.

Forty years ago, a friend quoted Gloucester poet Charles Olson to me as having said, "The landscape is what you see from where you are." That made immediate sense to me because I took "where you are" to indicate internal perspectivity—being situated in one's personal outlook. That, I believe, is where words and categories arise, in that sense of being personally situated in relation to the geography of one's mind. The concept of mapping is relevant to that geography in explaining where one is coming from in visualizing her landscape of sensory phenomena. In making sense of a situation, we map where we are in mental space onto the view we see from there. And perform the same operation in reverse, revealing where we are situated in order to visualize the landscape that we perceive.

Seeing the procession of auroral shapes in terms of recognizable features of my personal landscape tells me I am situated in my head as I look upon that phenomenal display. My reality is largely subjective. As it is in viewing a blowing trash bag as a crow, or hearing a squeaky hinge as a yowling cat. The crow-ness and cat-ness of those phenomena helped me make sense of my situation as meaningful in particular ways. My style of approach to the landscape is that of a tree-hugging, bleeding-heart naturalist for whom "nature" is the name of the real world. That's where I was coming from in order to entertain any landscape at all. Categorizing those streaming shapes and sounds, I did so according to my personal style of reaching out to the phenomena in my head in order to classify them as meaningfully as I could. In those shaded and echoing depths, I am the one who reaches for phenomena in that way to make them sensible to me. Meaning exists on that level of consciousness, and dictates any landscape which is to emerge as viewed from that place in the universe where I am located at the time. My coordinates in mental space grant me the privilege of seeing anything at all.

In seeing a figure in front of me on Fifth Avenue as presenting a rear view of Fred, I have to admit *wanting* to see Fred because I would find him meaningful in that place. He was my best friend in high school in Seattle, and having moved across the country, I missed seeing him. I unwittingly stepped into the path of a cyclist in Brattle Square because I wanted to enter the bookstore on the other side of the street. I stepped because I was motivated. I didn't look to my right because I was impatient to cross the street. Lives hinge on such homely shadows flickering in the caves of our minds. To see something meaningful, we actively choose from among those shadows, emphasizing one, ignoring the rest, sharpening attention, and dulling alternative views at the same time. To categorize sensory patterns is to put the stamp of personal attention on the world so we are sure to see what we want to see, to hear what we want to hear. I wanted to see Fred amid a teeming horde of strangers, not anyone else. I focused on him and let go of the rest—hundreds of non-Freds who didn't measure up to my motivated search criteria. Flit, I simply eliminated them from awareness so they wouldn't interfere with my pursuit of Fred.

Our lives are not destined in advance. We make them happen to suit our yearnings, proclivities, appetites, and motivating circumstances. Categorization is our tool for getting what we want. This and not that. We make choices in a few milliseconds, changing everything that follows—forever. The future is contained in this instant, and then this, and then this. We make ourselves happen through a succession of micro decisions we don't realize we are making, even though they change every other decision after that. I still remember seeing that trash bag as a crow, that cedar as a paint-scraping human, those auroral lights as a meaningful procession of familiar creatures. In my own way, I bring the landscape to life, looking for things I am afraid of, uncomfortable with, angry at, hungry for, or in love with, and so on. At the same time, I kill off alternative versions of that same landscape by shunning what I don't want to entertain as a phenomenon in consciousness. It is my move, now and forever. I am the decider, the director of my attention, to this, this, and this—but not that.

My situation is what I make of it. It is what I see-hear-smell-taste-touch-imagine-recall from where I am. Which is here at the helm of my attention, heading now this way, now that. Where are all those others on this Election Day, in what corner of their deepest minds? What landscape does their lust to see clearly drive them to portray? How do they choose to vote on this day of days? How do they categorize their situations in ways meaningful in the context of their personal life histories? Who are these voters—people looking from perspectives other than my own, leading other lives, making other choices, serving appetites I can only imagine?

Not privy to their minds, I can account only for myself. My business is to make my actions fit my mental coordinates as appropriately as I can. All the while knowing that others do the same from different mental perspectives in different mental situations for motives I cannot fathom. I am out for myself. They are out for themselves. Together, we people the Earth. Knowing that, who considers that larger whole in electing what life to lead? In asking, Who am I? Where am I? Why am I here? How can I best respond to this situation?

Everything depends on how we interpret the shades and echoes darting through the deepest corridors of our minds. It comes down to what we make of intuited phenomena flickering within us. By a momentary flash here and there, conscious life is illuminated in such instants. Introspection reveals how quickly they come, and then disappear, perhaps to recur, but more likely not. They don't stick around long enough for us to remember. To be fully ourselves, we must grasp each moment as it offers itself to us. That's what it means to be alive—to be alive to ourselves. To pay full attention to the only mind in the universe we can apprehend in its fleetness and fullness.

Categorizations are essays at approximating the import of sensory phenomena. The first criterion is to fix in our minds what matters most in our current situation. That is, to make something of this instant, and then this, and this. Not just *some* thing but the *essential* thing that makes all the difference. Which is why we use metaphors to highlight that quality of making a difference by singling out an unconventional quality in the moment for particular emphasis. Metaphors fairly cry, "This is what I make of it!" Meaning, how I see, construe, interpret, or categorize it. Recognition has a declarative function regarding the identity of the perceiver. I am one who views it this way; this is my intellectual property. Originality declares the personhood of the actor. Which matters a great deal in an age when persons are submerged (and ignored) in a flood of average tastes, interests, and expectations. In a crowd or mass audience, we all become anonymous residents-consumers-customers, when in each of our minds, particular in every detail, we are anything but.

To ourselves, we are all on one mission: to get ahead. That is, to make it through till tomorrow, and the day after that. We often distill that drive down to getting a paycheck enabling us to pay the bills, but what we're after is a long, productive, engaging, and happy life. Which governs how we categorize phenomena as helping or hindering us in that regard. We earn our categorizations and interpretations through past experiences, but we use them to project ourselves into the world of tomorrow in fitting style.

In my case, the only one I am intimately acquainted with, I consciously look ahead in trying to picture how my now situation will play out. I want to plan what to do next, and then next after that. That is, how to make myself happen in a manner appropriate to my situation as it might evolve into a different situation altogether. If I live solely in the moment, I might not make it to the moment after that. My categorizations are fueled by expectancies informed by the past, but which also look ahead toward the goals I've set myself for hoisting myself into the future.

Think of the long-term projects we commit ourselves to. Going to school. Getting a job. Getting married. Having a baby. Developing a career. Building or buying a house. Taking a trip or vacation. Making a movie, writing a book. Going on a diet. Giving up smoking, drugs, or alcohol. Getting out of debt. Learning tai chi, Spanish, to play the guitar. The mission of consciousness is to enable us to do these things—to learn through concentrated effort to be ourselves as we imagine ourselves being in the future on the basis of what we know and do now. And then to revise the plan as we move through uncharted regions ahead.

As we each reinvent ourselves over and over again, we categorize from the past into the future in an effort to make ourselves happen in a world where advancement is possible. We have trouble picturing ourselves dead or dying because that goes against our project of getting ahead. We will do almost anything to avoid coming to a full stop. We even invent a fictional category labeled "afterlife" to imagine ourselves in so we can pretend we don't really have to face the inevitable. There is no requirement that categories must be fitting, true, or real. We can be less than honest with ourselves by fitting novel phenomena never encountered before to the same old categories of yesteryear, becoming hardened ideologues leading fictional lives through fictional words and habitual actions. The world we make for ourselves is up to us. There is no way for consciousness to recognize one category as being true and another false.

I always picture the project I am currently working on as the best and most important use of my time. I leap through life from project to project, categorizing as I go, interpreting what happens in terms of what I set out to do, making myself happen as I fashion a fabulous (storied) world for myself, pulling myself ahead by pure will-power and imagination, construing events in light of situations I interpret from my singular point of view. That way, I remain immortal till I die an inevitably inconvenient death, which I will never recognize because it never enters my mind as a viable category. I cannot picture myself dead. That goes against the law of categorization, which is to use consciousness as a tool for turning past into future. When sick, I've always recovered. I haven't been dead yet, so how can I ever apply such a category to my image of myself?

Categories, that is, exist not in "real" time, but in mental time. Phenomena come and go, but categories persist in living memory— as long as it lasts. For a lifetime, we are more-or-less conscious, relying on categories for sorting segments of flowing experience into memorable and retrievable units, creating a sense of what's happening, what has happened, what is likely to happen in the future. In a very real sense, life progresses on two tracks at once, the sensory track bearing a succession of phenomena, and the categorical track enabling us to construe experience in terms of personal understanding, creating a third track of felt experience, the three together allowing a fourth track of meaningful action—all four pointing to a common terminal at their intersection with the horizon.

Switching metaphors from tracks to roles, just as actors play roles scripted by others, categories serve as roles for phenomena to play in the drama of making ourselves happen in the world. Each category is a miniature script interpreting the nature and import of a class of phenomena in one particular human life. The phenomena may be unique, grouped by identifying similarities, or even keyed to a distinctive feature or quality, but the category of all categories allows for a fit to each one in giving phenomena roles to play in individual consciousness and endeavors. Just as actors declaim, categories are a class of assertions, which is what *kategoria* means in Greek. While categories speak to us through the labels by which we know them, pure phenomena remain mute, simply being in the now. Categories endow those phenomena with meaning in reference to what we have learned and experienced before. Extrapolating on the basis of our assumptions and expectations, interpreted phenomena aim us toward our personal version of a possible or even probable future.

All of the above events occur—out of all locales in the universe—in our particular minds, and only there. Each of us being unique, the phenomena we recognize as meaningful in familiar ways are unique, the situations we picture ourselves in are unique, and the resulting courses of actions we plan and carry out are distinctively our own. If that sounds farfetched, I recommend you take up reading obituaries in the local newspaper. You quickly learn to tell the honest ones from the canned or ideological ones by the level of detail accounted for, and the metaphors resorted to in glossing over unmentioned particulars.

Better yet, consult your own stream of awareness. Sample the phenomena you actually reach for—the music you listen to, the sporting events you watch on TV, the books you read, the meals you eat. Don't neglect the moments your attention is on events that simply stream through your mind as if from nowhere; those moments come to you courtesy of the workings of your own mind. Pay close attention to them. Watch yourself watching them. They have much to tell you about how you occupy yourself and the inner world you actually live in. Too, check on how you categorize the results of your reaching for sensory experience. How you make the results meaningful in the context of your daily existence. Regard that context itself in terms of the situations you encounter and within which you act in making your way through the events of each day. Then track what you do in response to this flow of inner life at each moment as seen through your own eyes, heard with your own ears, felt by your own body. Then write the obituary of any given day of your life, telling what happened as you lived it moment by moment.

There you have it, a day in the life. The greatest adventure ever told because it's *your* adventure, a fragment of your life as actually lived. Now you have a sense of what it's like for me to be writing this book. Of trying to keep track of the thought kernels flooding my mind at every instant like a herd of fireflies winking on and off in the middle distance. If I capture even one or two it's a good day. Most are gone by the time I cup my hands in trying to catch them. Writing those fragments down is another matter—actually putting them into words, trying to be true to the original thought as it came to me, then quickly disappeared. To be followed by another, and another.

I gave up watching TV in 1986 because it so distracted me from the fireflies in my head. I am a nature lover, and I intend to spend my limited bodily energy learning about life in the wild, then telling the story. I have come to the conclusion that all good in my life flows from nature and the wild, wild Earth. TV flows from other minds for the purpose of directing my attention to commercials for goods and services others want me to buy, but I don't need and I don't want. Imagine the TV ads aimed at the American electorate in this midterm election, deliberately meant to interfere with how people cast their votes. Imagine the flow of money to pay for those ads. Imagine the minds behind the money behind the ads, paying to get us to put *their* thoughts in place of our own, to feed their desires. For what reason? To increase their influence in the governance of our states and nation, to increase their profits from that altered governance. A vote bought by such ads is a vote for the mind controllers, those greedy enough to try and stop me from thinking for myself and following my own inner sense of direction. There's a lot of that around these days, people trying to control the concerns others have in the twenty-first century, making it *their* century through purchase of the personal activities of the rest of us.

First we categorize the candidates for office by seeing them in a certain light, then we vote for the category—not the man or woman—who most appeals to us. If we surrender our vote to those who dictate how we categorize each candidate, all I can say is we get the government we deserve, but not the one best representing our personal interests—even though we may not see through the screen of words and images in time to realize the truth—and so vote against ourselves.

This is why I encourage everyone to undertake a campaign of introspection in self-defense. Introspection is a form of self-reflection, of taking yourself to be a worthy subject of study. It may be that no one ever suggested such an idea to you, telling you, instead, to do as you're told. But self-discovery is the essential basis of democracy, if there is to be any such thing in the universe. If no one will teach you to know yourself, how can you do it? For yourself, by yourself, that's how you do it. Indeed, there is no other way. There are no books, no videos, no courses revealing the secrets of self-study. You have to discover them for yourself, on your own, by committing yourself to learning everything you can about the mental processes—the seeing, the interpreting, the feeling, the understand-ing—behind your actions. The alternative is for you to give yourself away to the charmers who surround you, enticing you to do the right thing by surrendering yourself—mind and body—to them to use for their purposes.

Yes, this is a different kind of book, a book written by *me* with *you* in my mind. Not so I can control you, but so you can take charge of yourself and the life you choose to lead. I have no idea what a course of self-discovery will reveal to you, other than that it will be different from what I find in myself. Which is precisely the point. You are you; I am I. Both worthy human beings on a certain planet in a given era. Both with minds of our own, which others view as commodities to be bought and sold. Not so, says I. What do you say?

Next up, a look at the nature of human understanding as seen from the perspective of this particular understander himself. One who understands something stands under, supports, or commits to a particular way of looking at things, of interpreting or categorizing those things in order to be true to the workings of his or her mind in acting from personal conviction. Onward to Chapter 4 dealing with matters of understanding and self-knowledge, and how I understand myself and my world in particular. O

UNDERSTANDING

Just as my mind reaches for sensory input in terms of broad conceptual categories derived from earlier experience, so those same categories can be sorted into even broader categories of a more general understanding. I speak here of understanding instead of knowledge to stress the *process* above any seemingly objective quality of "knowing." "Understanding" allows for belief, doubt, revision, and even refutation—but not absolute proof. As I view it, there is an increasingly inclusive system within my mind that enables me to deal with experience on a hierarchical basis suited to the level of discernment I am concerned with at the time. Introspection tells me that since I think in terms of lower and higher levels of experience ranging from the concrete and specific to the abstract and general, some sort of three-tiered taxonomic system is built into my mind. This mental system ranges from concrete sensory figures, to generalized concepts, to understanding on an even more inclusive and interrelated level.

I didn't invent this hierarchy of mental processing, so I think it must be part of my basic equipment. Observing such systems in use by others around me, I conclude that they are a characteristic property of our minds. Being highly visual, I think in terms of diagrams showing how branching connections converge from the bottom level towards the top, or diverge from the apex to the bottom level. By way of examples, think of the chain of military command; the hierarchical organization of church officials; plant and animal taxonomies; food webs, family trees; organizational structure; and the organic order by which life is built from atoms into molecules into amino acids into proteins into cells into tissues into organs into organ systems into individual members of a species, into species themselves, into genera, and on up the taxonomic order. Solar systems consist of a central star orbited by planets, in turn orbited by moons. The universe is built up in a hierarchy of relationships between the bodies it comprises such as clouds of gas and dust, stars, star clusters, galaxies, supergalaxies, and so on.

Such a system is invaluable in helping me make sense of my experience by seeing how events are interconnected within my mind. I can quickly name ten items within the fruit category, and ten categories within my understanding of living things. Or I can list a variety of categories all of which include any individual item I can name. I can also decide if two items are on the same level of my understanding, or one is on a lower or higher level than the other.

Above the level of sensory phenomena fitted into categories, categories themselves are fitted into conceptual systems made up of related fields of concepts making up larger divisions of consciousness. Those divisions are multidimensional in containing various sensory figures, categories, feelings, emotions, levels of discernment, situations—all as a platform for undertaking planning and subsequent programs of action. Understanding, then, consists of multiple dimensions of awareness in more-or-less orderly relationship one to another, an order that can be analyzed in terms of its component parts, or regarded as a distinct subsystem of mind such as a field of study or disciplined practice.

I can look at my personal consciousness as functioning on six primary levels: 1) outlook and expectancy, 2) attention, 3) sensory figures, 4) feelings and emotions, 5) conceptual interpretation of sensory figures, and 6) understanding based on related concepts organized into a coherent field or system encompassing (in addition to interpreted patterns) feelings, emotions, levels of detail, together with their interrelationships. Each such system of higher-order consciousness makes up a situation within which planning and analysis take place in regard to a limited realm of understanding to produce actions appropriate to the makeup of that particular situation as portrayed in consciousness. The only evidence I have for supporting this model of my mental activity comes from thirty years of watching my own mind grapple with the eternal question of what to do next in taking my life to the next stage, and the stage after that.

I deliberately chose relatively simple incidents of not-seeing or wrong-seeing to include in Chapter 1 because, right from the start, I didn't want to take on the whole of consciousness as suggested in the paragraph above. Not only would I lose my audience, but I would lose myself in an impassable tangle of details. Nor will I attempt to deal with such details in this or subsequent chapters. In my case, if I tried to keep up with the activity in my mind, I would have neither time nor energy for living my life. I am doing us both a favor, worthy reader, in deliberately restricting the findings of my introspective investigation to topics I can deal with in chapters of eighteen to twenty pages, as opposed to a multi-volume encyclopedia devoted to the study of but one human mind. My plan is to touch upon the emotionally-charged high points, and leave it at that.

Category errors are a form of misunderstanding within such a hierarchical system of classification. It's not that we see one thing as another, but that we interpret a lower-level pattern incorrectly. In perception, there are answers, but not necessarily *right* answers. In seeing what we call a "rose," we are looking from a certain perspective grounded in earlier experiences. Roseness is not on the bush but in our minds, and in our minds in a variety of ways. What we perceive depends on what we are looking for or are accustomed to seeing, which is often a matter of habit or convention, not truly seeing what our eyes are focused upon (or of hearing what we are listening to, etc.).

Roses live within categories in our minds as plants, flowers, natives or exotics, wild or cultivated blooms, traditional or hybrid roses in *my* garden opposed to those in *your* garden. What we mean by "roses" depends on the distinctions and groupings we make in consciousness, which can be deep or shallow depending on our heritage of experience. That is, on how we have trained our memory to view roses in different categories. Looking at a rose today, we see into the past—our personal past history with rosy phenomena. It is one thing for me to encounter my first rose, and a very different thing to see a rose on a bush I planted and have been tending for decades. Your rose is not my rose, and my old rose is not even my rose of today. A red rose is not a pink rose is not a white rose is not a black rose is not a yellow rose.

Claiming a rose to be a rose or a spade to be a spade reflects categorical perception at its broadest. Things are seldom that simple. Roseness and spadeness are not in the world waiting to be discovered; they are in our minds, subject to how our memories reach out to patterns of potential experience. And that depends on how we have been calibrated by our culture to regard roses and spades, and how our personal history dealing with the patterns presented by specific examples of roses and spades has fine-tuned our attention. Our understanding of roses and spades comes down to how we construe the situations in which those matters come up, and that is subject to a great variety of influences from our expectations, current states of mind, and our respective stores of both semantic (referential) and episodic (autobiographical) memories.

Which is why I say all understanding is self-understanding, for the knower's mind makes all the difference in how perceptual attention is brought to bear on everything in conscious awareness. In looking for the missing mustard jar, I was looking for one image of a jar of a certain size, shape, and color as seen from the side—as if on a supermarket shelf. But the jar was hiding in plain sight by presenting its bright red, round top instead of the qualities I was looking for. I must have looked straight at it several times in my search, but didn't see it because the categorical concept I entertained in my mind was not affirmed by the perceptual pattern I had to work with—so I dismissed it as irrelevant. It simply wasn't there. Except it was.

On the other hand, Fred was there in front of me on Fifth Avenue—except it wasn't Fred but a stranger in a Fred costume, walking with a Fred-like gait, wearing Fred-like shoes. This morning I looked at a towel folded on the rack in my bathroom—and saw a princess wrapped in an ermine cloak. No, I'm not out of my mind; in fact, that's precisely where I am. My mind determines who I am and what I see. To me (that is, to my mind) it makes sense to interpret the fibrous texture of a towel as a cloak around a fibrous face peering out, wearing a fibrous crown on its head. If I can accept rays of light passing through strips of film driven at twenty-four frames a second behind a projecting lens as a depiction of moving events, or a beam of electrons streaming row by row across a cathode ray tube as a newscaster at a desk, or the map on my wall as a representation of the island I live on in Maine, it is no great trick to see a princess in a hanging towel or a gorilla in the patterns swirling in my linoleum floor. I perform such feats of magic (or delusion) every day, and, I suspect, so do you. We look through magazines and see not arrays of colored dots but pictures of car crashes, the rich and famous, and places we've never been.

The world as we understand it is not the world as it is in-and-of itself. Rather, it is a world of our own making or taking, concoction, categorization, interpretation, understanding, and so on. The world we so deeply believe in is, in fact, the world we were taught by others to see as the one-and-only real world, but *seeing as* is not seeing things in themselves. It can be more a wolf dressed in sheep's clothing to make a favorable impression on gullible minds. For proof I offer Santa Clause, Humpty Dumpty, Mickey Mouse, the Tooth Fairy, the Angelic Host, Zeus and other gods, and the Easter Bunny as evidence that the world we understand in our heads is but a rough approximation of the world that bodily supports us during our life-long journey spiraling around our neighborhood star as it carries us along on a journey of its own.

Seeing as presents us with a world—not as it is—but as we understand or believe it to be on one level of generality or another. That is, for whatever reason, in a given situation, we discover the world as we *would have it be* in light of what we take to be the evidence of our experience. This applies to questions concerning the nature of the universe, as well as lesser question such as, "Where do babies come from?" or, "Is there a Santa?" While I was shoveling out my car in the wake of the last blizzard, the local taxi driver shouted over to me, "Gotta clean up all that global warming." It was clear what mindset he was coming from. Understanding is not a passive act of taking the world in as it is. Rather, it stems from committing ourselves to a program of interpreting phenomena in light of our before-the-fact grasp of how the world works. Within individual minds, interpretation is guided by a personal point of view upon the current situation as each one construes it for herself, facilitating and even predetermining specific acts of categorization. It was clear the taxi driver was trying to induct me into the belief that global warming is not real, much as in 1897, editor Francis P. Church of the New York *Sun* tried to reassure eight-year-old Virginia O'Hanlon that, "Yes, Virginia, there is a Santa Claus," writing, in part:

> The most real things in the world are those that neither children nor men can see. . . . You may tear apart the baby's rattle and see what makes the noise inside, but there is a veil covering the unseen world which not the strongest man, nor even the united strength of all the strongest men that ever lived, could tear apart. Only faith, fancy, poetry, love, romance, can push aside that curtain and view and picture the supernal beauty and glory beyond. Is it real? Ah, Virginia, in all this world there is nothing else real and abiding.

In the course of rhetorical arguments, our discernment often shifts from one level to another without our knowing. Rhetoric is the art of persuasion. It is often easier to follow thoughts expressed in sweet words than the plain truth, as it is easier to swallow bitter medicine soaked in sugar syrup than the straight stuff.

In everyday life, ascribing a cause to account for a certain effect where such a cause is metaphorical or fictitious—or denial of such a cause where it can be proven to exist—is often the primary work of human understanding in fitting an interpreted phenomenon to a prior system of belief—that is, in assimilating novel events to a preexisting (or attractive) understanding of the world. Such personal outlooks give character to our minds in wrestling with the nature of events and situations as we come upon them. If we do not want to believe that the mounting concentration of carbon dioxide and other greenhouse gases in the atmosphere is our doing as the cause of global warming, then we will seize upon every scrap of seeming disproof (such as snowy winters) as supporting our disbelief. I remember a man trailing an oxygen bottle insisting that a window be opened because he had trouble breathing when, in fact, his scarred lung tissue was the cause, not any lack of air in the room. In spite of the tube running from his nostrils to the green canister, he remained adamant.

Our word universe comes from Latin *universus,* one turning, in reference to the circumpolar motion of the stars, when in fact that apparent motion is due to Earth's spinning on its (fictional) axis. It is we who are turning, not the stars, yet no amount of argument can convince us otherwise because we have no sense of ourselves turning in space. Even if we know better, we still refer to the "rising" and "setting" of sun, moon, and stars, not the continuous settling of the eastern, or rising of the western, horizon.

For thousands of years, in every culture on Earth, life has been associated with the rhythm by which we take air into our lungs and exhale it, cycle after cycle after cycle. We think of life as beginning with an infant's first cry, and ending at a codger's last gasp. Breathing and being alive are synonymous in our minds. Through artificial respiration, we bring the soon-to-be-dead back to life. If no moisture condenses on a mirror held under the nostrils, the subject is believed to be dead. In a physiological sense, there is no doubt that the human metabolism depends on oxygen being taken into the lungs, where it is dissolved in arterial blood, distributed to individual cells, to be replaced with carbon dioxide, in turn circulated back to the lungs and exhaled. Indeed, human life depends on that fundamental gaseous exchange. The question is, what makes us breathe? In fact our bodies are equipped to breathe, and contain elaborate systems for assuring that we do, for as long as we can keep it up.

But in beginning times, in days before we developed an accurate understanding of our own bodies, breathing was ascribed to an external agent that bestowed it upon us as the breath of life. Raising the question, where does that vital power arise, the very gift that enlivens us? The Latin verb *spirare* means to breathe, and is related to the objectified form *spiritus,* referring to breath, air, wind. And to spirit itself, as a kind of psyche (from Greek *psukhe,* breath, soul, life). Regarded as an object, spirit or soul became the gift itself, the ultimate cause of our awareness and our being, which enters us at first cry, and departs with our last breath. And God (as an illy defined concept high in the order of human understanding) became the bestower of that gift. This, then, was once the leading edge of human understanding concerning the miracle of life. Our early ancestors believed that men and women merely begat human bodies; it took the gift of spirit from the air to bring those bodies to life. So we are told. And when it departs, each spirit returns to the air itself, where it circulates as a kind of ghost or disembodied soul, to be recycled in other bodies, or is perhaps released from the cycle of birth and death by taking refuge in heaven or enduring punishment in hell.

The history of our language is the history of our most fundamental understandings and beliefs, from primitive times up through today. Old metaphors get forgotten, and are given new life as literal terms such as spirit, soul, and psyche. Words are old soldiers that never die, they just fade from one form into another, moving up in the hierarchy of understanding, taking on revised meanings in light of the needs of changing times, providing a bountiful font of irony that, like entropy, grows ever more abundant as time passes.

Understanding is a matter of supporting what we believe in—as the scientist believes, the preacher believes, the teacher believes, the politician, the economist, the industrialist, the general, the criminal, the judge, and all the rest—each trusting interpreted phenomena he takes to be evidence in support of his respective understanding of how the world works. People have given their lives in defense of such beliefs—and taken the lives of countless disbelieving others in the process. For thousands of years, to rid the world of wrong belief, different groups have destroyed the physical bodies, brains, and minds of those who do not agree with them that the world runs according to a master plan as they understand it in their minds.

Witness the felling of the Twin Towers, and the aftermath. There is no rigorous way to account for belief systems grounded in interpretations of personal experience. And since we are each different one from another on the deepest levels of experience, there is no end to the horde of disbelievers, heretics, infidels, pagans, and others of offensive persuasions whom we will see as taunting us without ceasing. Inevitably, our understanding of the world will be different from that of the majority of Earth's human population because their experience differs so radically from our own.

Our actions depend on the situations we find ourselves in, the sensory patterns we entertain in those situations, the ways we understand (construe, interpret, recognize, categorize, identify) those patterns among others at different levels on our hierarchy of understanding, the attention we invest in incorporating that understanding into awareness, the judgments and decisions we make as a result of fulfilling that awareness, the plans we formulate as a result of those judgments, the skills we possess for turning plans into actions, and finally the actions themselves as we are able to execute them on a particular occasion. At least that's the overall scheme I discover in myself as revealed through a thirty-year program of self-reflection.

When I became a Quaker in 1995, I did so not to be closer to God, but because I saw Friends as one of the most constructive forces for good in a troubled world. I joined the religious society as a secular Friend. As such, I interpreted two of the chief axioms of Quakerism—1) belief that there is that of God in everyone, and 2) that revelation of God's will as a source of wisdom did not die with the prophets but is available to seekers even now—as professions suited to times long past. My practice is to turn those tenets around in seeing prophecy as a revelation of deep personal understanding, and the goodness in each breast as a nugget at the core of our humanity. I am not being perverse, just applying my personal understanding to the collection of seventeenth-century metaphors that gives Quakerism its quaint and otherworldly flavor. My view is that the beliefs I have mentioned were appropriate to the century in which the *King James Bible* was introduced, a time when common citizens in England did battle against the four powers of suppression—church, monarchy, courts, nobility—while nobody stood for the people. But now I see the metaphor of the "God within" as fatal in denying the essential autonomy and dignity of those claiming to follow dictates from a higher power, when it is our own personal judgment and strength we need to develop in meeting the challenges of our time. Claiming to follow God's will leads to passivity in waiting for the call to come in, while what is needed in our times is for all people to take the initiative by, as Gandhi put it, becoming the change that we seek, which is the essential message of my findings through introspection—that it is I, not any high-order abstraction, who makes myself happen in the world. Human understanding, compassion, and dissatisfaction, not the gods, constitute the engine of social change. I say the same regarding the human economy, which so many worship as the god of these times, but I view as yet one more fatal metaphor in assuring the liquidity (and ultimate liquidation) of both natural and human resources. The wealth of nations inheres in the minds of each and every member of the populace, not in profits, money, investments, trade, or material production. We do better as a nation of poets than drudges, singing the beauties of nature than converting Earth to a wasteland like Mars.

Essentially, my understanding serves as a platform for more-or-less effective action in a world scripted by the assorted fables others would have me believe or which I tell myself. The test of my personal understanding is in how well it serves as a ground for appropriate action, not in the fables recommending one such course of action or another. It's not what I *tell myself* as a rationale but what I *do* with my physical body that proves (or disproves) my understanding. What did I do when I saw a dying crow ahead? I thought to wring its neck, but as I drew closer, I was disabused by the increasing refinement of my vision, so drove by, relieved it was not a sentient being but merely a trash bag.

Raising my arm to clap Fred on the back, I caught myself about to assault a total stranger, and in that instant realized I had been pursuing a false vision for several minutes *as if* it were true. Crushed, I stood on the sidewalk as the crowd streamed by me, then gathered my wits according to a revised situational understanding, and went my way. In the case of the crashing plane revisioned as a TV antenna, I aborted the call to 911 and continued my original errand.

How I act in the world is predicated (based on) a series of events in my mind, so the action itself is predicated on my personal understanding—the set of my mind—at the time. Here revealed is the syntax of my personal speech acts and behavior. Where do words come from? The same place every act arises, from my personal construction of situations as I understand them. I am always the subject performing the act on another, who in turn serves as the designated receiver or object of the action. The action itself is how I project myself into a world I can never be sure of. Any action is an assertion or predication that I know what I am doing in categorizing a sensory figure a certain way. Which, I am embarrassed to admit, would be wholly inappropriate if the situation were other than I construe it in the heat of the moment—as when crow reverted to trash bag, plane to antenna, Fred to unwitting imposter, cows to bikers, paint scraper to northern white cedar. This is the whirling, fluid mentality revealed through introspection, the base from which I make myself happen in a world I have great difficulty picturing, much less understanding with any degree of confidence.

Understanding *before* the act and *after* the act often turn out to be two different things. Which is why so much of what I truly understand results from trial and error—the most effective teacher I have ever had. All else is based on assumptions, suppositions, habits, guesses, hearsay, rumors, misinterpretations, errors of judgment, deficient skills, and arrogance in acting before I am adequately prepared. Look out, world, ready or not, here I come. Which, I suggest, is why the world is in the terrible state it is now, and has been throughout much of my life. I, with considerable help from my friends and neighbors, am responsible for the confusion and chaos I discover around me as a projection of the raw, uncertain state of my mind. I take full responsibility for the collective harm I have inflicted on spouses, children, friends, students, neighbors, and countless casual acquaintances, which, over the course of my lifetime, has been considerable. Mea culpa, that is the teaching of self-reflection and introspection. And considering I am but one human agent out of seven billion, the carnage resulting from the homonid takeover of planet Earth through time is humbling, to say the least.

If nothing else, self-understanding is about truth and reconciliation. It's not all those others who are the bad actors we should blame. That approach takes us nowhere beyond where we are now. No, I picture each one of us as a flawed actor driven by an imperfect process for turning our dreams and assumptions into actions appropriate to our earthly situations. Evolution has tailored us to the Stone Age, not recent times. All knowledge is self-knowledge because in each case what we do is backed by a network of complex mental factors driving us to make ourselves happen in ways that seem sensible to us at the time, but later turn out to be largely the result of near-perfect ignorance of our true situations, compounded by impatience and unjustified arrogance. I'm thinking here of what I have learned about myself, which, since I can't imagine I am the deviate of all deviates, I am happy to share with my earthly brothers and sisters. I speak for myself here; do I speak for you?

But back to my personal history of misinterpretations and misunderstandings. In the case of the clip-art cat (Ch. 1, Incident 9), upon hearing what was really a complaining hinge, I took it as the yowl of a cat whose tail I had just stepped on, so on that premise, I leapt up to relieve the insult, while picturing in my mind a bluish-gray kitty looking mildly back at me without anger, blame, or resentment. That is, I reacted not only physically to the squeak, but also mentally in conjuring an apparent (and fictional) source of the noise. My faulty understanding of the situation made me do it. And since situations don't interpret themselves for my convenience, that interpretation was solely my own doing. I justified my leaping up by creating false evidence in my mind. Mid-air, I fabricated Exhibit A, as innocent and convincing a plaintiff as ever portrayed.

In stepping into the path of a bicyclist I didn't see coming against the one-way traffic in Brattle Square (Ch. 1, Incident 1), I placed blame for my not looking squarely on him, and shouted my displeasure by hoping he would rot in hell for assaulting me. Again, I adjusted the facts to suit my misunderstanding, acting in public on the basis of illusions in my head. I was so overwrought, if I'd carried a gun, I might have dispatched him on the spot. I have served my time as a hothead, and have known more than a reasonable share of ill temper, which I frequently directed at those who displeased me. My contribution to world peace is backed by the fact that I have never owned a gun in my life.

In the case of my not seeing my partner's sunflowers, I was intent on retrieving my camera bag, so having eyes for nothing else, I was functionally blind. The same is true for different reasons in my not seeing the mustard jar in the refrigerator. There I was looking *for* the wrong sensory pattern so aggressively that the pattern the jar actually presented was invisible from my point of view. Not seeing can be a side effect of trying to be efficient in saving time and energy by serving a particular world understanding.

In not recognizing the Rockies when I saw them for the first time, my blinding was more habitual than intentional, because in upstate New York, I wasn't used to seeing snow on higher ground without there also being snow in the foreground. It was late August, not February, so I was expecting to see clouds, not snow. It takes energy to suppress or inhibit one pattern for the sake of seeing another. That was the action I took that resulted in my not seeing the Rockies, or the mustard jar, or the sunflowers, because I was committed to seeing what I expected to see in each situation, not what was there to be seen.

Understanding, that is, exists in the context of a situation which determines to large extent the possibilities for how phenomena and interpretations are likely to complement each other, and how unlikely to fit at all in other ways. In that sense, understanding is highly perspectival and subjective pretty much all the time. And our actions in the fabled world based on that understanding are equally perspectival and subjective. As for universal understanding common to all of humanity, as well as absolute understanding of what is good and true and beautiful—such ideals are not going to be attained in this lifetime. Rather, they are matters each of us must decide for herself, and then recognize as convenient fictions rather than grounds for acting in concert out of feelings of good or ill toward all humankind.

This primary complementarity between phenomena and the interpretations which embody them in our subjective understanding is a fundamental feature of consciousness that has tremendous implications for the fabled world of everyday reality. On a daily basis, newscasters supply us with bulletins about "the economy" as if it truly existed, and everyone knew what it was and how it worked while, in fact, there is only the experiential economy as each individual portrays or "understands" it from his limited point of view, and every such portrayal is a unique smattering of the vast generalization of what the economy might be to all who are affected by it one way or another. "The economy," that is, is a fiction of convenience so that we all use the same term in discussing our personal affairs *as if* our words referred to the same entity in reality, which, given the subjective nature of language, they cannot do. The same mythical trust in our great generalizations (peace, love, justice, truth, God, etc.) is based on a similar complementarity between sensory phenomena and their interpretations in the minds of the people, in no two minds the same. The upshot being that the concepts at issue can represent all things to all men and women, and represent very little that could be considered real in itself.

When strong emotions cloud mental understanding—as when people grow fearful of or angry toward their governments; toward other religious groups; or strangers who look, dress, and talk differently than they do—it is easy to assume that they are driven by the same sense of dissatisfaction. But in truth, the objects of such anger are often entertained at such a low level of discernment in anyone's mind, when seen from so many different perspectives they don't mean anything at all. What we know is that people are disgruntled for reasons we do not and even they may not know. Speaking in generalities, they can't say exactly why, nor can anyone else. The fitting complementarity of sensory phenomena and their interpretations is as important between people as it is within any one mind.

The nature of human understanding has implications that are entirely ignored in treating all people the same, as is commonly claimed in so-called democratic systems. Where this is particularly evident is in the varied levels of discernment on which individuals understand sensory patterns, and by which they attempt to fitly interpret them as a basis for subsequent judgments, decisions, planning, and action. Some people take more (or less) sensory information into account than others do; some have a wider (or narrower) range of possible categorizations in their repertory than average. With the result that our respective understandings of events and situations constitute a spectrum of different possible interpretations, some more discerning and detailed, some less, than the rest.

These differences have consequences in that a few individuals may be experts in their respective fields, while others are more naïve. I see this spread in my own self-reflections. In some matters I have broad and deep experience, while in others I am either shallow or narrow, and so my understanding in such areas is handicapped. My understanding of photography, estuarine issues, horseshoe crabs, celiac disease, and my own mind, for instance, is in each case fairly rich and detailed, while my understanding of such important issues as politics, insurance, economics, warfare, and nuclear physics amount to practically no understanding at all. Which, unfortunately, does not imply I don't spout opinions on such matters. Ignorance has rarely stopped me or anyone else from having his say.

It takes a great deal of dedicated living in terms of personal experience and hard work to develop expertise in any human discipline. Practice really does make perfect—deliberate, attentive, conscious repetition of routines until the required level of skill can belong not only to the likes of Mozart, Rembrandt, and Babe Ruth, but to those who work hard to achieve it as well. It is not just a matter of putting in the time. The quality of that time is crucial to success. Rather than complain about the state of the world, we do better to turn our passions into disciplined behaviors through strict concentration. That is what it takes to build strong neural connections and mappings in our brains sufficient to turn the untested model we inherit at birth into a customized mind suited to understanding the challenges of today's world. To realize our personal dreams, there is no substitute for concentration and hard work. In the end, we get good at what we consciously apply ourselves to over and over again.

To develop skills, timing, judgment, and understanding, we have to do whatever is required to build high-resolution maps in our minds. Whatever we train our minds to do, they will be more likely to perform on demand. That is the amazing secret of human understanding. Treat our minds in humdrum fashion, our minds will see to it we lead humdrum lives; but challenge our minds to do all they can, they have no choice but to return the favor in kind. Expect little—that's exactly what we will get. If we ask for the moon, we must build that moon crater-by-crater over time into our minds; then when we ask, there it will be—our very own moon. On the other hand ten thousand hours spent, say, flipping burgers leads to a burger-flipping life.

Through the course of evolution, consciousness has been naturally selected for by the survival advantage it provides in giving us a tool for working our way out of those tough, unanticipated situations we keep getting ourselves into that reflexes and habits are no equal to. What, we ask children, do you want to be when you grow up? Fireman? Astronaut? Rock star? NASCAR driver? Consciousness has evolved to enable us to set goals such as these. And beyond that, to work our way through the arduous training and hours of practice that will modify our bodies and minds accordingly, putting our goals within reach. Once suitably stimulated, our minds will give us the skills to match our performance to our desires, or perhaps some worthy equivalent. Ice-age minds are good for understanding and dealing with ice ages; but modern challenges require more up-to-date minds capable of understanding and dealing with global warming, sea-level rise, periodic economic bubbles, eternal warfare, over-population, over-consumption, wastefulness, corporate personhood, power reserved to the elite for their exclusive benefit, greed, racism, sexism, and other challenges of similar magnitude. If there is to be a better way of running the world, we've got to build that way into our minds by facing up to and understanding the myriad situations affecting our lives in modern times.

Understanding is made up of an array of anticipated sensory patterns matched to a repertory of available conceptual interpretations, all at higher and lower levels of discernment, making those patterns acceptably meaningful in certain ways. To meet the challenges inherent in changing times, we can no longer rely on the teachings of yesterday concerning how best to interpret—and so understand—our situations. We must press ourselves to see our times in a new light by reaching toward altered situations with renewed understanding. That update allows us to fit a new set of interpretations to the sensory patterns we meet in awareness, and to bring a new set of tools to bear in acting appropriately within changing situations as we now understand them. That fitting of our minds to unfamiliar situations is called *accommodation,* or learning.

The alternative is to force new situations to fit the repertory of interpretations we already have on hand from prior learning, as if our understanding was universal and absolute, thus worthy of any situation we might encounter anywhere, anytime. That forced-fit approach is called *assimilation,* by which old ways of understanding are taken as good enough for any and all new situations, much like pouring new wine into the musty old bottles we have in the back room. The status quo is good enough, we say; it worked before, we figure it will work again.

But no child ever became an astronaut by meeting the challenge on his or her current level of understanding. She had to grow into the job, not simply put on a Halloween costume and expect to lift off from the backyard. The speeding treadmill on which we leave old situations behind and become the match for whatever novel ones lie ahead is crucial to making ourselves fit to deal with an ever-changing bioenergetic reality in terms of energy flows and transformations we cannot fully grasp. Which is a metaphorical description of the human condition. Always off-balance, we stumble ahead as best we can, never sure where we will end up, but doing our best to get there—wherever *there* turns out to be.

By another metaphor, we find ourselves tugging hard on our own bootstraps to raise our understanding to the next higher level. The point I want to make in twisting the old saw out of shape being that it is the effort that matters, not forcing our feet into the same old pair of boots. Or in the case of the treadmill, you think you get off where you got on, but the effort expended has taken you to an entirely new place, if not externally, then internally, where blood is now coursing through your arteries and veins.

Metaphors are ways of understanding new situations by posing novel theories as stabs in the dark based on intuition. That's pretty much how my mind works. I reach for the new in terms of the old slightly skewed out of shape. Upon closer look, most human understanding is metaphorical in nature. We go back to Old English, Old French, Latin, or Greek roots—or even to hypothetical Indo-European roots—to understand what the words we use today might mean, or what they might have meant in the past, and where they came from. Understanding is build up in layers like an archaeological dig. The words we learned as children lie at the core of our vocabulary today, and beneath that, the situations in which we first heard combinations of sounds uttered by our elders, and we intuitively put the two together, each situation serving as what specific sounds meant to us in an experiential sense at the time. Historically, a *phenomenon* refers to that which clearly appears; a *concept* is something conceived (or made pregnant) in being grasped by the mind. I use *understand* (to stand under) in referring to a clear grasping of sensory patterns by a repertory of concepts, narratives, or interpretations on various levels of discernment. And beyond that, to an active commitment to that understanding as a coherent landscape of interpreted sensory patterns comprising a situational or even universal domain of personal experience.

That is, in my inner world of consciousness, I picture a sensory pattern standing under (supporting as evidence) an interpretation to produce an understanding made up of both sensory and interpretive aspects of awareness. Taken collectively, such understandings then provide a platform for reaching into the world. This suggests how hard it is to use words commonly addressed to a fabled external world in talking about aspects of experience which truly exist within consciousness itself. In working inside-out as the mind does, the standard is set *as if* fashioned by consciousness as it applies its arts to an outside world extrapolated or implied beyond sensory phenomena as they present themselves in awareness.

In conveying understanding from one mind to another, words, numbers, and other meaningful gestures are essential. But in the case of my one mind trying to understand itself, I find beneath the words—standing under them—thought kernels or nuggets that are wholly nonverbal in themselves, while they embody the essential meaning borne by my choice of words. Too, I experience redness—the quality of being red—without having to think of the word "red," and experience the qualities of roughness, heaviness, sharpness, bigness, complexity, and so on, apart from those words themselves. When I saw a dying crow by the side of the road, I didn't think, "Oh, there's a crow," or "There's something flapping up ahead." I *saw* an interpreted sensory image without benefit of words. The words came later when I tried to describe my experience. To have the experience in the first place, I had no need for words. What I had was a series of unconscious mappings from one part of my mind onto another, and since the interpreted sensory image was revised, revised mappings must have traveled back the other way so that my understanding changed from crow to trash bag blowing in the wake of passing cars.

The point being that, as I have maintained, all understanding is self-understanding, all knowledge is self-knowledge. The self is so heavily invested in its own doings, all experience is self-experience as constituting the mental world of but one individual. And yet in taking for granted that we are mere vehicles of experience done unto us, we look upon the outer world as if *it* were responsible for what passes in our feeling bodies and minds. We may say, for instance, "You make me so mad!" while the other person is only an apparition in our minds over which we madden ourselves. Everything, but everything, is our doing—a product of our personal understanding—yet it is far easier to see consciousness as the world's doing than claim it as the child of our own creativity. The shortcut on my desktop is not the program, and even what I call "the program" is really many lines of code turning streaming electrons off and on under certain conditions. Even when I go to the movies, I don't see a film—the film is in the projector modulating light passing through a lens onto the screen I am focused on. What I see is a fast-changing pattern of colored light which I interpret as a film, much as I saw the cartwheel aurora as a parade of animal forms. It takes a great deal of concentration and experience to understand even the simplest things as they are.

I could very well have dispatched the eighteen incidents in Chapter 1 depicting category errors and misinterpretations to the graveyard of stupid mistakes. Introspection requires nothing if not close attention to seemingly trivial events and details of events. Nothing seems to be happening except everything is happening in unexpected ways. Dispatch any of it and I am throwing my life away as so much packing material.

But attention and expectation are not packing materials—they are the real thing, along with doubt, uncertainty, questioning, ambiguity, and other modes of reaching *for* understanding. These are what we use in the two-way coupling between sensory patterns with concepts in our minds, building an understandable world around us in the process, as sensible as we can make it under prevailing conditions in the situation we are currently engaged in. Shopping, fixing lunch, doing laundry, reading an article, having sex, writing a book—these are the projects we work at in living a sane, sensible, and understandable life. If we lose sight of these everyday activities, what do we have to show for our days on this Earth? Time passes; life passes. End of story. With introspection, at least, we have some understanding of where our lives come from and go.

Both deliberately and inadvertently, our families shape our understanding by calibrating our sensibilities through the quality and amount of attention they dole out before we have a chance to develop minds and mental habits of our own. Aside from our families, the culture we are born to also calibrates what we do to get love and attention from others, which is certainly one of the main functions of schools and religions in shaping us as acceptable members of society. That is, seeing to it we conform to others' expectations of who we should be and how we should act. Schools certainly lay the groundwork for habits that future employers are apt to find useful: dutifully doing our assignments; being punctual, neat, and orderly; not disturbing others; showing respect, or at least not being so outspoken as to offend. As we progress through the grades, we dutifully acquire the characteristics of productive workers in a world run by our elders, until we discover we are elders ourselves in relation to those behind us, and we get on the school board, become teachers, or parents in our own right, and do unto those behind us as we had done unto us—calibrating their impressionable minds by letting them know what pleases us by meeting our standards and what doesn't.

Calibrating a thermometer, we stick it in ice water and make a little scratch on the glass to mark the height of the indicator column, then put it in boiling water and do the same, dividing the distance between the two scratches into our units of choice. Eureka, we read off the temperature corresponding to the height of the column of red liquid. In being calibrated by others, we are put through our paces— the standard experiences by which others get to know us—and our responses are noted in other minds as well as our own, so we are calibrated in their terms and in ours at the same time. This is how we get to know ourselves as foils to others' likes and dislikes, expectations and desires, strengths and weaknesses. Success means feeling approval; failure means feeling displeasure. It's that simple, yet can affect us for a lifetime.

Of course we don't feel the quality of the attention directly—it is conveyed by a smile or frown, a hug or a spanking—leaving us to interpret our phenomenal version to understand what it might mean. I felt uncomfortable when the visiting sex educator singled me out of the crowd in attendance at her talk. Why was she speaking directly to me? I thought there must have been a message in her fixed gaze, but I couldn't guess what it was. In such situations, I usually imagine the worst, but in this case I read no displeasure in her face, so was at a loss in trying to figure out how I might be significant from her point of view. It turned out she approved of me because I looked like her son.

Which is exactly how I treated the cartwheel display of aurora borealis—as a surrogate for the parallel parade of recognizable shapes and creatures I entertained in my mind. I didn't see patterns of flowing light, I saw whales and snakes because that's how I understood (stood under) what was happening. I was calibrated to see meaningful forms, not pure phenomena, as the speaker was calibrated by her experience to single out her son's look-alike in the audience. She mapped her son's face onto my features, much as I mapped animals in my mind onto the fluent aurora.

Which leads me to conclude that human understanding exists in seven billion parallel universes. Unless we are calibrated by undergoing a program of similar exercises with "right" answers (called training or education), we go it alone in a universe of our own making—as I did in experiencing the aurora, as the sex educator did in giving her talk. As artists everywhere do in expressing aspects of their self-calibrated, inner universes in their works—their drawings, paintings, sculptures, music, songs, dances, dinners, and many other forms of creative expression.

Having read through this manuscript several times, I now see that my serial argument taken as a whole goes beyond my piecemeal grasp of the matters I deal with in each chapter. With the result that my understanding of my own mind verges on the realm of creative imagination and transcendence. Human creativity reveals each of us to be unique and capable of performing in ways that others—and even ourselves—cannot anticipate. Proving in each case that we do not understand our own powers very well. For, indeed, our self-set standards determine what we expect of ourselves, and the broadcasting of such standards as limits to our expectations does an injustice to the full potential of our conscious minds. We are neither clones nor robots, models nor paradigms, uniform standard products nor hollow ideals. We are who we are, such as we are, which we can best discover through self-reflection and self-discovery if we want to understand and enjoy our unique and all-too-brief stay on this Earth, accompanied by the cohort traveling with us—those whom we have any hope of understanding in relation to how we regard ourselves. Whatever our situation, we have little choice but to press ahead in being fully engaged as only each of us can be. Where this takes us will be revealed in what we accomplish.

In this chapter I have ranged through my thoughts on understanding and self-knowledge in relation to sensory patterns and their interpretation. Which leads me to think about two of the oldest questions in the world that I paid a great deal of attention to in writing my doctoral dissertation: What does it mean *to be* or *exist?* And what does it mean *to know* one thing or another? Introspection naturally leads to such considerations. It is no accident these issues are the topic of the next chapter. Please turn the page when you are ready. O

CHAPTER 5

BUILDING A WORLD INSIDE-OUT

Introspection is the subjective study of personal experience. In my personal practice, I discover several strands of awareness whose interplay determines the various qualities I discover in my mind. Sensory phenomena, their interpretations, and understandings which accrue over time are three among them, leading to judgments, decisions, plans, projects, and actions.

We introspectors believe that experience is what the mind makes of it or takes it to be. In that light, I offer the following anecdote from a different mind altogether, that of Miss Elizabeth Andrews in the form of a childhood reminiscence cherished for almost eighty years as told in a letter to my mother in April 1981.

> Still vivid in my mind is the day I stayed after school in the first grade to 'help' the teacher. In awe I watched her make rather a clumsy sketch of a crescent moon on the blackboard. Beside it she lettered 'moon.' I rushed home to tell my mother that I had already learned the spelling word for the next day: 'm-o-o-n, banana.'

The crude crescent on the blackboard formed a sensory pattern that opened onto a number of possible interpretations. The teacher intended her drawing to illustrate one particular instance of categorization, while the young student saw it differently. The spelling word for the day might have been "curve," "claw," or even "fingernail clipping," but she inferred it was "banana," because that's how she read (categorized) the sensory figure in her mind.

This little story presents a cohesive understanding in one mind becoming unraveled in another, in this case by the figure interpreted in the teacher's mind as a moon becoming unstuck in the child's, so that the sensory figure and its intended meaning float free of one another—allowing a more experientially vivid or personally salient concept to barge past that of "moon." The schematic nature of the drawing invited this to happen through its lack of telling detail such as size, color, time of day, location, luminosity, and so on. The impoverished visual detail led the child to construe the simple crescent as a sign pointing to "banana" rather than "moon." Her mistake was not one of misperception so much as inadvertently defying the conventional sound-symbol relationship in her language community between the pronunciation and spelling of one English word. In her mind, she was right in labeling the crude shape "banana" because that was the interpretation her memory of prior experience led her to put forward as most likely that day after school.

As children, we are calibrated by the experiential and linguistic standards preserved by the culture to which we are born as novice human beings, so that we come to share in the assignment of conventional meanings to the repertory of phenomenal figures we are likely to encounter as adults. And in mastering these assignments— in making them ours—we have strong feelings of pride and accomplishment in seeing ourselves become competent members of our speech communities.

But sometimes it happens that we are able to catch ourselves having an experience in which a meaning or label becomes detached from a sensory figure, and we recognize the doubleness of that experience, just as the enthusiastic scholar in the anecdote might have been caught and corrected by her mother.

As children, all of us have known similar disjointed experiences—and continue to have them as adults. Who among us has not identified a familiar figure walking ahead of us—only to discover the familiar stride, coat, or posture to be flaunted by a callous imposter? Who has not struggled to make sense of hurriedly-read material in which such innocent words as "physiologist," "conversation," or "through" have been demonically confounded with "psychologist," "conversion," or "thorough," respectively? Who has not misidentified a tree or roadside plant, a haunting tune, or a well-known mug shot in the paper? Who has not known a Wednesday that felt like Monday, a May that acted more like March, a tomboy or a precocious youth? Some of us are "prematurely" gray, or are prone to fits of "childish" behavior. When traveling we become refreshingly aware of quaint airs and novel customs, or else take offense at a lack of looked-for routines and common courtesies. All of us have muttered, "It's only a game!" when fervor or disappointment got out of hand, or, "It's only a movie!" when the scene became too graphic or the plot overly grim. Who has not felt terror at falling—to wake up on the edge of the bed, the "precipice" a figment from a fading dream? Who believes that rabbits reside in magician's hats or that pretty assistants truly suffer the knife or the saw? We know they're tricks, that appearances are deceiving, and it's all done with mirrors, wires, hollow wands, and sleight of hand. Speaking of tricks, who has not been told that "Beauty is only skin deep" and "Handsome is as handsome does"? Who has never known fallen hopes or undeserved victory? Who has never been surprised by a joke or turn of events, caught in a lie or mistaken belief, been betrayed by a pal or the weather, disillusioned by seasonal fashions or random fads, slipping wigs or padded shoulders? Are we not all human after all, subject to the richness and complexity of our experience—and the fallibility of its judgments? Do we not take pride in our skills in detecting fraud and deceit, yet find ourselves frequently gullible in holding to our beliefs and convictions? Is not our daily experience ruled by efforts to understand the flood of sensory images we are subjected to, only to find meaning in events that others take differently than we do? Are we not divided between Democrats and Republicans, capitalists and socialists, Christians and Muslims and Jews, Harvards and Yales, blacks and whites, males and females, old and young, rich and middle-class and poor, the lapsed and the born again? To be human is to evolve strategies for interpreting existential appearances, and when deceived, to try again. If we mistakenly believe "m-o-o-n" spells "banana," do we not remember it all our lives, along with other times our judgments have been found out of joint? Do we not learn from such experiences, and is any experience not centered on a motive to attach meanings appropriately to the sensory figures we discern all around us? Can "to be" acknowledge more than the presence of an existential figure of stimulation within experience; can "understanding" make greater claim than to interpret those figures as prompts pointing beyond themselves to referential concepts or interpretations as "meanings"? Can experience itself be anything more than a ceaseless exchange between sensory phenomena and the interpretive categories we fit them to under the circumstances? Finally, when we face into the full significance of our mortality, does anything remain but a faint track on the road we have traveled, which we entrust to our heirs in hopes they will fit that track to some sort of meaning in their own hearts and minds? Can we be anything but restless patterns to one another, fibrillating phantoms who come together in harmony or discord to generate interlocking figures in which to read the meaning of our lives and attachments?

All of this seems too steep a crescendo to build on the one theme of a little girl running home from school to tell her mother that she had learned the spelling word for tomorrow. The world did not sprout from an acorn, nor can the interplay between sensory figures and their interpretations be grounded in a single example. If introspection is to serve as a productive method for detailing the nature of human consciousness and understanding, such interplay must be substantiated by millions of examples taken from individual lives as actually lived. Fortunately, as suggested in the preceding paragraph, everyday life abounds with such examples. The point of introspection is to tease apart discrepancies between awareness and understanding to reveal the dynamic interplay by which we build the worlds we live in for ourselves. Self-revealed disparity (as in the incidents I relate in Chapter 1) is the basis of the empirical method of discovery through reflection on daily experience. Probing the category errors we commit gives us a means of taking responsibility for the workings of our own minds so we do not reassign our mistakes to others. Appreciating the working of our minds, it becomes easier to gauge the situations within which we act, and to make ourselves happen appropriately within the personalized system of consciousness at the heart of inner life, which for each of us is tantamount to the real world.

That last sentence is a mouthful, which I mean to chew more thoroughly in this chapter. To give an example, in 1755, Samuel Johnson included the following definition of *oats* in his first English dictionary: "A grain, which in England is generally given to horses, but in Scotland supports the people." That backhanded slur, perhaps more subtle than a typical limerick or ethnic joke, serves as an example of humor by playing on the loose coupling of sensory figures and their interpretation in experience. Bringing the conventional English practice to bear on how Scots use the same grain, Johnson heaps scorn on those north of the border as seen by one in the south. Such an attitude is the unstated content of the distinction made in Johnson's definition: there are those who feed oats to horses (the sensible English), and those who eat them as food (the deviant Scots). How you are likely to take the joke depends on which side of the border you live.

This illustrates how local attitudes become taken-for-granted as normal or conventional everyday practices, highlighting foreign customs as deviant examples eliciting ridicule or biting humor. Both humor and metaphor reflect the doubleness of experience precisely because they deviate from standard expectations in dissociating a sensory figure from its conventional interpretation. If jokes do not violate the niceties of social custom, they do violence to other conventions governing language or experience. All customs, habits, fads, traditions, institutions, prejudices, and attitudes are vulnerable to humor because they represent an established habit that asks to be tested and stretched to determine its coefficient of elasticity and durability in the service of local opinion. This helps us refine our discernment between the true and the false, the sane and the suspect, the routine and the unconventional—in short, between the expected and the novel.

Through such exercises we explore our experience, jabbing it here, tickling it there, tweaking it somewhere else, laying hands on conventional "reality" to see how it will react, grasping for something stable in the flux of experience to call a world, and, by indirection, to tell us who we are and to which groups we belong. Humor is one of the ways we probe experience, trying to demonstrate the truth and validity of our opinion. If sensory figures were too loosely coupled to their usual interpretations so that they could be stuck or unstuck according to any whim or desire, meaning one thing today and another tomorrow, or one thing for me and another for you, then any stable sense of self, world, other, or culture would be impossible and the sensory, existential side of experience would continually slide past the meaningful, interpretive side, causing experiential earthquakes as devastating as slippage along the San Andreas fault.

There are some conventions, however, we are not willing to call up for review. These are the areas of experience wherein we find no margin for error, the havens of our sacred beliefs. All of us are zealots in one way or another, fighting to preserve some core of unquestionable truth. When the concrete, sensory patterns of our lives are set in stone and their meanings ossify within our brains, then experience loses its resilience and humor concerning the sacred topic is taken at best as a show of poor taste, at worst as a sure sign of heresy. At the far limits of human endeavor, suicide bombers will never be acceptable to those they threaten or assassinate, any more than pilots of armed drones will be forgiven for killing civilians as so-called collateral damage.

But when the damage is only linguistic, as when new place names are needlessly appended to old ones whose meaning has been forgotten, then we are apt to shake our heads in wonder at our folly. The notion of man, the computing computer, is funny in the same way that the name of a place would be funny if it were named after itself. The humor arises because the new name gains no forward motion, the joke being on the namer. Such absurd redundancies are not as rare as we might think. Isaac Taylor points out that "Trajan's bridge over the Tagus, is called the *La Puente de Alcantara*," where "*Al Cantara* means 'The Bridge' in Arabic, and *La Puente* means precisely the same thing in Spanish." He cites several other examples of redundant naming, such as: "In the name of Brindon Hill, in Somersetshire, we have first the Cymric *bryn*, a hill. To this was added *dun*, a Saxonised Celtic word, nearly synonymous with *bryn;* and the English word *hill* was added when neither *bryn* nor *dun* were any longer significant words." Thus Brindon Hill, just like Pendle Hill in Lancashire, means hill-hill-hill (*Words & Places,* 1864).

In his essay "Songbirds," E. B. White tells how a copy of Roger Tory Peterson's *Field Guide to the Birds* affected his busy household in Brooklin, Maine, turning it upside-down when the spring warblers came through. White does for the institution of bird watching what Samuel Johnson does for the Scots on the topic of oats: parade the foibles of an opposite persuasion by contrasting it to the local way of making meaning. As in metaphor, humor focuses on alternative ways of interpreting sensory phenomena. It describes a situation and then tells us what it means as seen from a particular but unanticipated point of view. By separating existential patterns of being (warblers on the wing and on the page) from their categorizations (species identifications), humor helps us appreciate the compound nature of experience by placing us in the tension between two related functions of consciousness, holding us there with suspended meaning until the humorist redeems us through his deviant yet acceptable punch line or point of view. If we don't get the joke, or scorn it as unacceptable in violating our attitude toward birding, then it is a bad joke that leaves us where we were before, at A, which may be funny in itself if we expected to be transported to a more exotic B. Shaggy dog stories make no forward motion whatever, despite a great show of trying; they are jokes that amuse because they defy our conventions concerning humor itself, just as Chinese humor (translated, say, by Robert Graves) is likely to do, or that of young children.

Children go through a brief stage, before they develop effective categorizations, of breaking free from their immediate concrete perspectives by relying on random cues within their environments to direct them toward appropriately outrageous predicates in calling people names. "You're a" (with much looking around the room) "a ... a lamp shade; a ... dirty dish; a ... a car in the driveway!" All followed by riotous laughter at the spontaneous creation of such adult-sounding humor (He's a turkey, pig, weasel, skunk, rat, commie pinko, fairy; she's a sweetie, honeybun, doll, chickadee, bat, witch, shrew, etc.). Playing with categorizations leads to mastery in labeling sensory patterns as we choose to depict them by mapping meanings onto existential figures in awareness.

Children's play is a similar stage on the way to eventual maturation. The existential pattern of a finger-pointing hand serves as a suitable gun, as a stick becomes a sword, a stuffed animal a pet, and a doll the child of its "mother." Playthings allow children to experiment with attitudes and points of view by serving not as concrete objects but as artifacts of meaningful experience. The hand is not a gun by itself; it takes a child to make it one, to *mean* or *intend* it as a gun. To view a stick as a sword takes a point of view by which the meaning bestowed upon the existential shape is that of sword. Given the proper attitude, anything can be designated as anything else. Chessmen, checkers, even pebbles, can assume the burden of good guys and bad, white queens and black knights. Adults often play as children do, bestowing meanings upon baseball teams and games of cards *as if* they filled a need for tension or excitement, social contact, or a sense of belonging. Songs, dances, films, videos, computer games, literature—all offer sensory phenomena to make meaningful through rapt participation.

Naming a baby, pet, boat, car, city—these, too, offer chances for projecting our meanings onto patterns of existential being. As we move about on the surface of the Earth we carry our longing for familiarity with us, designating places we settle according to our earlier attachments: China, ME; Boston, MA; Salem, OR; Ithica, NY; Memphis, TN; Moscow, ID; as well as New York, New London, New Orleans, New Brunswick, and Nova Scotia.

Nowhere is this transference of old meanings to new phenomena more evident than in the assigning of names to the constellations. If there is indeed a dog (Canis), lion (Leo), crow (Corvus), swan (Cygnus), wolf (Lupus), or even a fly (Musca), in the heavens, it is because we placed it there (along with centaur, dragon, and phoenix) to satisfy a yearning to make the strange familiar in order to incorporate the nearby universe into our scheme of things, the brightest stars providing the syntax by which we impose our free-floating semantic categorizations.

William James speaks of perception as being a state of mind—or it is nothing—and our perception of order among the stars is similar to the order we discover in his mock French phrase, *Pas de lieu Rhône que nous,* when we approach it from the familiar English standpoint provided by "paddle your own canoe," or *Gui n'a beau dit, qui sabot dit, nid a beau dit elle?* as a translation of "When a body, kiss a body, need a body tell?" Thus do we project order onto what would otherwise be nonsense. From my childhood, I well remember, *"Mairzy doats and dozy doats and liddle lamzy divey, A kiddley divey too, wooden shoe."*

The most human of behaviors, devotion to a transitory fashion, clearly illustrates the same dynamic of coupling meaning to being. There is meaning in wearing Madras shorts or miniskirts when they are in vogue, and that is expressed in such phrases as "keeping up with the times," "being smart" or "with it," or "staying in with the crowd." All social groups put their members to a test periodically to weed out the stodgy and independent ones who don't play social games. Fashion does for society what metaphor does for language: it keeps the whole institution vital, stimulating, dynamic. Old ways of being are discarded and replaced by others that stand in distinct contrast to them. If lapels were formerly broad, now they are narrow; if green was in last year, this year's color is purple; if pants were flared, now they're pegged, or perhaps piled up like bellows around the ankles, down to the finest detail—shoelaces and eyeglass frames, belt buckles and social jargon. The old fashion is dead; long live the new (at least for a season). New styles are always billed as daring and exciting, no matter how silly they are. In fact the excitement comes from throwing aside standards by which silliness is judged, so what was once thought outrageous is now the current thing. The meaning stays the same ("I am on the forefront!"), but the concrete display by which that meaning can be achieved keeps changing. Just as the vocabulary and syntax of our speech must be appropriate to our group to be meaningful, so must the syntax of our dress. If our shirts are cut to the wrong pattern, or our hair to the wrong length, we present ourselves as unacceptably deviant, or on the outs. The trick in fashion is to deviate from the old fashion in a novel manner, but in an acceptably conventional novel manner, far enough out to be noticeable, but not so far as to be tasteless (being without taste is the ultimate blunder). Here again is that familiar tension between being and meaning, sensory figures and their categorization, just as in metaphor, humor, naming, and consciousness itself.

Travel to foreign lands—which may seem exotic to us—fills us with novel sights, sounds, and foods that refresh our appetite for stimulating sensory figures. We encounter strangeness and novelty on every side—manners of dressing, greeting, eating, speaking, living—in short, ways of being that are new to us. Our understanding lags. We do not know why the little Japanese lady bows to the speeding express train as it roars through the station, why she sews fishhooks into her son's clothing when he sets out to find a job, or why her family reveres dragonflies and fireflies. We partake of food chopped into unidentifiable bits, delicately arranged in myriad bowls, but have slight idea what it is we might be eating. By encountering these unconventional ways of being, we develop new appreciation for those we are used to, like C. G. Jung struggling southward from the Mediterranean to the oasis city of Tozeur to enhance his view and grasp of European civilization by looking through new eyes.

One of the strongest attractions of travel is the sensitivity to beauty it awakens in us. Back home we take a largely functional view, evaluating things by the meaning and utility they have in our lives because habits have us live more conceptually than existentially. There is another kind of meaning in which the relation between the parts of a sensory whole is of primary importance, not matters of cost, function, or reference within a field of abstractions. This is the realm of aesthetic judgments in which harmony and discord determine the quality of experience. Travel alerts us to this dimension of consciousness because we see so much we cannot understand; we simply have to abandon the familiar frame and open ourselves to sensory qualities having little meaning beyond themselves—to colors, shapes, textures, motifs, materials, patterns, accents—to life and nature as artistic forms of being in the world. Here arrangement and coherence are everything, the way things *are* simply by being taken as themselves. When approached in this way, the entire world becomes an eternal sunset, a display of subtle colors, forms, and patterns that never fade. Kodak, Agfa, and Fuji have made billions of dollars, Marks, and yen by allowing travelers to capture some of the details of such worlds and take them home for display in albums or shows cast on screens as treasures to share with family and friends. In the digital age, we now point our cellphones and shoot, then email the raw results to anyone we think might be interested.

These remarks concerning metaphor, humor, play, naming, fashion, travel, and photography are only a sampling of experiences dependent on our making sensory figures meaningful, a process central to consciousness itself. The world may provide the raw matter and energy that stimulates our senses, but the significance of the resulting phenomena in awareness is up to each of us. The emphasis here must fall more on the *process* of making meaning than on any notion of meaning as a seemingly static feature of experience.

Two related processes appear to be involved: one by which coherent sensory figures reach out for meaning, and another by which the repertory of conceptual meanings simultaneously seeks realization in sensible being. Though being and meaning can be thought of as different aspects of experience, discussion in terms of processes and functions directs us to the complementary kinetic aspects of experience as ongoing activities responsible for the simultaneous coupling of being with meaning. Just as metaphor is fueled by a tension between the novel and familiar, the kinetics of experience depend on a similar tension by which meaning is recognized or discovered in particular sensory figures.

To return to the case of the chalkboard moon taken as a banana, it is fair to ask, what is the dynamic by which an existential shape on the blackboard assumes the meaning of a banana in the mind of a child? It strikes me that two processes must be going on simultaneously within the girl's experience: the concrete crescent is cuing the meaning "banana," while at the same time the conceptual category "banana" is facilitating recognition of the familiar crescent shape. There is an interaction here, a mutual collaboration in which a meaningful episode of experience is synthesized. It is impossible to say which has priority; the drawing was required no more than the meaning, and no less. There appears to be a looping pathway that links the phenomenal and semantic aspects of experience, a mental route by which a two-way exchange takes place, each direction informing and affirming the other. One pathway seems to invite (cue, call-forth, or otherwise incite or activate) a meaning, an intending pathway by which the cue points beyond itself in reference to a repertory of possible objectifying interpretations. At the same time, another pathway seems to convey a perspectival expectation in guiding recognition of the cue as a token of a certain type. These two paths, operating in concert, allow a sensory cue to elicit a meaning, and that meaning to embody itself in a fitting existential figure.

Another clue to this process is given in the wording of the anecdote by the phrase, "I rushed home to tell my mother." Here we have an indication of excitement, arousal, and affective involvement. The girl had learned something in school and was eager to share that learning with someone whose praise she eagerly anticipated. Not only was a meaning triggered by the crescent, but, too, a sense of importance, releasing a corresponding rush of energy.

I view the girl's excitement as akin to the happiness Proust's protagonist in *Remembrance of Things Past* discovered in a spoonful of tea bearing a crumb of madeleine as an echo from his childhood, or the pleasure Thoreau discovered in breaking ground for his cabin in Walden Woods. If such experiences were less provocative, mothers would never be told how to spell "banana," great books would go unwritten, and cabins in the woods would remain idle dreams. These works require expenditure of energy, and arousal beyond the routines of everyday life. Rendering existential patterns meaningful takes both motivation and anticipation of some sort of reward. Learning touches us at a very primitive level, at the depth of our loving and fighting and fleeing, of writing from the heart, and running home to tell mother. Strong emotions are felt as a mediating presence in activating the looping pathways between sensory discernment and intentional retrieval from memory—between sensory figures and their categorization, between being and meaning.

Similar recognition must be paid to memory itself and its essential role in keeping concepts alive as vital members of the interpretive repertory. Its role in maintaining the interpretive loop (as the conjoined pathways might be called) is fundamental; without it there would be no repertory, no "banana" to summon into presence, and a crescent shape on the blackboard would remain forever an empty curve with no capacity to cue a meaning by pointing beyond itself.

How did the young girl come to intend that crude crescent shape as a "banana" as if it were an object in the world, and take responsibility for that object as the true meaning of that particular shape? What was the mental context that made all this possible? Here I have to consider the situation that might have influenced the actual viewing of the crescent as an intentional effort. But I can probe no further because I lack access to the mindset determining the girl's particular reading of her teacher's blackboard drawing. In truth, the only person with access to that mindset is the girl herself. Which I take as justification for the extra work that introspection imposes on us in coming to full understanding of our own minds. The moral is, no one else can do that work for us; if it is to be done, that job is ours alone.

To experience the fabulous world requires us to bring some image of world structure (as perceived) into conjunction with some aspect of personal memory, tuning them to each other as best we can. The resulting story we tell ourselves—the narrative of an interpreted event—is our way of understanding that particular episode of our being in a world we cannot experience directly. When being and meaning come together, both we and our world are born to each other in that moment. Which leads to the next meaningful moment, and on to the next after that. Life is the fable we tell ourselves of our passing through the corridors of consciousness.

But what do we really know of life and the world? Only what we tell ourselves as experience flows into and beyond awareness. We are observers of being and meaning coming together in our minds, interacting more-or-less smoothly, then separating to make room for further such couplings. Who am I? I am a reacher toward coherent phenomena from my repertory of categorical interpretations and, at the same time, a reacher for meaning from the perspective of my being in the moment. My mental activity happens so quickly, it is gone almost as soon as I notice it. I have to pay attention if I want to capture any of it long enough to hold in memory so I can tell it to someone or write it down later on. Expectancy and attention set the stage—not for action itself—but for remembrance to act. They are the gatekeepers of memory that decide what is worth keeping and what isn't, what matters and what doesn't. Getting praise matters; learning spelling words matters; bananas really matter because they are food. A beating heart cannot wait long for food or oxygen, any more than a restless mind can wait to match up sensory stimulation with meaning, meaning with looked-for sensory stimulation. *Slow down! There's a deer in the road ahead, don't you see it? Do you want us to get killed?* Attention and consciousness are on duty all the time, except when we are dozing or asleep. And even then—when we cannot effectively engage our surroundings—we have our moments of arousal when we can rehearse coupling meaning and being in our dreams.

M-o-o-n is a kind of dreamlike spelling of banana. A young girl's putting the one with the other is nothing mysterious. It is the coupling of two aspects of awareness as an item thought, through inexperience, to resolve the very reasonable question, What is the spelling word for tomorrow? The crescent consisted of two intersecting curves on a blackboard—very much like a sketch of a banana. The lines may have been intended to represent a crescent moon, but their moon-ness was given by the word spelled out on the board, not by the lines themselves. To a non-speller, it made sense to reach toward that sketch as a banana, taking it through her eyes into her mind as a banana made flesh, reconstituting it according to a life-long familiarity with bananas. The resonance between the teacher's drawing of a moon and the girl's image of a banana was not quite exact; they were a little out of tune with each other. But the shape animating the schematic crescent was so apt to the meaning radiating from the notion, "banana," that the girl "saw" them as one and the same.

On that occasion, there was not enough of the moon brought into play to alert the student to her error. On a summer night she never would have pointed to the moon and said, "banana." She was so eager to understand the spelling lesson that she converted a minimal cue into a ripe banana without asking the right questions with her eyes, and without knowing that the teacher's crescent could not give sufficiently detailed answers even if she had. The similarity between the concrete figure rendered by her visual system and the abstract shape of a conceptual banana led her to leap to an unwarranted conclusion, or, at best, a hasty one.

Identification of the moon on a summer's night depends on some combination of details such as its position in the sky, brightness, phase, surface mottling, color, size, together with modifications made by clouds, city lights, atmospheric effects, the presence of trees or buildings, its reflection in water, and remarks made by one's companions, among other factors. The sensory evidence provided by the hasty blackboard sketch lacked all such details. There was nothing in that impoverished symbol to check up on in seeking verification. The one relevant clue provided by the context—the lettered "m-o-o-n"—was not available to the girl because for her it was the unknown in the whole equation.

The experiential calculus underwriting consciousness, then, is the process by which individual interest and attention make possible the balancing of a sapient potential for meaning against a sentient potential for being, the two swinging slowly around the still-point that eases the tension of uncertainty, resolving it with a judgment of equivalence between being and meaning—between a sensory presentation and its conceptual or categorical identity as interpreted.

I do this a thousand times a day, don't you? Well, maybe without knowing it, but that's as good a description as I can give of the process I discover through introspection—the same process enabling me to grasp the workings of my mind much as I daily assume I grasp the workings of the world I live in from the standpoint of how I choose to live my life. I put it that way because looking in and looking out are both operations of such daunting complexity as to challenge anyone foolish enough to try to understand them. But those of us who take reward in tackling the difficult, seize that challenge as a dare. Which we as a species seem condemned to do over and over again, using whatever methods and vocabulary are available to us while grappling with that challenge.

All of us subscribe to a host of interpretative schemes with varying degrees of conviction. At any one time we experience the pressures brought by conflicting disciplines and authorities, and must select from among them the one that best answers our doubts and questions at the moment within the context of our current situation. In one situation, a given scheme may enjoy absolute authority, while in another it may serve as only one candidate out of many, and in a third it may be wholly inappropriate. Education is not only a matter of acquiring a serviceable repertory of interpretive schemes, but of acquiring the judgment to choose between rival systems of understanding recommended to us by competing authorities. Trial and error allows us to sort the drove of competing authorities into ranks of probable suitability and, in addition, to choose between rival claims upon our loyalty and credulity. Gradually we refine our judgments, so become more able to suit our schemes for grasping experience to our situations by learning how to bestow the most likely interpretations upon the sensory figures that concern us.

89

Accidents still happen, however (as in the case of the "m-o-o-n, banana," and the assorted incidents of not seeing and inappropriate seeing I give in Chapter 1), and we frequently misjudge our situations and invoke inappropriate interpretive schemes, which should remind us how difficult it is to build a world around our minds, and to make ourselves happen in that world in keeping with our respective styles of interpretation and skills for putting them to good use through deliberate courses of action. I will begin the ending of this chapter with a vaudeville routine:

"Who was that man I saw you with last night?"
"That was no man, that was my husband!"

And one more:

"Why did the teacher draw a moon on the blackboard?"
"That was no moon, that was a banana!"

Tricky business, fitting being to meaning, meaning to being. But since life depends on our getting good at it, it's worth taking the time to do as well as we can. After all, meaning doesn't reside in some external reality composed of objects, people, plants, animals, and minerals—it is something we make for ourselves, inside our own minds. Whatever meanings we discover are *our* doing. There are dog people and cat people and gerbil people and teddy bear people—you name it. Our attachments and affections, preferences and understandings, go where we send them because we are who we are. Which is why there is so much friction in the world between those of us who see it differently, as each of us does.

Picture the scene as the first-grader rushes in to tell her mother she has learned the spelling word for tomorrow: "M-o-o-n, banana!"
"No, dear, that can't be right. Where did you get that idea?"
"Teacher wrote it on the board. She drew a picture of a banana, and wrote beside it 'm-o-o-n.'"
"Show me what the picture looked like."
"It was a banana, like this:" (draw, draw).
"Oh, I see, it does look like a banana, but I think she was drawing a crescent moon, like you see in cartoons to show it is night-time."
"A crescent moon? Is that what it was, not a banana?"
"I think that must have been it."
"So that's not how you spell banana, that's how you spell moon?"

"Yes, m-o-o-n spells moon, not banana."

"I was being silly?"

"You weren't silly at all; it wasn't that good a moon."

"Mommy, mommy, I know the spelling word for tomorrow: m-o-o-n spells moon!"

"Not banana?"

"Silly, I don't know how to spell banana. All I know is m-o-o-n spells moon. I learned that after school."

"Yes, you did, and I'm proud of you."

"It wasn't easy."

"I know dear, it was hard."

Who we are as children or adults is told by how we categorize our sensory impressions in coupling being to meaning, meaning to being, in the process of constructing both the worlds we are to live in and who we are as inhabitants of those worlds. O

CHAPTER 6

FEELING AND EMOTION

I am a self-made empiricist dwelling wholly within the confines of personal experience. The idea of empiricism is suggested by the Greek word *empeiros* meaning to skillfully press ahead in a situation of some peril, that is, to experiment through trial and error. Which accurately sums up the method I am using to compose these chapters based on self-reflection, and then to gather them into a book—a risky venture, indeed. First I compiled a blog of 201 posts as a kind of scratchpad for random reflections about my personal consciousness; then I teased out fifteen major topics covering what was on my mind; I put the topics in sequence, and, devoting a chapter to each, set up a basic narrative on introspection as a means of describing what I discovered. So here I am, staking my mental life—not on what I have been taught by others—but on subjective experience. How risky is that? Yet I know no other way to make sense of myself, my acts, and the unknowable world but by keeping close watch on the one mind in which events accord with my personal awareness. How else am I to know myself except inside-out? To me, introspection is the essence of empiricism. To know myself as an instrument of awareness is a prerequisite for knowing anything at all. I have no choice but to continue pressing ahead into the perilous unknown. The peril lies in being superficial, doing dumb things, getting it wrong, the big It—life itself. To climb a ladder, it's best to go one step at a time.

It is comforting to know I am not alone. A great many articulate people have shared their personal journeys into the interior of themselves. Where do music, poetry, fiction, and autobiography come from if not the depths of the human mind? Consider, for example, this entry Thoreau wrote in his journal on November 21, 1850—160 years ago to the day I am starting this chapter:

> I saw Fair Haven Pond with its island, and meadow between the island and the shore, and a strip of perfectly still and smooth water in the lee of the island, and two hawks, fish hawks perhaps, sailing over it. I did not see how it could be

improved. Yet I do not see what these things can be. I begin to see such an object when I cease to *understand* it and see that I did not realize or appreciate it before, but I get no further than this. How adapted these forms and colors to my eye! A meadow and an island! What are these things? Yet the hawks and the ducks keep so aloof! and Nature is so reserved! I am made to love the pond and the meadow, as the wind is made to ripple the water.

In relating this episode from personal experience, Thoreau is inventing a means of suspending (holding in abeyance) his understanding of things in order to focus on the sensory patterns through which he experiences Fair Haven Pond. That is, he is viewing the scene before him without interpreting what it might mean. Taking in the sensual elements of that scene as they are related within the space of his mind, he notes both pond and island, a meadow between island and shore, a strip of still water out of the wind, and two hawks overhead—basic relationships between clumps of his visual experience. He is dealing strictly with existential patterns uncoupled from their tentative interpretation. He judges everything to be exactly as it should be. That is, he is convinced that his seeing is authentic. Then comes the first of two "yet"s. With his understanding switched off, he does "not see what these things can be." Reduced to forms in awareness, these apparitions have no meaning beyond their appearance as sensory figures. Probing the scene, he asks, "What are these things?" And answers himself with another "yet" introducing the unbridgeable distance he feels between the raw, uninterpreted scene and himself. Without claiming it as his own by categorizing it into one cognitive bin or another, he finds the scene is not truly his; it remains distant and reserved. And then he discovers that he is reaching out to the raw scene with love—even without judging what that scene might be or somehow depict—wishing the scene would explain itself, which it cannot do because meaning is a project of the mind, not the world of phenomena.

Thoreau's journal entry offers a concise illustration of the empiricist's dilemma in uncoupling meaning from being in order to view phenomena in their raw, uninterpreted form by deliberately abstaining from doing violence to them in claiming them from a cultural or habitual perspective. It takes tremendous willpower to let things stand as they are without imposing human values and conceptions upon them. By this view, no wetlands would be converted to golf courses, no River Fleetes turned into sewers, no rainforests felled to make room for cattle and cash crops. Without categorizing and interpreting from a subjective point of view, humans would bring industrial civilization to its knees, and walk the Earth in a perpetual state of bewildered awe, yearning, and unrequited love.

Thoreau's discovery in his risky empirical exercise at Fair Haven Pond is that he is "made to love the pond and the meadow" just as they appear without human intervention. That is, his internal order on that occasion is both more aesthetic and affective than rational. If he had engaged that scene by applying one of the customary categorizations he learned at Harvard, he might have glossed over the feeling that lay underneath. Which is clearly a present danger in placing excessive reliance on rationalized thinking and systematic categorization by which wetlands are converted to golf courses as the "highest and best use" of their acreage, and all other human "improvements" are inflicted on a natural world that supports us all in the most fundamental way possible.

I introduce this striking quotation at the beginning of a chapter on feeling and emotion to suggest how the affective dimension of experience can be made visible in spite of the overlay of rational categorizations we are taught in school *as if* they were properties of the world itself and not our own contributions. Introspection lets me, as an inner empiricist, step out from under that overlay and reach toward sensory being from the perspective of one who, like Thoreau, is openly moved both emotionally and aesthetically by the pure arrangement of things in nature without having to stifle their beauty beneath a load of politically (economically, intellectually, culturally, religiously) correct categorizations. To use but two examples I am familiar with, Thoreau was a journalist, I am a photographer; how we feel about the sensory arrangement of phenomena draws us to our subject matter. Our job is to sweep conventional interpretations aside in revealing the inherent order of nature—both in ourselves and, by imaginative extension, in the fabulous world beyond.

Excessive reliance on categorizations to dress sensory patterns in culturally acceptable terms risks smothering the deeper emotions which might well recommend against many of our shallow and self-serving interpretations. Myself, I feel more comfortable as a voice crying in the wilderness (any mind is a wilderness) than I would crying in a park or city street, with the great shift in underlying assumptions I'd have to make to bring that about. By closely observing my mind, I know how I *actually* feel; in a park, I'd know how I was *supposed* to feel.

How did I feel in those incidents I introduce in Chapter 1? In the first one (being felled by a bicycle when crossing Brattle Square), in a brief span of time I felt shock changing to fear changing to anger changing to chagrin changing to regret, all within a five-minute period during which I kept reviewing what had happened. I felt shock at finding myself sprawled in the street; fear in seeing a truck bearing down upon me while being unable to move; anger at the bicyclist whom I seized on as the "cause" of my predicament; chagrin at realizing I was struck down because I hadn't looked to my right; and regret after I'd crossed the street that I couldn't go back and apologize to the biker and trucker for not only being a fool, but for entangling them in my folly. My emotions, that is, colored how I interpreted what was happening. I was no impersonal observer of events in my own life. I was emotionally involved. Which gave me an autobiographical perspective on events very different from the perspectives of the bicyclist and trucker.

Most striking to me was how quickly fear had hardened into anger, leading me to lash out at what I was afraid of, even though I was the one who hadn't looked both ways when stepping into the street in the first place. But it took me a while to accept responsibility for that lapse. I soon came to see that my initial vulnerability had quickly morphed into an offensive (verbal) onslaught toward the biker, even though I had been the aggressor in blindly leaping into his path. It was I who had imperiled him, not he me. I had never coupled fear and anger before, but observing myself in action, I realized there was an undeniable link from one to the other, summed by the formula: We hate what we fear. Anger is fear twisted around, redirected through hate toward a convenient enemy. Safely on the other side of the street, I was chagrined at realizing I had made the first move, and then felt the stab of remorse. It was all so emotionally complex, these fierce states of mind tumbling in such quick succession that I seemed to experience them all in a jumble of confusion. It took me a while to sort it all out, and I don't think I have reached the end of it yet.

The point of having emotions is the same as having consciousness, to act personally and effectively in the world. In the heat of the moment, at least, reserving the right to refine our actions later on. Emotion urges us either to keep doing what we are doing, or to change course and try something else. If a rhinoceros rumbles out of the brake straight toward me, not knowing what to do isn't good enough. Emotion kicks in with a surge to get me moving one way or another. Think of road rage erupting when another driver cuts you off, putting you at risk, making you afraid—then uncontrollably furious. This is a life and death matter. You swear, lean on the horn, and chase after him to teach him a lesson. Emotions override everything our mothers have taught us, or we were supposed to learn in school. They put Plan B into effect, which often rides roughshod over the public personas we've cultivated over the years, leaving us strangers to ourselves, trying to understand or explain away behaviors we didn't think we had in us.

When the ancient skull I was uncovering along the Columbia River abruptly turned into a turtle shell, I was embarrassed to catch myself thinking I'd be a hero for finding a burial site no one knew about. I had the scenario all worked out in my head—and it fell around my ears like a tin halo. The false pride I'd worked up burned with white heat, searing the lesson into a memory I'd never forget. I can feel it today, and even see sunlight glistening on the river, cumulous clouds in the sky—backdrop to how disappointed I felt with myself.

Which is similar to how disappointed I was when the great doctor told me he didn't know what I had after five days of intensive diagnostic testing in the hospital. Out of the emptiness I felt then, I now cherish a rage at the white-clad authority quacking at his ducklings in the hall outside my room. I never thought to get a second opinion by having another doctor review my test results because the pattern of disappointment had been burnt into me by earlier visits made to at least ten other doctors who had no idea what my problem was. That was it; I was licked. Disappointment was to be my lot in life, together with a simmering anger at the medical profession. Doctors! You know how they are—fancy diplomas on the wall, fancy cars in reserved spaces, kids in fancy schools—as if under their white coats they were smarter than the rest of us. That's the tight little knot of bitterness at the core of my disappointment in learning that my stay in the hospital had been for nothing. I was as ignorant of having celiac disease as I'd ever been.

Through empirical self-reflection, I see I have hung a diploma of my own on the wall of my self-examination room, giving me the right to quietly seethe for the remainder of my life. Seethe at myself for being prideful, and at others whom I view as paragons of pride. I am doubly calibrated by my own emotional experiences in trying to understand myself and my world. Recognizing that fact—characterizing myself as that sort of person—I at least have the option of taking responsibility for warping my personal perspective, skewing my outlook, clouding my judgment concerning certain loaded issues. Introspection is a humbling occupation. Sadder but wiser, we empiricists earn the right to stumble, recover, and lurch ahead one more time. So do we learn through memorable—because painful—experiences.

I was also disappointed to find that the figure I thought was my friend Fred was not Fred but a stranger I was trying to catch up with on Fifth Avenue. Pulling even with him, I recognized immediately I had miscategorized an anonymous figure as my friend. Disappointed for a moment or two, I recalled where I had been going, and went about my business. But the fact that I've remembered that mistake for fifty-five years now tells me something, though I'm not sure what it is. There's more to it than simply mistaking one person for another—I do that all the time without making much of it. Intuition tells me it's about not getting closure on a friendship that was important to me during three years of high school, and for five or six years after that when I'd moved to New York. A lot of my brain is dedicated to memories of Fred and myself exploring together. His mother had an old 1931 Buick in the garage in Seattle, which Fred drove once in a while when he'd convince her to lift her standing ban on his driving the car. I still remember lurching along dark streets in that rigid old box—we called it cruising—wondering where we could get hold of some beer, complaining about the state of the world in 1949. That's the only time I remember listening to popular songs on the radio, when I was a junior or senior in high school. I think my mind was specially equipped to remember sights and sounds during my coming of age—that was my special time, my special world. The later incident of finding that Fred wasn't Fred takes me back to that world. It stands for the last time I think of us together—the end of an era. I can't recall the last time I actually saw Fred, so my mind clings to the last time I *thought* I saw him through a kind of emotional transference patched together in hindsight. At least that's what I now make out of a non-event proven to be so memorable.

Three incidents seem related in my being thwarted one way or another in not being able to do what I wanted to or find what I was looking for. The older I get, the more I hate being thwarted. When slices of a carrot I am cutting cling to the blade of the knife, migrate toward the handle, then drop onto the floor; or tissues tear as I yank them from the box, or else wad up and jam—I get really mad, curse, and for two seconds rail at the universe for balking me in trying to do some simple thing. I felt that way in not seeing the snow-covered Rockies when I had so carefully calculated they should be in clear view. I really, *really* wanted to see those mountains that first time, and I couldn't understand why they didn't leap into view when we were obviously so close. They should have been there, but they weren't because the snow was costumed as clouds in my mind, and the mountains themselves as purple shadows under the clouds. Why weren't they there? Why couldn't I see them? I got pretty wrought up—not because the mountains didn't show, but because my mind unwittingly took them as perfectly ordinary clouds and shadows. Only when I realized the clouds and shadows were fixed in place did I convert them to snow-covered mountains. I'd missed that detail for half an hour, then it struck me—and relieved, I saw them. When much younger, I'd known that same feeling when waiting for somebody to call, or a package to arrive parcel post. I'd sit by the phone, or wait by the window watching for the mail truck. Now it would be the UPS or FedEx truck. Having great expectations is a setup for disappointment and a sense of being thwarted in doing something that feels important to me.

The older I get, the less nimble I become, the more prone I find myself to breakdowns and interruptions in my loop of engagement. I cuss and mutter under my breath, taking offense at not being the man I once was. Being peevish is a sign that an engagement I counted on is now off, or at least takes more concentration than it used to. Now I use such situations to take note of my inner workings, much as a mechanic would listen to the engine in my car to diagnose why it wasn't running properly. When I suffer the peril of frustration, irritation, annoyance, or interruption, I listen to myself moan and groan, sputter and spout obscenities, and am sure to discover what is interfering with the smooth running of my loop of engagement. I try to do this before my annoyance boils over as anger and I lose it, which would only make matters worse.

The case of the missing mustard jar was terribly thwarting because it should have been in the refrigerator where it usually was, but it wasn't there. I was in the middle of making lunch, and I'd reached the point I couldn't go on without mustard. In my scheme of things, the time had come for mustard to walk in on cue—and it didn't show up. My routine fell apart because of that one missing element. I looked everywhere I could think of, and did a slow burn as I was thwarted again and again. I don't like to repeat myself because it shows that the world isn't paying attention. If I put myself out, the world had better hop to! That's how it feels. But wishing doesn't make it so, any more than getting agitated. That's a hard lesson: If things are going to happen, I have to make them happen myself. That is my responsibility, not the world's. But when things aren't where I put them the last time I used them, or are presenting a novel side of themselves I don't recognize because it differs from the generalized image I am looking for, then there's simply no reasonable explanation, and I get that old feeling of being unjustly treated by the big, bad, old world. It's fine to say, "It's better to light a candle than curse the darkness," but if I don't have a metaphorical candle, or a match to light it with, or a flashlight—then that old feeling of being thwarted by the universe sets in. Truly, the times are out of joint. My stars must be crossed. Maybe somebody's put a hex on me. Witches, that's it. Find someone—anyone—to blame and burn their house down; make 'em suffer. As I say, I'm not a rational person.

The scary thing about my own mind is it can get unruly when things don't work out as I hope. Unruly means not governable by rules, law, or discipline. When emotion gets the better of rational thought, which in my case it often does, then my mind jumps out of its habitual track and goes hurtling through the landscape wreaking havoc all around. I pride myself in being a sensible, reasonable person, so when that is obviously not the case, my tidy world crumbles to dust. Is my headstone really going to read, "Done in by a mustard jar"? Sometimes that's how it feels—like the world is against me, when in my right mind I know the world is of my own making, so I am conspiring against myself. Again, a hard lesson to learn.

Deleting the quarry photos before I saved them to my hard drive was a crushing blow to my professional self-esteem. I went from reveling in the pictures I'd taken to bemoaning their loss—and I had no one to blame but myself. To find that I am my own worst enemy is thwarting on a very deep level of self-disappointment. I was stunned because I couldn't imagine myself doing such a thing, which all evidence showed is exactly what I'd done. I was in denial for about a minute, looking in the trash, seeing if there was any trace of the pictures in my camera—to no avail. Then it sank in. I did this impossible thing: I deleted the photos on my own, deliberately—not realizing what I was doing. Beyond incompetent, I was stupid. That's a hard swing to make, from being—if not the greatest—then certainly the worst. But there it is. At least I had wits enough to see there was only one thing to do—retake the pictures. Which I knew I couldn't do, but I had to make an effort to salvage the situation however I could.

My situation at the time was that in making a PowerPoint on quarrying in Sullivan, Maine, from 1830 to 2010, I'd been unable to find any photos of quarry work actually being done in the 1880s and 1890s. The historical images I'd found all showed quarry workers in aprons standing with their tools on their shoulders, posing for the few seconds it took out of the year to get the image on film, while all the work they did went unrecorded because cameras were too slow in those days to capture the action. I'd vowed to take detailed sequences of work in the one Sullivan quarry still in operation—and I'd blown it all on my own. I let myself be shattered for about two minutes sitting motionless in my chair, then I put a fresh battery in my camera, drove the thirty miles to the quarry, told the quarryman what had happened, and continued where I'd left off earlier that day.

Negative feelings are strong teachers. Don't ever do that again! Take pains to do the job right; if you don't, you might as well not do it at all. Or lower your ambitions: Get a job washing dishes in a restaurant. These are powerful lessons. Submitting to my chosen methodology of the empiricist's relentless trial by fire, I get such messages fairly frequently. That is, I give them to myself. No one asked me to live my life as I do; it is *my* expectations I am trying to live up to. How I deal with my mistakes is precisely my business. That's our social contract: you tend to yours, I'll tend to mine. That way the human world may continue to revolve a while longer.

In two of the incidents I related, I felt a strong sense of relief, as if a load were lifted from my shoulders. When I realized I was agonizing over a trash bag blowing in the wind, not a moribund crow, and the crashing jet was more accurately a sweptback rooftop antenna, I was disburdened of having to wring a tough bird's neck, and of calling 911 to report a catastrophe. Whew! Which is why business as usual has such strong appeal. Boring, yes, but with the charm of complacency. Commotions and alarms may add excitement to dramas, but their rowdiness takes a toll in stress and anxiety. When the hoarse voice shouting "Fa, Fa" clicked in my auditory brain as "Fire! Fire!", I jumped out of bed, saw flames across the street, and called the fire department in one coherent move. One of my mind's main jobs is to tell true alarms from false. That takes a lot of trial and error if I want to get it right next time on the first trial.

In the sink-song episode, I felt a yearning for the song that proved so elusive, which may have been more about lost youth than any particular song. It was a reminder of the era when Fred and I were buddies, and we both had lives to look forward to. Today, that song is from a forgotten past so deep I only know there was such a song, but have no notion what it was. These days, I yearn for the song only as a sign there was a deeper past when it might have held some meaning for me. Yearning for something to yearn for—that's a sure sign of old age.

The discomfort I felt when the sex educator singled me out of the audience was at being put on the spot for I knew not what. What'd I do to make myself stand out in her eyes? Nothing behavioral, as it turned out; it was a case of inadvertent resemblance—which came across to me as feeling like mistaken identity. Imagine being in a police lineup and having someone finger you as the perpetrator of a crime. That's the stuff nightmares (and memories) are made of, and my mind considers worth filing for reference.

I don't know if fascination is an emotion, but that's what I felt while watching the cartwheel display of aurora borealis. I couldn't take my eyes off it. It was like the first day of school in seventh grade when a girl in my class showed up with breasts giving new shape to her sweater. Who could have imagined? When she was in the room, I pictured her vividly, even if she was behind me. My awareness took on a new dimension, as it were. Which is pretty much what the aurora achieved. I didn't know such displays were possible. I liked it, I liked it. That, too, I remember.

Consciousness, I am saying, like food preparation, combines several ingredients in producing a coherent experience. Introspection, like dining, is a matter of appreciating the contribution of each one that went into making the recipe, as well as its fittingness to the hunger of the moment. Feeling and emotion are two of the ingredients of consciousness, along with sensory figures, their interpretation, the grasp of the two when taken together as understanding in the presence of affect, all constituting an episode of meaningful being—the meal itself—as a mindful event. In fact, I suspect that the underlying emotion makes the combination possible by joining both the existential and meaningful aspects of experience within a loop of mutual expectancy fulfilled in felt and motivated awareness. Looking within myself, I identify these facets over and over again in everyday awareness, particularly of the more lasting and memorable episodes such as the incidents on which these findings are based.

Feeling, emotion, and affect are often used interchangeably in referring to the passionate aspect of consciousness. To gain a sense of its vitality, imagine life without passion, excitement, sentiment, affect, emotion, or feeling. Why bother? Exactly! What would be the point? Which suggests that life without passion would be a kind of living death—a contradiction of life itself. Yet our educational system often underplays the role of the emotions in everyday life as somehow unessential, as if a state of pure reason were the desired end of humankind. Introspection tells me otherwise. What school has ever offered a class in sentiment, passion, lust, or affection? We train rats by punishing and rewarding them; what do we suppose these are if not affect-arousing stimuli of a particular polarity? Yet we often go out of our way to suppress mention of any similar dimensions in our experience. For myself, I uncover powerful emotions at the core of every memorable episode of my conscious life. Life without emotion would be an oxymoron—at best a contradiction as the ultimate unthinkable thought. Not an ideal but the most cruel punishment I can imagine.

I find it convenient to think of feeling (distinct from emotion) as a dipole with opposite polarities, one positive, one negative. I use the term valence (or polarity) to distinguish between those states of mind we seek and those we try to avoid (even though they find us whatever we do). I think of the valence of an emotion as its goodness or badness from a personal point of view. To some, jokes can be *offensive,* so *not funny!* Other affective dipoles include: pleasure-pain, confidence-caution, elation-dejection, love-hate, glad-sad, liking-loathing, pride-guilt, beauty-ugliness, care-neglect, rapture-rage, joy-sorrow, tenderness-harshness, desire-avoidance, and so on.

When I was in eighth grade, I looked for the scariest rides a carnival offered, and would ride them until the lights went out, sometimes for hours. In my thirties, I had a change of heart, and have avoided Ferris wheels, cable cars, ski lifts, and high-flying jets ever since. Activities I used to take pleasure in became pure torture. Whatever changed as I aged, the upshot was that the valence had shifted from excitement to fear, and that was all there was to it.

I now own up to a well-developed fear of high places having no visible means of support. Mountain trails are OK because they are solid. I trust granite to hold me up. But when there is air between me and the ground, I get out of there a.s.a.p. Someone once told me how great the Top of the Sixes was, the bar and restaurant in the penthouse at 666 Fifth Avenue. Without thinking, I decided to check it out. The elevator wasn't so bad because I couldn't see the shaft stretching beneath my feet. Some 480 feet up, the doors opened onto a bar on the right and floor-to-ceiling windows straight ahead. I strode manfully to the windows, glanced down forty-one floors toward the street, turned, walked back to the elevator, rode down, and that was my trip to Top of the Sixes. Immediate retreat was my only option. But I could see how the bar might sell a lot of martinis to people like me who were stuck there.

Lighthouses have the same effect—the ones with open grilles in the steps so you can see all the way down. Maine has some great lighthouses, but I've never made it up one of them yet. Jet airplanes terrify me when I think of myself as a potential passenger. I remember one turbulent flight over Montana in the 1950s when the plane yanked up and down for half an hour. I thought the wings would fall off. For thirty minutes I was terrified. Yet small, single-engine planes don't bother me. I like riding the wind, as if it were holding me aloft on great wings, like an eagle or hawk.

My most painful memory of high places was taking the elevator up through the arch of the Gateway to the West in St. Louis. I sometimes wonder if the arch was part of a scheme to smear the reputation of Lewis and Clark. It is run by the National Park Service, which led me to trust it against my better judgment. The elevator is a train of little capsules hitched together like peas in a pod, so I was crammed into a hot, airless ball with five sweaty stranger who were probably as scared as I was. The ride began underground, and crept up slowly, slowly, creaking and rocking as if about to break down—leaving us (in my imagination) stranded with no way to get down. I could picture my progress with X-ray vision through the arch as if I were outside looking in. There's Steve the idiot, trapped in his death bubble. After what seemed like five days—or was it years?—we made it to the top of the arch. From there, the deck curves upward, with windows on either side. Tricky windows because they lean out at an angle so you can look straight down. I walked to the center of the arch, took one look down—into emptiness, then a pavement of red bricks far below—and crept back to the death cars on bent knees. I got in and waited. And waited, alone in my cramped peapod universe. It took forever to fill each car so we could beam down to Earth. But there was no beam, just a slow, wobbly descent into hell. If I was in charge of the CIA and wanted to torture terrorists, I would replace Gitmo with Gatemo, and get every one of them to squeal on his best buddies.

That was an instance of emotion not merely underlying experience, but being on top as the major component all the way. Similarly, when I listen to music or make photographs, my aesthetic sense is on top. Aesthetics is the placing of emphasis on sensory qualities of phenomena—on size, shape, color, direction, proximity, texture, spatial or tonal relationships, motion, continuity, symmetry, and so on. Leaving conceptual categories and meanings to fend for themselves. This is a huge part of my consciousness unearthed in the course of personal introspection. Some of it is innate, some acquired through training. I took two courses on aesthetics in college, but they did nothing for me because they were all about ideas, and in my mind, aesthetics has little to do with ideas. Aesthetic schemes deal with the structure of being—of sensory relationships giving characteristic form to existential figures. Studying aesthetics in terms of words and ideas is like studying architecture without walking through buildings. Aesthetics deals with the architecture of phenomena, of existence itself. Logic deals with the architecture of thought and ideas—another topic altogether. But because experience is so fluid, both architecture and logic are too rigid to serve as adequate models of either sensory awareness or its interpretation, both of which flow through the mind, resembling rivers, clouds, or changing seasons more than some form of mental engineering.

What I call valence, I now believe, is a primitive (fundamental) gauge of how feelings are shaped by comparisons in the brain in an effort to get clear on deciding how to regard a situation and act appropriately within it. Reality, whatever it might turn out to be, is more a continuous flux of radiations, shadows, reflections, gradations, and interactions than we commonly suppose. It is not only complicated but ever-changing. Visualizing it—the portion we are interested in—is more difficult than we often admit. And deciding how best to act appropriately to it, more difficult still. Yet we do it every day in comporting ourselves in respect to the notions we entertain in our heads about what is happening around us and in determining how best to respond. Living is based on what we believe is going on, and what we think we should be doing about it at the time. Feelings help us do this by giving us a sense of direction, which is what the valence—the desirability or undesirability we read in a feeling—suggests to us. That is, feelings in consciousness are interpreted, just as sensory phenomena are. They are edited in compliance with the teachings of past experience, then put forth in summary form of good or bad, right or wrong, yes or no, to guide us in deciding what to do in a particular situation. Reality, then, is crafted by our minds to accord with our current desire and prior experience. Nothing is more personal or subjective than that.

The gist of that paragraph came to me in a slight fraction of a second, yet it took me over a minute to read what I wrote out loud, and considerably longer to expound in those 257 words. Consciousness and action in the world progress at very different rates because of the delay imposed by having to realize awareness in terms of mental planning and physical execution. Saying a word, for example, is much faster than having to spell it out in order to write down in the context of a continuous sequence of thought and expression. The valence of a feeling gives us a head start in translating thought into action. In providing a sense of direction, it starts us off with a particular goal in mind. Attaining that goal, however, depends on the skill with which we are able to make ourselves happen by actualizing our intentions. Valences, then, are a shorthand form of preference for acting in certain ways. Seeing that rhino emerge from the brake, we have to act fast, and the valence we feel at the moment gives us a head start. If we hesitate, we are in serious trouble.

Feelings, emotions, phenomena, and interpretations are different dimensions of consciousness distinct from subsequently committing ourselves to one form of bodily action or another, just as daydreaming is different from being in the world. And taking drugs is different from daydreaming. In a practical sense, reality has more to do with how we actually act in the world than how we might conceive of ourselves acting in the world, or sensing a vague preference for acting this way or that (as the valence of a feeling might indicate). Caffeine, nicotine, alcohol, opium, cocaine, marijuana—these and other mind-altering drugs affect the workings of consciousness itself, changing the clarity, nature, form, and salience of phenomena, and the rate at which, and means by which, they succeed one another. I include drug-induced states among such affective modes as feelings, emotions, pain, pleasure, valence, aesthetics, depression, elation, attraction, and so on. The chemicals we ingest alter not only the way we see the world but how we act in seizing on that world, changing the world by altering how we choose to live in it. Diet does the same. Not all foods are equivalent in how they nourish our bodies and minds. To take an obvious example, I am not the same person either physically or mentally when I eat products containing gluten (the protein that gives wheat its cohesiveness) that I am when I abstain from it entirely. As for alcohol, I regret almost every act I committed under its influence. It made me a far unhappier person than what I consider my normal, sober self. I idly wish I could undo the harm I did to others—and the consequences for myself—when I drank to excess.

Then there is the affective side of sex, marriage, childrearing, and all the other aspects of human sexuality. You don't have to read Freud to know that sexuality—a big part of human experience—is charged with feelings and emotions, often the deepest and most powerful we experience in a lifetime. In some situations, sexual urges can have a very positive effect on experience; in others, a squelching effect that stops us in our tracks. That valence is determined not by the phenomena involved but by the mind entertaining them as it struggles for clarity in order to act appropriately in emerging situations. Feelings are an important facet of consciousness in alerting us to a yes or no, go or no-go, signal before we commit ourselves to a course of action. Feelings arise when we ask ourselves, should I or shouldn't I? Which human cultures, in answering such questions for us, package into teachings of virtue, sinfulness, and morality—usually of the "Do as I say, not as I do" variety. Just saying "no" avoids the whole dynamic of desire, temptation, and arousal, which I find through introspection to be an attractive part of daily life. Not that I am committed to the pursuit of personal gratification, but developing sensitivity to and appreciation for the allure of the moment provides a spark of excitement, telling me I am engaged on a meaningful level of existence, which is right where I choose to live. If young people (living by the prohibitive word of their elders' advice) don't learn to live on that level, they are not being adequately prepared for an adult life filled with a wide range of harsh and tender emotions.

I sometimes wonder if the masking of Islamic women's charms is not a public denial (literally, a cover-up) of sexual urges men find too hot to handle, so pretend those urges do not exist by projecting them onto women, blaming them as temptresses who must be hidden beneath shapeless layers of cloth. How we present ourselves as sexual beings is a sensitive issue in every culture. Largely because the relation between the sexes is the fundamental reason we have cultures in the first place. This is the sort of concern that led nineteen men from a foreign culture to board four airplanes on September 11, 2001, with deliberate intention to inflict as much harm as they could on a people with a history, when working, serving, or traveling in the Middle East, of (inadvertently) offending the manhood and cultural beliefs of their hosts.

This was an incident in which males from one culture took a stand against a different culture for, as they viewed it, flaunting its ways and beliefs in an insensitive, arrogant, and offensive manner. When manhood is threatened, watch out!—a punch in the face is sure to follow. Few in America saw the blow struck on 9-11 from an anthropological or cultural (rather than criminal or military) perspective. But the outrage felt in response to how Americans conduct themselves abroad *as if* to elicit some kind of reaction is, indeed, more an intercultural than a military matter. If nearly 3,000 innocents had not died, two landmark building been leveled, and the headquarters of the US military not been violated, in such a case we might not have lashed out by bombing Afghanistan and subsequently trumping up excuses for invading Iraq. But that havoc did occur; the valence was too strong for the tender American mind to resist.

After ten years of war, we can reconsider whether or not that was the most appropriate response we could have made. Certainly some of the families of those who died in the destruction of the Twin Towers are unlikely ever to change their minds. But the families of soldiers and civilians wounded or killed in the aftermath might wonder why their sons and daughters bore the burden of revenging the first wave of deaths. Once begun, where does the carnage stop?

When loins are girded and weapons primed, how do we un-gird and un-prime them? Once offense is taken, can it ever be forgiven, much less understood? More likely by counsel from the seasoned and wise than the ardent or angry.

Time and again on the world stage, emotional valences in individual minds have inflicted lethal consequences on those who view things differently. Hatred against others who trespass on ingrained sexual customs can lead both men and women to terrorize people calibrated to deal with their sexuality according to radically different traditions. When cultural institutions (legal, educational, religious, for example) judge individual sexual valences in terms of right and wrong (decent and indecent, proper and improper, natural and unnatural), they mean to achieve social harmony by declaring certain valences as normal and thereby correct. But such declarations do little to lessen the variety of affective states that unique members of the larger society experience within themselves. In my lifetime, French-speaking Acadians in Maine have been forced to speak English, left-handed children forced to write with their right hands, gays and lesbians forced to pretend they were straight—all being made to deny major determinants of their inner lives for the sake of conforming in outward appearances to the prevailing, one-size-fits-all norms of the society presuming to judge their behavior. When social institutions do violence to individuals in establishing such norms, is it any wonder that sometimes those individuals rebel and fight back against an oppressive society?

Yes, personal feelings have consequences. No enemy is worthy of death but thinking and feeling make it so. To deliberately kill other persons, we must first kill them in our minds, convincing ourselves that as inferior beings, they deserve to pay for offending us. If we fear what is strange or different simply because we are unaccustomed to it, and that fear hardens into hate, then anger at confronting the stranger can support outrageous behavior directed at destroying that which discomforts us. It is irrational to blame others for the valences we experience in our minds. But humans are not known for being rational. That is a myth we recite to set ourselves up as the good guys in every conflictive situation. Our norm is to excuse ourselves in order to blame our troubles on outsiders—the team from Away, those who are not members of our in-group, that marauding gang from the next block or far side of town.

In the early 1900s, my mother spent time with an aunt who lived in Boston. Coming into the street one day, she met what she called a "Chinaman"—the first she'd ever seen—passing on the sidewalk. She burst into tears and ran back into the house. That was all it took to terrorize a girl who'd grown up in Maine without ever seeing such a person. But her terror was her own; the stranger was no terrorist. What if she'd strapped on a belt of explosives and asked the way to Chinatown? Farfetched? Exactly. But because of the emotional valence inherent in such an experience, the terror seems real and wholly justified to the one who experiences it.

Anger is fear twisted around, redirected through hate toward a convenient—and hopefully appropriate—enemy. Many jobs in law enforcement and the military are fearful jobs—hateful jobs. When fear stirs up anger, we should not be surprised at any aftermath of brutality. Training troops for combat duty, we want to believe that they will revert to their pre-training selves upon returning home. But combat emotions are memorable for good reasons: in dangerous situations, abrupt signals can save lives by triggering evasive actions on cue. The aim of military training is to convert learned behaviors into reflexes. It makes no difference if the signal is from hostile fire or a backfiring car; the point is fast action. Which can lead to battlefield feelings and responses being carried over to civilian situations where they are inappropriate, leading to stress and conflicting feelings of desire, fear, hate, anger, remorse, guilt, among others. Emotional reality gears us for immediate action; it is no respecter of altered locations or situations. An ongoing practice of introspection would help to familiarize us with the eddies and backwaters of our minds as a reminder not to be overly hasty in categorizing cues and situations without thinking, and to be wary of demonizing those who are demonstrably different from ourselves.

On the other hand, many child abusers are members of an inner circle they share with their victims, gaining access of convenience, which others may not view with sufficient caution. Barring the door is no protection against those already inside. Family living is an exercise in trust. Am I to be trusted? Are you? The first way to find out is for me to ask the question, seeking the answer through intensive self-reflection—and for you to do the same. The worst thing to do is deny that our affective states could possibly bring harm to anyone else. The appetite of American industry for unending war provides all the evidence I need to claim the danger lies in us, not any lurking enemy. Some prefer to think of it as the "defense" industry. Which is like justifying a first-strike capability as a manly form of self-defense against fictional chemical, nuclear, or biological attacks. Putting our troops in harm's way is a meaningless slogan when, despite the best of intentions, we are the aggressor bent on doing harm because our economy and vanity depend on it.

America, I feel, needs a good dose of soul searching before it sets out again to save the world from terrorism (or immigrationism, for that matter). Such soul searching would entail personal introspection on a national scale. I don't know about you, but my ancestors were immigrants to these shores, largely undocumented. If they'd been sent packing at the time, their families broken up, I wouldn't be here today, and Native Americans wouldn't be called Indians.

The affective dimension of the human mind is one of the most telling of our attributes. It governs or influences everything we take to be real, everything we think, everything we do. I can't speak for anyone else, but personal introspection tells me this is true in my case. In the next chapter, I will deal with the loop of engagement between my conscious mind and the fabled world I live in. I have now reached the point I can make some sort of sense of the ongoing interaction between how I externalize my inner life in a world I can't know directly, coupled to how I take events from that world into my consciousness as signs of how the world receives what I think I am doing. Just as my digestive and circulatory systems facilitate exchanges of food and gas with my environment in support of my metabolic activity, so my nervous system facilitates a similar exchange of sensory and motor signals in support of my conscious and unconscious awareness. Here, again, I take full responsibility for that interaction in connecting "my" mind to "my" world—the mind that I am with the world where I claim to live. O

CHAPTER 7

LOOP OF ENGAGEMENT

Thirty years of personal introspection tell me I interpret my sensory world in order to act more-or-less effectively in a situation as I construe it, even though I can't directly confront that situation apart from how I render it in personal consciousness. I characterize that situation in terms of sensory figures, interpretations, and understandings as influenced by the affective valence steering my attention at the time. In planning and acting within that felt situation, my mind sets up a looping engagement with a world I cannot know in itself, enabling me to trade overt physical gestures for sensory input, followed by a series of adjusted gestures and revised inputs, mediated by personal feelings, judgments, values, goals, and prior experiences.

That is the gist of my argument to this point. My thinking in writing the foregoing paragraph stems from my 1982 dissertation, *Metaphor to Mythology: Experience as a Resonant Synthesis of Meaning and Being* (University Microfilms International, 1983), in which I wrote regarding my "schematic circuit diagram of sensory pathways in the brain" (*see* Appendix, page 272) based primarily on animal research published between 1970 and 1981:

> [T]he external milieu [or "world"] serves to close the loop between behavior and sensory reception, between discriminative attention and sensory perception, the *inter*-active or dialogical loop by which the individual maintains an ongoing exchange of gestures with others and with a world (pages 274-276).

That is the origin of what I am writing about in this chapter, the loop of engagement incorporating the physically active self on one hand and the existentially perceptive self on the other, an idea I have been developing for the past thirty years. As I picture it in my mind, such a loop represents a process linking personal consciousness to the hidden and unknowable world on the far side of my sensory receptors (which translate ambient energy into neural signals). My actions are addressed to that world, which returns stimulation to my senses as the basis of phenomena (flavors, odors, sights, sounds, and tactile impressions) and valenced feelings interpreted in a meaningful way by my personal consciousness. Those sensory figures feed forward to further planning and action on the basis of my current understanding of the world as construed in my mind, and to further sensory awareness as subsequently updated and refined.

Round and round go the pulses coursing through my nervous system, *from* action, *through* the gap of the world, *to* felt and interpreted sensory figures, their reconsideration, refinement, adjustment, and subsequent action. All of which can take place on several levels of discernment at different rates of mental consideration. The *reflex* level of processing is the fastest, so when someone throws a fistful of sand at me, I shut my eyes, turn away, and duck down—all in one swift motion without having to think. The *rote* or *habitual* level of mental processing is almost as fast, so I can automatically sharpen a pencil or ride a bike without having to think, taking only a split-second pause to consider my options. Acting on the level of *assumptions and ideology,* nervous processing may take a brief moment to kick in, but once activated, allows for prompt action. Most such hastily planned actions take place below conscious awareness. On the level of *full conscious deliberation,* however, when various aspects of an issue are to be considered, action may be delayed for seconds, minutes, or weeks while I consider and eventually decide what to do.

The loops of personal engagement by which I see us reaching out to our worlds through various gestures, and those worlds reaching in to us as parties responsible for such actions as we have taken or are considering—these loops exist in our brains as molecules, ions, neurotransmitters, and pulsing electrical charges coursing across cell membranes and through networks of nerve fibers. Wholly oblivious to this rush of neural traffic, we entertain only a flow of sensory phenomena through our minds, which we duly interpret, understand, emotionally probe, compare, remember for a time, and even feed forward to the planning areas of our minds. In due course we answer the world by making a physical response appropriate to our grasp of the situation we think we are in.

All this mental processing takes time and energy, which are factors in our deciding which level of processing to employ in devoting ourselves to the issue of the moment. What feeling tone and urgency do we feel? Are we interested, involved, engaged? What is being asked of us? What are our options? Are we being threatened, assured, invited, condemned? Decisions, always decisions, which are the essential business of consciousness to make in fitting each of us to our respective worlds, and those worlds to us as we present ourselves at the moment. Consciousness is nothing if not fraught with choices to make before we act. I propose loops of engagement as the theater of mental operations in which those choices and decisions get made, either consciously or unconsciously, but made personally by each of us nonetheless in response to discrepancies arising between our actions and relevant sensory stimulation.

In this chapter I want to address the felt and dynamic nature of such loops of engagement, together with a few of the implications for how I behave in making myself happen in a world I know more by repute or inference than through immediate experience. And on a wider screen, I want to consider the relation between the parallel universes of our personal experiences—yours and mine—as we do our best to make sense of our respective lives as situated in our subjective worlds so we can simultaneously specialize and cooperate in order that our personal courses of action truly complement one another.

I will begin with a tale of a botched loop of engagement that came to me early this morning in a dream:

> I was driving north on a two-lane road for some twenty miles at night over bridges, through tunnels, facing glaring headlights coming against me. The problem was I could see to the side, but not ahead, so kept wandering out of my lane, terrified, not able to stay on my side of the line. Looking askance, I could see approaches to bridges and tunnels, but only the glare of oncoming traffic, not the vehicles themselves. I pulled over to see if I could find what was wrong, but couldn't, so pulled back on the road. At one point I drifted into the oncoming lane and saw a shadowy school bus coming at me, then at the last second veering into my proper lane to avoid me in my improper lane. Having to make the trip for desperate reasons, I kept going, fearful the whole way. I steered by looking in the rearview mirror, trying to figure out where I was on the road by watching that reversed image. Reaching a small town, I pulled over and got out of the car. I finally saw the problem: two large opaque panels lay against the windshield, blocking my view. I'd driven the whole way looking to the rear, gauging

where I was on the road in relation to headlights glaring behind me, not ahead. Policemen I seemed to know (as aspects of myself, after all) gathered around the car to consider my situation. Earnestly, they examined the opaque panels, and made clear to me, as a menace to society, I was heading for prison. I would never drive again. I wanted to call someone, but there was no phone. I realized I was dreaming while walking down a long corridor toward a door behind bars.

I have often had the thought that my sense of days ahead is rooted in past experience, so that I expect the future to be an extension of bygone days, not something wholly new. What is behind me, that is, provides the stance from which I look forward. Ironically, my outlook is trapped in the past. The dream seems to translate that temporal idea into the idiom of space. Not seeing ahead, I am guided solely by what is aside or behind me. Hindsight, that is, is my chief instrument—my compass—for looking to the future. That is a terrifying realization. I am locked into the same old, same old. Back to the future, indeed!

Such is my loop of engagement with a world I cannot know in itself. I lurch ahead expecting to find more of what I already know. And I find myself in the wrong lane facing a dark bus bearing down on me. It is clearly the school bus driver's move if the crash is to be averted for I am helpless, totally dependent on him—the bus driver part of myself. Luckily, the driver swerves at the last moment. Not so luckily, as the penalty for endangering him and his passengers, I am to be taken off the road and sent to jail. That is the world's response to my driving essentially blind, much as I was felled by a cyclist while attempting to cross a one-way street while fully awake, yet not seeing.

That interpretation highlights two complementary modes of expectancy within a dream situation, one spatial, one temporal. The spatial mode applies to changes resulting from my personal actions in weaving across the road or walking down a corridor; the temporal mode applies to changes I am not responsible for—the bus swerving out of my path at the last instant. In the dream, which is wholly *my* dream, and in my interpretation of it, both modes play out in an apparent unity of time and space as the medium of consciousness itself. In dreams, we cannot really perform the acts we seem to, nor truly perceive the events which happen to us, leaving the medium of consciousness free to explore how we might act and the world might respond to our hypothetical, poetical, or fanciful gestures. A great many of my dreams are about getting from one place to another by one means or another under circumstances of great difficulty. Typically, I am lost in my dreams, doing my best to find my way by bus, car, subway, or on foot. I make a move, and the world (really, the world memory construes for me) makes a countermove that invariably surprises me. I see dreams as a metaphorical kind of game like chess or checkers where I keep violating the rules, and suffering emotionally-charged penalties as a result. I always end up more lost and forlorn in each dream episode than when I started. If the tension becomes unbearable, I wake up. I think I have really one basic dream played out in myriad installments, all exercises challenging my presumptive mastery of time and space—of dealing with interacting self-changes and world changes—all revealing what a rank amateur I am as a conscious being.

Implicit in such dreaming is a fundamental disparity between where I am and where I want to be, between what I can do and what I can't manage on my own. These nocturnal comparisons seem to generate error signals from the fact I can neither act nor perceive appropriately because, in fact, I am asleep, leaving me dependent on habits, affective memories, and motivating drives or appetites to do their best in carrying on while I am incapacitated.

In waking life, space is the medium in which I act; time is the medium in which the world makes its response to my acting. Round and round we go, my world and I, always testing each other in trying to achieve some kind of accord in time and space, the here and now. Wherever I am, I am always *here*. Whatever time it may be is told by assorted worldly agents as they affect my presence in the *now*. Space is a measure of my acting in the world; time is a measure of the world acting on me. Both modes of consciousness giving me a sense of being in the world, of the world being in me. Eureka, my spatiotemporal reality.

Could it be that our minds and dreams alike are aroused by comparisons between outgoing and incoming neural signals resulting in a valenced discrepancy that stirs us to consciousness? Binocular vision does, in fact, give rise to a sense of depth resulting from the slightly different phenomenal scenes produced by our left and right eyes in viewing the world from outlooks some three inches apart. Rapid eye movements (saccades) between fixation points of clear seeing are steered not only by visual feedback but by auditory, tactile, remembered, and vocal signals as well. And in the cerebellum, comparison between motor intent and sensory feedback produces refinement of subsequent behavior. Could a disparity between actions as performed and sensory figures bearing witness to the results give rise to consciousness itself as emergent awareness of the difference between what we hope our muscles will achieve and what our senses tell us actually happens? I know for myself I am mentally stimulated by novelty and put at ease (if not to sleep) when everything runs according to plan.

Such conjectures may sound like nonsense to you, as anyone's inner turmoil must to the extent it differs from your own. But I wonder if our methods for deriving our respective senses of space and time—qualities of consciousness itself—are really that different. In my case, spatial dimensions of my experience in feet or miles—my calibrated sense of left and right, north and south, up and down, in and out, far and near, tall and short, and so on—are derived from my sense of physical exertion as I move about right here where I am. Time, on the other hand, is given me in reference not to my own exertion but to something noticeably changing outside and apart from myself—ultimately, by the apparent motion of the sun through the sky, which traces back to Earth's rotation on its axis as humanly calibrated on a scale of twenty-four hours. Whether electrical, mechanical, digital, or otherwise, clocks mimic that rotation, "keeping" time for us, so when we ask the time, there it is on the dial for us to read out for ourselves. I do that for myself; you do that for yourself. We are calibrated in much the same way. That is, our personal actions and the actions of others are similarly calibrated in our minds in terms of the measuring systems our culture provides to us so that we can talk about such events in the same words *as if* time and space were in the world and not in our minds. But even using the same vocabulary to talk about internal and external changes, the actual experience of such changes is in our respective streams of consciousness, and we use the same words in talking about different things altogether—as is the case with *my* dreams and awareness here and *your* dreams and awareness there.

I offer my getting hit by a bicyclist while crossing Brattle Square as an example. I acted first, looking across the street and to my left (but not my right). The world responded by informing me (via sensory phenomena) that a truck had turned the corner, which I, in turn, took to be far enough away that I could safely make it across.

Stepping off the curb, I collided with an aspect of the world I had not seen coming toward me, and was sent sprawling onto the pavement. To which the world responded in the person of the truck driver putting on the brakes and coming to a stop just short of where I lay too stunned to move. Recovering somewhat, I waved a grateful salute to the driver. Looking to see what I had run into, I saw the bicyclist standing by the curb. When our eyes met, he said he was sorry (a detail I left out of the original telling). I told him through clenched teeth I hoped he'd rot in hell. The truck waited, the driver motioning for me to cross (another detail). Looking both ways this time; seeing no traffic, I limped across the street, reaching the far curb somewhat later than I had expected to.

The situation unfolded in stages of acting and subsequent awareness as an active exchange of giving and taking in my personal consciousness. Containing factors I had not considered, the *here* turned out to be more detailed than I had supposed. Three bodies were moving in relation one to another, a more complicated equation than I had imagined. But in the end, through interpersonal negotiations, I crossed the street, the truck driver moved on, and the bicyclist continued his errand. I have long regretted blaming and yelling at the cyclist. And been grateful to the driver of that truck. Here I am decades later replaying that scene because my memory won't let me forget it. There is something important in that incident I do well to remember.

A situation is an experiential event in which personal space and impersonal time conjoin in different minds to produce a more-or-less coherent happening in the minds of those involved. Situations unfold as influenced by the tensions and emotions between actors, this happening, then this, and then this. The overall process taking place in the mind of one participant or observer is what I refer to as a loop of engagement. That loop is nothing less than one person's spatiotemporal reality. Which is bound to be different in each case. Some notice more sensory details than others, some are more emotionally invested in the process, some interpret or categorize phenomena differently, some are impatient, some distracted, some bored, and so on. Recordings and videos made on the spot will suggest some of what happened, but what really happened is the looping engagement between each individual and the world event as he played a part in it—no two loops alike.

One situation, one engagement after another, my life goes on. I play my part by doing the best I can; the world plays its part by changing on its own, supplying rhythms of years, months, seasons, weeks, days and nights, and cultural gradations of hours, minutes, seconds, and fractions thereof. We divide circles into 360 degrees in keeping with early estimates of how many days it takes to fill a year, our measuring systems harmonizing with one another in our minds, much as our counting system dances with the fingers on our hands. We project order onto time, space, words, and numbers in keeping with the harmonies and rhythms that please our minds. Our loops of engagement, by which we connect to a world we cannot know apart from its impact on sensory experience, tune us to our worlds, those worlds to ourselves. The apparent "one turning" of the starry universe keeps to the one turning of our home planet as it spins around an imaginary axis of our own making, an axis pointing to an imaginary hub at the North Star (as seen from the Northern Hemisphere). From any other planet that apparent turning would be different. Without any memory-equipped observers at all, there would be no axis, no wheeling about a center, no universe, no sense of time or space. Thank you Microsoft clock in the corner of my computer screen for reminding me what time it is. Thank you, universe, for setting the clock. Thank you, consciousness, for coming up with the idea of clocks that time may be replicated for our convenience.

Because we are creatures of our home planet and interact with it, and because we have minds that notice and remember changes and discrepancies, we give ourselves to our planet through the media of space and time in order to calibrate the changes we make by acting, and the changes we notice by observing, connecting overt action and sensory reaction in our minds so we can get to work on time, build pyramids, and place astronauts on the moon, showing that we have gotten some things right, at least, before we leave the scene. Hunger comes upon us as apparently not our doing, so is therefore a sensory indicator of time. The same for yawns, sexual urges, our aging bodies—all saying what time it is, and cuing actions we might perform as appropriate. Space is told by deliberate actions mapped in our heads during the planning stages before we execute them. To make a move, we need to know where we are located—where on the master maps in our minds.

Wittgenstein detected an echo of thought in sight; I find echoes of time in unintentional changes that seem to enter consciousness on their own through sensory perception, as well as echoes of space in planning and executing intentional actions. My looping engagement with my surroundings alternates between states of acting and states of waiting for some kind of response, space and time seeming to take turns, like players in a game—a tennis match where opponents alternate hitting the ball back and forth. Hit; wait; hit; wait—so goes the game, switching between giving and receiving, trading my changes for your changes, my moves for your moves in response, space and time alternating in our respective awarenesses. Our minds keep track of the valenced discord between the expectancy with which we act and the resulting sensory figures we form as a result.

When rats rise up and sniff the air with their whiskers inviting scents toward their noses, they are asking their surroundings to act upon them while holding still to make sure they don't influence the results. Getting the picture through pheromones—the olfactory lay of the land—they can tell who's been in the vicinity, how far away they were, roughly when they were there, and what shape they were in, all told by sniffing while otherwise keeping still. Then they rely on that collection of interpreted phenomena in deciding what direction to head, and scamper off with a purpose, putting effort into moving, not sniffing.

Which is similar to our taking time to move our eyes about a scene while staying still, exploring our situation by turning our heads to the side or up or down, watching, listening intently, sniffing the air, savoring food and drink, paying attention to what our bodies are trying to tell us, even introspecting to find out what is on our minds—all ways of inviting changes and discrepancies to enter awareness while we are not distracted by trying to do something else. When we move about, accurate perception gets harder because we must subtract the effects of our own motions in space from the changes we detect in our environment to maintain a clear picture of our current situation. Are these discrepancies our doing or do they reflect changes in the scene around us? We must tell the difference in order to take responsibility for disturbing our own awareness.

Conversations follow a similar pattern of alternation as participants take turns speaking and listening. The idea is to find a topic of mutual interest, then to develop it cooperatively by each party sharing relevant observations, experiences, or perhaps questions in response to what has previously been said. When listening, if time is spent rehearsing what to say next, the rhythm of the exchange is broken, and perhaps the loop itself, leading to a one-sided exposition from a single point of view, more lecture than conversation. The art of conversation is not in one party taking control and shining above all others, but in each contributing to a common sense of understanding and enjoyment shared among participants. All the while our pauses, ums and ers, and mindless interjections (like, y'know, I mean) give us time to gather our wits for the next round of engagement so we can keep up the flow of focused attention and activity.

Even a game of solitaire is a looping engagement with the world, shifting between actions such as shuffling, laying out the game, playing a card from the deck, putting an ace aside, moving a card from one pile to another, turning up a card—all revealing the possibilities inherent in a particular shuffle of the cards and their random arrangement in the seven piles as laid out. The world acts through those possibilities as they play out in the cards, each game likely being different from all others. Players stay engaged as long as a particular arrangement of cards holds their attention. When the random arrangement seems somehow deliberately stacked against the player so he cannot make a move, interest tends to wane. Several such games in a row lead players to start looking for something else they might do that would be more rewarding, such as reading a book, making cookies, or going to bed. Games of chess are similar engagements, with an opponent, not a shuffled deck. Both chess and solitaire are highly visual, islands of avoidance and opportunity appearing on maps in the mind *as if* on the board or among discrete piles of cards.

Dreams often seem similarly reactive, but the loop of action and discovery is wholly internal to one particular mind, so they illustrate loops *within* that mind, not between it and the world. As such, dreams offer a particular form of introspection in which every action and every discovery results from that particular mind's own activity, so sheds light on its workings when the external loop is broken, both acting in the world and the world making a response becoming highly unlikely. What is possible in such circumstances includes emotional arousal, desire to act, and situational possibilities drawn from memory and the unconscious. In my dreams, I am typically trying to do something in a particular setting such as a school, subway system, or neighborhood, and am thwarted at every turn by my inability to act effectively in reaching the goals I have set for myself.

I find evidence for my looping engagement with the ambient world of energy and matter (which stirs sensory figures within me) in the many disconcerting occasions when my personal loop breaks down, leaving me stymied and at a loss to know what to say or do next. Whether thwarted by a car that won't start, jar lid stuck in place, password I can't recall, or some other obstacle to my earnest intentions, the sensory feedback I get tells me my expectancy is no match for the occasion and I'd do best to make a fresh start. Which I do, once I figure out an alternative route for getting my plans back on track. Or not, in which case circumstances force me to give up. Words that come to mind for describing such occasions: balked, bothered, frustrated, interrupted, spooked, failed, disappointed, stymied, dashed, annoyed, thwarted—in a word, defeated. I have lost the game, opening me to a host of strategies for doing better next time, which I vow to adopt, or at least consider in healing my wounded pride. Indeed, the more I am invested in a particular engagement, the more I stand to lose if it fails. Loops of engagement entail peril, which, I propose, is why we have them—to keep us abreast of our standing in a given situation we can view only subjectively, inside-out. If things go our way—the car starts, the lid comes off, the password comes to mind—then our vocabulary shifts and we speak of our achievement in glowing terms: success, victory, triumph, breakthrough, progress, recovery, winning, overcoming, moving on, getting ahead. Things fall into place and we can move on to the next round of the loop—graduation, advancement, the championships. Or at least get dinner on the table after picking the chicken off the floor and rinsing away the grit. The play's the thing. The loop will go on. Single-mindedness turns out to be the loop's preferred mode of action, which leads to persistence and jobs getting done. Interruptions lead to double-mindedness, confusion, hesitation, dashed dreams, broken hearts, and forlorn hopes.

Even during waking hours, loops of engagement are driven by feelings of expectancy. Why else bother to exert yourself and pay close attention? Expectancy is a sure sign of engagement extending from the past into the now, and pointing ahead toward the future— the coming, but not yet. Why play solitaire if not to put shuffled cards back in order by suit and by number (which is what it takes to win)? Why play chess or tennis if not to enjoy—and try to succeed at—a difficult exchange with an opponent of comparable skill? What is the issue in holding a conversation? Learning something new, perhaps, or telling a story, updating a relationship, finding companionship, being actively engaged, having fun. All looping engagements require certain sorts of skills, of being active in fulfilling ways, of trying to reach certain goals—such as winning, learning, telling, doing, making. The skills are every bit as important as the particular goals held beyond reach at the end of expectancy, as are the partners we choose in being ourselves in those skillful ways.

Partners are people we engage by agreeing how to set our relationship up so our respective loops of engagement complement each other rather than compete or collide head-on. Taking turns is one way (games, doing chores), having one take the lead while the other follows (dancing, ice-skating), or specializing (I'll make dinner if you'll do the dishes). Such agreements are reached by negotiating the terms of the partnership (marriage, team play, duties within the firm) in advance.

Even in combat to the death, we sometimes compete within rules of engagement agreed-to beforehand. Increasingly, however, asymmetrical conflict defies any such conventional agreement as might level the battlefield (opening the way to piracy, gorilla warfare, suicide bombing, torture, and other horrors of conflict between unequal forces). Similar tactics are evident in political and economic combat.

In domestic political campaigns, the fact that incumbents have an easier time raising money, and all power goes to the winner, has brought about a reckless, Machiavellian mindset aimed at winning no matter what because, once in the race, a candidate simply cannot afford to lose. If victory is not a sure thing, what's the point? These days, office is purchased by millionaire candidates, with help from their corporate friends, skewing electoral engagement. Now, corporate funding of political campaigns can be seen as an investment in future profits by making sure taxes and regulations are kept low, profits held high. To some, good governance has come to mean no governance and no oversight. If such thinking is broadly applied, America's touted democracy based on diversity, freedom, and hard work has been taken over by a corporate money culture that values a one-way loop feeding high profits into selected bank accounts, a parody of free speech by which the point of every engagement is for the few to hoard wealth, not promote the general welfare of the people as a whole.

Meanwhile, back on the personal level, the several dimensions of my unchartered loop of engagement as revealed to me through introspection are the subject matter of this book. First comes expectancy, then attention, followed by sensory figures at a useful level of discernment, interpretation making such figures more-or-less familiar, the big-picture understanding in which each interpreted figure has its place, all made relevant by the values that motivate me and feelings that alert me to how my engagement is going in a particular situation. Then the challenge of deciding what to do next by judging the foregoing dimensions of my loop in order to move my projects and relationships ahead to the next stages of planning and action.

Looping engagements are a kind of adventure, of putting ourselves out there in ways that challenge and affirm us. Of reaching into the world as ourselves and none other. Of being who we are with skill and confidence. It is no accident I take my camera with me almost everywhere I go; I've been taking pictures since I got my first camera when I was four years old. I became a still photographer in the Signal Corps when I was drafted, worked for a catalog fashion studio, a university public relations office, a college astronomical and astrophysical observatory, briefly published a journal of photography, then taught photography, and now use photography to monitor an estuarine ecosystem and share the results via PowerPoint presentations. Photography is a thread running through my entire life. I am a highly visual person, and photography is one of my most reliable mediums for being who I am. If I could, I'd take photographs of my mind at work. Instead, for thirty years, I've been directing attention toward my inner frontier, looking to see what's happening in my stream of consciousness, with the results I—still the same person—am reporting in this book in terms of my looping engagement with my current situation.

Loops of engagement combine skillful action with careful attention at a level of discernment which deepens with practice and experience. Based on expectancy, they are never a sure thing in producing predictable results. They are adventures in being who we are, where we are, with perpetual willingness to do better. Reduced to routines, such loops settle for the status quo, with nothing ventured, nothing learned. Or, worse, as ideological statements, they inflict foregone conclusions on the world in place of wonder, curiosity, and experimentation. Such loops betray the essence of expectancy in accepting only responses that are predetermined to be politically desirable and correct. The types of engagement I have been writing about cannot produce standardized results. They must allow room for novelty, surprise, improvement, and new learning. Just as the teacher who expects the same rote answer from every student probably is a better trainer or disciplinarian than a teacher, the mind that always insists on getting the "right" answer when it queries the unknowable world is probably that of an ideologue and no independent, original thinker. An ideologue is one who knows the answers before any questions are asked, or else shapes all questions to elicit the one acceptable answer already lodged in his mind.

The best way I have found to test an idea of the world against the world itself is to hand the problem to my unconscious mind before going to bed so that, when I wake up relaxed and refreshed in the morning, I find either the answer waiting in my introspective in-box, or a suggestion for how I might go about finding such an answer. The ultimate reward of my committed program of introspection is trust in my mental faculty to do whatever job I *ask* of it, not *assign* to it. There's a big difference. Asleep and awake, I have to live the process myself, not hand it off as if to another. That way, I am truly surprised to discover my mind has solved the problem overnight. To earn that trust, I have to do as much of the work as I can, then take a break, urging consciousness to carry on—as it evidently does in dreamtime when I am not officially on duty as my normal self. If I am stressed, harried, or overwrought, those same qualities become properties of my mind. I can't expect miracles, but must do my share of the work for the, say, 10,000 hours it takes to get good at doing anything out of the ordinary. Then my dream crew will handle the rest.

Introspection is a full-body, full-time commitment. There's no such thing as a part-time introspector. If I want to get to know myself, I have to live with my mind the whole distance, the whole time. That way, I have a good chance of finding out who I am. No lesser effort will do that for me. With only one life to live, I've got to get it right the first time through. Till now, many others have had their way with me: my parents, siblings, relatives, teachers, co-workers, supervisors, friends. Can anything be more important than showing what we can do on our own? In your case, the only qualified mind gazer is your singular, first-person self, as I am in my case.

Having said that, I will return to the stories told in Chapter 1 to see what they reveal in light of what I have written about loops of engagement. I've already considered such a loop as exhibited in the tale of my crossing the street in Brattle Square. In a variety of ways, those incidents reveal a strong undercurrent of expectant attention flowing through my several engagements.

When driving west across eastern Colorado with my family, I expected to see mountains ahead, but inquiring with motivated eyes, I was answered only by a row of low, phenomenal clouds, with not one mountain in sight. The place was right to see mountains, but the time was not right for me to see them because it was late August and the Rockies were covered with snow, while I was expecting to see bare, summer mountains. The snow appeared in my eyes to be a line of low clouds floating above their own shadows, which were actually the mountains below the snow line—the very ones I was seeking but could not see. Because I resisted seeing snow, my loop of engagement was broken by my demand to see mountains without snow, and what I saw was clouds that made a better fit with what I thought I wanted to see. I was almost right, I was convinced I was right, but in terms of that particular situation, I was dead wrong. Expectations wrought in the past were no match for my current situation, so my looping engagement with the landscape before my eyes was troubled and I simply would not let those mountains form in my awareness. The harder I tried to make them fit my expectations of how mountains should look, the better clouds I made of the snow which covered them. Despite my best efforts, I forced those clouds onto the mountains I was looking for, hiding them from view. The harder I looked ahead, the less I could let them appear. In such cases, the past rules the present every time. Until in this case I noticed the clouds stayed exactly the same for half an hour—which no self-respecting clouds would ever do. This was a new discovery, changing everything. If they weren't in fact clouds, what could they be? Reframing the question from *where* are they? to *what* are they?, I was answered with snowcapped peaks—the Rockies, indeed, right where they should be, right where they had been all along.

This tale tells the difference between assimilating the world to preconceived expectations, and accommodating expectations to the world that is there. The landscape that I saw reflected past situations I had been in. My outlook was rooted in my earlier experience, which I cast ahead of me into the void of the unknowable-in-itself world. And then in a flash I updated myself, never to forget what I learned on that day in that place—how the snow-covered Rockies actually appear in late August as phenomena to be interpreted in my mind, which was all new to my then thirteen-year-old self.

I am sorry to beat that lesson so relentlessly, but writing depends on the same looping arrangement between what I want to say and what I experience my fingers actually typing on the screen of my computer, so it's hard for me to stop until I finally get it right. Writing is a looping, serial process, though it looks like rows of words piled up on the page. Perseverating the one idea, I mimic my younger self perseverating my expectation of what mountains should look like. Even so, there is more to be said. From my perspective, fixed things exist in the realm of space; moving, changing things exist in time. In the incident I am recounting, my expectations were fixed in my mind, which matched what I allowed myself to see—a set landscape of clouds and shadows. Only when I *changed my mind* did I allow myself to discover something wholly new and unexpected—those weren't clouds at all but snowfields on high peaks. Clouds, obviously, come and go, but I had held them fast beyond all reasonable justification. They couldn't be clouds; clouds don't act that way. I had to let them be snowfields on the mountains, a more accurate interpretation of the white shapes I was actually seeing. When loops of engagement get dammed up like that, pressure builds to remove the dam. Which, when it happens, comes as a sudden burst of revelation. Like Paul on the road to Damascus; like Archimedes and the crown of false gold, like young Steve allowing clouds to be snow.

Much the same argument can be made regarding my pursuit of Fred on Fifth Avenue in which I finally let Fred be not-Fred. I wanted that figure to be Fred, I expected it to be Fred, but Fred-ness evaporated the instant I came abreast with hand raised to clap him on the back, only to discover an un-Fred-like brow, nose, and chin. My expectancy crashed. Relenting, I let non-Fred go on his way without any knowledge of the drama he had stirred up in my mind, no longer a fixed image but an anonymous pedestrian striding into the distance, receding in both space and time, no longer my presumed friend.

The missing mustard jar is another example of my having the wrong gestalt in mind when time came to put mustard on the sandwich I was making for lunch. I reached into the world with a side or profile view of the jar in my eyes, but all I got back for my efforts was emptiness. It was like getting an error message: No jar of that description can be found. But I knew it was there, just as I knew the Rockies were there, and Fred was there—before my searching eyes. It had to be there. It was there yesterday, more than half full. It couldn't be gone in one day. Another pursuit, another loop, another block. And again, another case of errant expectancy cast into the void. Time stopped in its tracks. Lunch stopped. Patience stopped. Where could it have gone? Never questioning my search criteria, I went on as before, looking for the same profile image in different locations, never once doubting it was the correct one. Not on the table, in the living room, upstairs in either bedroom. Not on the kitchen counter. It had to be in the refrigerator. But it wasn't. It had to be. Opening the door one last time, I thought the jar might be behind the milk, so reached out with my hand to right the jar with the red top—which instantly turned into the mustard jar I was looking for. Time had come unstuck and I became conscious because my fingers unstuck my mind from its original assumption that the jar would be resting on its base, not its side. As usual, the solution was in me, not the world. Next time, I'd look for both presentations, and maybe throw in a bottom view as a possibility as well. Mustard jars, you know how they are—fickle, or at least changeable like the rest of us. That is, from time to time they change their appearance on their own, and no longer show up on spatial maps, with the result I can't find them anywhere because they've jumped media and now exist in time, not space. To find one, I have to understand mustard jars that change over time. I have to let them be what they are and not impose rigid expectations on them. Accepting them that way, I get along with them a lot better. They really can't help it.

The house-scraping cedar tree is more of a mystery. I wasn't looking for either paint scrapers or cedars, just as I wasn't looking for cows on the road to Bar Harbor, dying crows or trash bags, or either crashing jets or TV antennas. I don't feel I was looking *for* anything in these cases. It's more that in haste I mistook one thing for another because they both had a certain resemblance. The cedar had "shoulders," was about the right size to be confused with a man, and was blowing in such a way to resemble a man pressing with his hips while scraping paint. The cows I had in mind were black-and-white, like the bikers' rain gear, and the flick of an arm while donning raingear resembled the flicking of a tail. Both crow and trash bag were about the same size, black, and moved when cars stirred the air. Jet and antenna were both made of metal, shone in the sun, were angled downward, and had a swept-back quality. All true, but where, exactly did the paint scraper come from, the cows, the crow, the jet? Lots of things bear a resemblance without replacing one another in consciousness. What caused these perfectly ordinary things to morph into something else entirely when expectant attention was not the driving force?

Perhaps phenomena that appear only briefly are first approximations serving to capture the outline of a situation without filling in unnecessary details, which are to follow later. As such, I should expect them to change quickly as short-lived sketches of what's really there. Then again, their dreamlike quality might stem from a lack of expectancy in that I am involved in some other activity and, out of the corner of my eye, catch a phenomenon somewhat similar to what I am thinking about. Both ways, my seeing is within the range of metaphorical possibility, much as dolls and stuffed animals serve a child's metaphorical reality, or pointing fingers do the work of metaphorical handguns.

Since we probably don't sleep in order to dream, dreams are likely an offshoot of a state of inactivity and idle attention, a kind of irrelevant noise in the background, as some mutations are genetic noise, random exceptions that don't fit the overall plan. If the cows-scraper-crow-jet phenomena are not trial attempts to categorize novel or amorphous sensory signals aside from conscious expectations, perhaps they are so far out on the fringe of ongoing consciousness (driving along the road, walking downtown, creeping along on slippery ice) as to make them hasty irrelevancies. Sometimes things just happen as blips in the universe. I don't find that an appealing explanation, yet it might be the case in a complicated matter such as consciousness. I thought I saw something, but on second look it was gone. Just checking, that's all. What strikes me is that almost anything unusual can spark a brief glimmer of consciousness as a spot check on the current situation, which, I now believe, is where consciousness comes from. It takes a more substantial error signal, however, to sustain consciousness long enough to rouse what we call working memory, and a sustained novelty or irregularity to keep the loop going for more than a few seconds.

What I do know (or think I know) is that comparison between sensory figures and what I feel I ought to do about them leads to spurts of awareness, which may be inaccurate, but at least prompt me into a state of vigilant arousal and alertness. Disparity, that is, creates a need to pay attention, so novelty draws awareness to itself, sparking consciousness. I view my brain as a comparator, an organ for placing signals from different areas side-by-side in adjacent cortical columns of nerve cells to see how they measure up against one another. The lateral prefrontal cortex and posterior parietal cortex, for example, so-called association areas of the brain, both direct outputs (motor-linked and sensory-linked, respectively) to multiple sites throughout the brain aptly suited to serve as staging areas for action. Converging on the same sites, these outputs would allow comparison, and the degree of sameness or novelty to be fed forward to motor areas. John Hughlings Jackson long ago suggested that consciousness arises as a result of signals from such "association" (or in my view, *comparison-promoting*) cortices (Saper, Iversen, and Frackowiak, "The Neural Basis of Cognition," in Kandel et al., eds., *Principles of Neural Science,* fourth edition, 2000, page 363). I know my brain only from books, not personal reflection, but putting what I know through direct observation together with what I know *about* through reading and studying diagrams, I have become convinced that the valenced disparity between my intentions and sensory signals in my brain gives rise to my mind and, in specific incidents, its content of streaming awareness.

My thought is that, given the degree of consonance or dissonance compared to what I expect (am familiar with or used to), I experience a valenced signal that drives the adjustment needed to put me on the heading I desire. I steer my way by that signal much as a helmsman steers through fog by the deviance of his compass needle from his charted course. His mindfulness of that error allows him to turn the wheel to port or starboard to counter the error at each moment as he goes. In that simple image I discover the rise of William James' stream of consciousness, what others see as successive instants of working memory, and I see as my ongoing loop of conscious engagement.

Whether due to novelty, error signals, simple category mistakes, or dreamlike fantasies, one thing is evident: interpretations have multiple routes for connecting with phenomena, a long way via expectancy and evidence provided by the world, and a short way via two-way internal connectivity within the brain. Dreams indicate the internal route can take over when we are not able to connect with the world through either action or perception. Our mental screens don't go blank under such conditions; when random eye movements take over in REM sleep, they are associated with visual imagery emerging within the dreamtime brain, just as eye movements are involved in recognizing familiar faces or locations. If the cues fit a remembered pattern, recognition occurs. In the scraper-cows-crow-jet situations, perhaps the visual cues were faint, yes, but sufficient to trigger such interpretations as in a dream.

Hearing the voice in the night crying "Fa, Fa" was a clear case of my not being able to interpret what that sound might mean. To me it was just a noise (or meaningless auditory figure) breaking into my sleep. My sudden recognition of the word "Fire!" shouted by a weak voice over and over again burst into my stupor all at once with force and with meaning. What had changed in my nighttime consciousness to bring that about? I now think the repetition had a lot to do with it, leading me to question what purpose the voice might have had, the sound not being random but pregnant with some sort of meaning (which I had yet to discover). Just as in the case of persistent Colorado clouds turning to snowfields, that persistent sound turned into a man telling the world his house was on fire—and I heard not just a sound but his message. On the umpteenth round, my loop of engagement went into a questioning mode, allowing there was meaning in that repeated cry, and my job was to interpret it, which I did in short order. My attitude changed from being bothered while asleep to actively reaching for meaning. That's all it took to breach the dam.

In the case of my not seeing my partner's sunflowers in a vase, I didn't see them because, in being intent on retrieving my camera case, I never thought to look for them. I was in a hurry, and sunflowers simply weren't on my list of items to expect. My looping engagement with the world was highly focused on the gestalt of one little black bag. I managed to get up the stairs safely, to walk across the floor to where I usually stash the bag—there it was! I grabbed it, turned, and left, passing the sunflowers both coming and going. I was wholly ruled by the expectancy of getting that case.

So much for my seeing what is before me. I see what I intend to see, want to see, am determined to see. I see what I demand to see, not what is there. As in the case of the voice in the night, I eventually demanded meaning from that insistent cry, and in Colorado that time saw mountains only when I demanded to see them because I not only knew they were there, but accepted that what I had been seeing couldn't be right. Projecting openness into the world on the

130

outgoing leg of my loop of engagement, I allowed the resulting sensory figure that came to me to be interpreted a new way. The landscape I entertain in consciousness is what my looping perspective enables me to see—that and no more.

That memory feeds into such loops is told by the sink song I failed to remember two nights after I heard it. Where else do expectations come from if not memory? They are categories and fields of understanding waiting to be filled. Sometimes in specific detail as in an explicit episode from the past, other times more generally or schematically in terms of broad features composing a concept embracing a wide range of possible content. In brief, I often find what I am looking for to the degree it accords with my attitude of expectancy. If I am intent on a specific mission, or no such image as I am looking for presents itself, or I don't understand the language a signal is composed in—in such cases my loops of engagement are apt to be returned to sender, empty.

Or if not empty, as something else entirely, as in the case of the skull I was unearthing on the Nespelum Indian Reservation turning into the shell of a long-ago turtle. In that case, at a word from my supervisor, I suffered a severe bout of revisionism, and had to accommodate my outlook to his unexpected revelation. When I'm in the mood for assimilation, my loop is one of expectancy based on what I already know or believe. In that mode, I simply map my current understanding onto the phenomena that enter my awareness, and, right or wrong, that is that. When I allow for the possibility of having to accommodate to a larger world than I know, that loop can be one of inquiry meant to expand my understanding. If I am suspicious that something isn't right with the world, I cast suspicion outward with my gaze to see what turns up. And so on, my looping engagement with my current situation being largely determined by me. Casting my personal foibles and idiosyncrasies onto my world via a highly personalized net of expectations, I haul in what harvest of phenomena I am able to catch using that particular approach. The landscape, instead of simply being there, is what I am able to see (hear, touch, smell, taste) from where I am situated within my own mind. The study of geography or anything else depends on where every student in the room is situated in his or her awareness. Subject matter exists in minds, not books. It is what students reach for with their respective loops of engagement. And what they are able to bring back in terms of richly-patterned phenomena to categorize, interpret, and understand with feeling.

The scariest incident I relate in Chapter 1 is not the one in which I find myself lying in the road hoping an approaching truck would stop short of my body, but the one where I undergo a week of diagnostic tests to find out what ails me, and after a week of being a guinea pig, am told by the doctor he has no more idea what my problem is at the end of that hospital stay than he had at the beginning. His loop of engagement was one of inquiry, but as far as I could tell, he learned nothing except that his suspicions were incorrect. Instead of being the beginning of a new chapter, that was the end of the saga. For him, but not for me. I limped on as before, and only thirty years later found out I had celiac disease, and had had it my whole life. Finally, a breakthrough for me, but not the good doctor. He'd gone to medical school, so supposedly knew how to keep learning through personal inquiry, loop after loop, case after case. Except in my case he learned not a thing, even though that is what he was drawing a salary to do.

Which reminds me of the sex education lady giving her talk while looking straight at me as if I'd been her son, which I clearly wasn't, but that made slight difference to her, as my illness made no difference to my doctor. He was getting paid as a teacher, so he probably didn't see himself as merely a practicing physician any longer. He'd gotten beyond that point, and had his white-clad ducklings to prove it. He had stature, he had tenure. He had his set loop of engagement to tell him if he couldn't fix it, it probably wasn't broken. Next case.

In the case of the cartwheel display of aurora borealis, I was so captivated by that cauldron of novel shapes stewing at the zenith, I couldn't take my eyes off it. I just let it play, giving it my best attention for more than two hours. It was so inventive in weaving light shapes together, I vowed to keep up with it as long as I could. It was a once-in-a-lifetime opportunity to connect with the universe in a personal, non-intellectual way. How could I turn it down? Which I ultimately did, but not until I found myself sleeping on my feet, my loop lagging behind while my eyes were shut. Sometimes novelty invites engagement, while an excess is likely to shut it down.

The sensual lure of phenomena is a powerful attractive force in my life, drawing my restless attention, leading my interpretative faculty on and on and on. How better describe my lifelong interest in, and commitment to, photography? That pretty much captures who I am. At least until I finish this book, which is really more of the same, except now my attention is turned inward upon the aurora-like, dreamlike display in my mind. Ultimately, everything I am writing about—the source of all these words—is that looping continuum of life between my ears and behind my eyes and nose—my version of life on Earth as I live it every day in my unique experience. I am given that display in my little vault in the universe to watch and watch over. If I don't rise to that challenge, no one else will do it for me because no one else can. On that I am perfectly clear. Once given a life, who am I if I don't explore its many dimensions and live it as deeply as I can?

Who am I? That is the question of questions. Photography has been my chief line of inquiry in the past; now I am looking inward, tracing my dreamlife to its source. I'm getting closer every day, I can feel it. Preparing to write this chapter, I made pages and pages of notes—which I haven't looked at once. The text is inside me, already inscribed in my experience. My job now is the same as it was in facing into the cartwheel aurora and translating the effects of solar radiation into a form I could grasp. My engagement with the unknowable world is like that radiation, which can only tell where it comes from, but knows nothing of its effect on even one human mind. None of us is destined for anything; we are what we make of ourselves. I am making myself happen before your eyes. Keep your attention on these spilling words while they live in your mind, for engaging that space is also my aim. Together, let's see what happens next. Appropriate phenomena are the basis of appropriate interpretations are the basis of appropriate feelings and understandings are the basis of appropriate planning and actions in the world are the basis of appropriate engagements with the one and only planet Earth. If we can keep to that journey, then let's see what actions we can perform as citizens in good standing with our home planet in the vastness of space.

In the next chapter, I deal with situations, the sensible milieus our loops of engagement struggle to define, and within which our mental faculties, if they are to be realized, grapple for understanding as an appropriate standpoint allowing effective action in the mysterious world. ◯

CHAPTER 8

SITUATIONS

L oops of engagement extend the influence of individual consciousness into the earthly milieu serving as its current situation. Within that province of localized activity, each such loop contributes to the flow of ongoing events. That flow, in turn, alters the situation itself in various ways as told by energies falling on participants' senses, leading to the updating and reformation of sensory phenomena. These revised figures lead to revised interpretations and comparisons within that situation and, in turn, to revised feelings, understandings, plans, and programs of action. That is, situations evolve, and participants' minds do their best to keep up with events as they develop. In this way, through participation in situations, individual consciousness contributes to its surroundings, and those surroundings shape sensory phenomena at the core of consciousness in return. This is our contract with the universe, that those of us who participate in a given situation will mutually interact with one another in fundamental ways. We are participants in and citizens of earthly situations. Existence is what we, together, are able to make of it.

Think of the many ways we do this every day of our lives by watching televised football games, listening to music, surfing the Web, walking through woods, reading books, attending lectures, playing games, preparing food, eating, having sex, talking with friends, staring blankly into the middle distance, sleeping, dreaming, shopping—making ourselves happen in genres and venues through which we conduct the business of personal consciousness. That is, engage ourselves in getting the stimulation we need to be ourselves by directing our attention to what matters most to us at each moment of daily life.

In the preceding chapter, I left out the affair of the clip-art cat because I found it the most problematic of the incidents I related in Chapter 1. Where did that cat come from, the one whose image stayed with me the rest of the evening, and I can still recall to this day? There I was in the homely situation of putting dishes away, when a hinge squeaked at me—and there was this cat underfoot, howling in pain. So it seemed at the time. Actually, the cat was a figment of the creative imagination by which I catified a squeaky hinge, causing myself to quickly lift my foot, bringing to mind the image of a ruffed, blue-gray cat looking mildly up at me, if not from the floor (I don't have a cat), then from the floor of my mind. I made the whole thing up in keeping with the instant interpretation I laid on that shriek. Definitely a cat, not a hinge. Immediately a cat, no expectancy was required. A charged situation that fed into an illusion. Telling me there are mental routes to action that bypass the planning stage and go straight to the muscles, literally, as a kind of knee-jerk response. But why did that direct route make me jump? I had no expectation that a cat would appear while I was putting away dishes. It was entirely my contribution, which I plucked out of the air because it was a ready response in my bodily possession beforehand. I activated it to suit the occasion, again, literally, leaping to an unwarranted conclusion. The situation I created in my mind had to have been prepackaged, ready to spur a jump without warning or rehearsal. Shriek—jump! Just like that. A reflex, not a conscious decision.

My behavior in that situation was worthy of a lab rat trained to avoid electric shocks as motivated by fright and fear of pain. How did any such rash expectation get into my loop of engagement while putting dishes into a particular cupboard, something I'd done every day for ten years? And there's still my personification of the cat-that-wasn't-there as the innocent victim displayed in my mind. Was it a psychic Band-Aid so I wouldn't feel completely foolish? A massaging of the facts so I wouldn't feel guilty? The situation that put me in the kitchen had been made passé, abruptly replaced by having to deal with the clip-art cat. That cat was a rationalization of what had just happened. A kind of after-the-fact explanation. Maybe that was it. If expectancy can balk the loop of engagement, perhaps guilt and regret have a similar power. Denial, that's the name of that persistent cat. An excuse for a cat in that there was no cat—I had leapt up reflexively upon hearing a cry made by an outraged hinge.

I have underplayed the expression on the cat's face, which was mild and totally accepting, not accusatory. That cat was there to forgive me, to get me off the hook. I put it there myself, or my mind put it there to make it—the situation—all better. That feels right. The clip-art cat was not underfoot, never would be underfoot. It wasn't angry or hurt. It was the picture of innocence, forgiveness, total acceptance. It was clearly meant for my eyes only; no one else could see it. It was my reward for jumping quickly to spare a cat that wasn't even there. Good boy, Steve, good boy. A metaphysical trick I played on myself. I wasn't a bad person for stepping on the cat, though the experience had that accusatory valence. I was a good person precisely for not stepping on the cat because the cat wasn't there—there was no cat. Which is what the cute little blue-gray image came to tell me. See, I'm not hurt. How could you possibly step on the tail of a cat that doesn't exist? Just as the unchanging clouds over eastern Colorado told me they weren't really clouds so I could let them be snow, that unchanging cat stuck around to free my mind so I could see it as a pretend cat—a metaphor or category error. The fact that it persisted for hours suggests to me that synapses were being built up in my brain to make sure I would not forget the lesson of that event.

That looping drama had a typical beginning, valenced muddle in the middle, and ending (this time on a happy note). That's how situations play out: 1) the scene is set; 2) difficulties arise; 3) resolution is attained one way or another. That plot is built into our brains. It's the basic scenario for learning from experience. Don't cross the street without looking both ways. Don't judge dying crows and crashing planes prematurely. Be careful not to mistake strangers for old friends. Don't think mountains have snow only in winter, or mustard jars must always look like you expect them to. Don't think every bone in the ground represents a human burial. If you come late to the opening scenes of a movie, you have to sit there for a while to figure out what is happening—to enter the loop. The same is true for every situation—you have to let it unscroll. Otherwise, motorcyclists in the rain are apt to turn into cows, men calling "fire" in their dialect can't always be understood.

What I've learned is, if an experience is to be had, it is best to give myself to it as it develops in its own fashion. Hasty judgment might lead to *mis*judgment if I jump the gun. Consciousness is an exercise in problem solving. There are just too many unknowns in any situation to see a rush to judgment as anything but a first approximation. The situation might develop differently than I expect it to, or I might change my perspective, so view things in a new light.

"What's happening?" we want to know when we enter a new situation. "What's going on?" "What time is it?" "Who's ahead?

"What's the score?" Essentially, we participate in events by under-standing them in meaningful ways as we go. In that sense, situations are occasions for applying our interpretive, comparative, and nar-rative skills so we can follow the action. This happens, then this, then this. When I listen to sports news on BBC and hear the latest cricket bulletins, I hear the words but have no idea what they mean, so it's all gibberish to me. I always laugh and say, "What was that all about?" The joke's on me because I'm outside the loop.

Speaking of feeling like an outsider, I haven't been in a barber shop for forty-five years, but my memory is that the talk was all about baseball and sex. The first one I ever went to had a brass spittoon next to the chair. The only entry requirement was a suffi-cient level of testosterone. Garages are much the same, featuring calendar pictures of nude women reduced to objects on display among hanging fan belts and wrenches. Venues are places where people with certain interests gather to join in activities that attract them such as sporting events, concerts, conferences, crimes, or (originally) military campaigns—a venue being a place where people gather for an attack. Certain kinds of situations are likely to develop in particular places. We go there because that's the kind of people we are and we want to be in our preferred loops to feel like ourselves.

How we are accustomed to directing our attention has a lot to do with the situations we seek to engage. Genres are categories of human interest, excitement, and concern, that is, of situations likely to draw our attention. We all have our preferences. Some of us, for instance, read mysteries, thrillers, romances, how-to books, cook-books, histories, biographies, or science fiction. With high expec-tations, we direct our loops of engagement toward venues and situ-ations likely to fulfill yearnings of a certain sort. Going to a res-taurant, we have first to decide what sort of food appeals to our appetites at the moment: Chinese, Japanese, Italian, Greek, Scandin-avian, Indian, Pakistani? What about Vietnamese, or French? We don't know yet what we'll order, but we do anticipate what sorts of choices we'd like to make—what sorts of cookery or cuisine we want to engage with, what sorts of comparisons with our hunger.

Are you a dog person or a cat person? An urbanite or a back-to-the-lander? A vegan, vegetarian, carnivore, or organic fanatic? Mak-ing yourself happen in the world, what is your preferred idiom? Such questions are meant to detect echoes resounding in our darkest interior, where existential preferences are established. Which do you prefer, crossword or picture puzzles, brass or string ensembles, board or mind-teasing games, people who wear solid colors or plaid shirts, heavy metal or folk guitar, jazz or country and western?

Too, we can look at the sorts of situations we go out of our way to avoid. Likely conflict between rivals, high levels of aggression, gatherings of young (or old) people, places where it's too noisy or too still? I hear people say, "I never go bowling," or "I'm just not a golfer!" Whatever we do, we declare our preferences for certain valences within our loops of engagement. Which keeps comparison at the forefront of awareness, always asking: Was that the right thing to do? Could I have said that more positively? Am I being honest with myself? Or sometimes congratulating ourselves: I am the greatest! Or more likely, Not as bad as I thought it would be.

I work my way into situations so to make them extensions of my familiar self. In school, I always twisted assignments somewhat to jibe with my personal interests. Putting my stamp on writing assignments, I always worked harder than I would have on less personalized topics. Writing about the local national park (*Acadia: The Soul of a National Park*) where I worked as a part-time ranger, I managed to write more about my enthusiasm for the park than about the park itself. That way, by narrating my experiences based on sixty different hikes, I projected my soul as a hiker onto the park, which gave me a certain authority in claiming that the soul I discovered was more the park's than my own. If not perfectly honest, that technique got the book written and published, the very assignment I had given to myself. This current book, too, is written the same way, inside-out. These words are the testament of my valenced, situated experience. There is no way to be dispassionate or objective in writing about introspection. This time I am being as upfront as possible about both my method and subject matter. If others return from a similar adventure of their own, I expect their findings to be different from mine—as different as their minds are from my mind. After a thousand books about introspection appear, then a review can be written about the common features of them all, which will make their comparative similarities and differences all the clearer.

Today I awoke to a new situation: the world I went to sleep in last night was covered by four inches of new snow. Without thinking why, yesterday I had placed my two snow shovels near the front door. I knew the time was coming, I just didn't know when. Today is the day, it turns out. Lying in bed at 6:00 a.m., I heard something I took to be a plow blade scraping against pavement. That sound announced the change. I knew from then on, we would be playing by new rules. Temperature, 26° Fahrenheit. Barometer, 29.03 inches. Wind, from the north-northwest at 20 miles an hour. Checking the tide chart, highest tide of the month today at 10:39 a.m. Keeping track of high tides and coastal erosion is one of my self-assigned monitoring tasks. Roads would be bad, but at least I could walk to the town pier and take pictures of an extreme tide at full flood. I made breakfast, wrote for a while, taped a gallon plastic bag around my camera, lens facing the opening (cutting a hole for the viewfinder), donned boots and winter coat, and walked into the storm. Immediately, a paragraph I'd written about a hike I'd taken along Acadia's Seaside Trail on March 5, 1997, came to mind:

Being the first one out after a snowstorm is one of life's greatest joys. With roads and walkways erased, there are no rules governing where you can go. The world has been made anew, and you are the first to witness its beauty. Usually, creatures of habit that we are, we get out the snow shovel and start remaking the world as it was. But if we resist that urge and give in to the wonder of the moment, we find ourselves made anew as well, as we were as children awakening to a day when school was called off because of a storm. I remember lying in bed without opening my eyes, listening for sounds from the outside world that would tell me what kind of day it was. Better than the scrape of shovels or the whump of loose tire chains clattering against fenders was the eloquence of a town muffled beneath a foot of new snow, the news conveyed by absolute silence. I did not have to look out the window to know a revolution had swept over the world in the night, and I had been dubbed emperor while I slept (*Acadia: The Soul of a National Park,* p. 158).

In such situations, change is initiated on the sensory side of the loop of engagement, not the action side. My job is to adjust my mind to new appearances, new interpretations, new understandings, new feelings, and take appropriate actions in response to my altered situation. The older I get, the harder I find having to adjust to changing seasons. Seasons don't just change, they keep changing. August is one thing, September another, then October, November, and now December. I don't want to think of January leading to February leading to March. Fact is, that's how it is with the seasons, and always has been since I first became aware of them in upstate New York in days when winters were winters and summers, summers. Even in those days every month changed into its successor without my being able to do anything about it. Living requires continual adjustment to altered situations, that's just how it is. Which is why, as survivors, we are able to do it. Those who can't adjust simply put up with it, fall by the wayside—or move to Florida, Arizona, or some other state where life in the brochure appears easier, the pace slower, golf courses stay reliably green (says the chamber of commerce, which would never lie). Yesterday, I heard it was colder in Florida than in Maine.

Except, perhaps, for the old and moribund, the human mind has proven itself adaptable to whatever comes. Our ancestors lived through ice ages and survived. Not many made it to the end of the Stone Age, true, but enough did to keep the story going. Without changing situations, as without feelings and emotions, life would be dull as colonial print wallpaper just begging kids with crayons to mark it up a little. We've gotten good at dealing with change and imminent disasters because we've had to. Particularly at dealing with catastrophic changes—earthquakes, tidal waves, great storms, fires, pandemics, invasions, slavery, legal decisions promoting corporate personhood, and the rest. There's turmoil for a while, but the living bury their dead, then get on with it. We are survivors, the children of survivors, who were children of survivors all the way back to the origin of life. Improbably, yes, but we are here nonetheless—which is what it means to be a survivor. Each of us is unique with a unique set of skills and abilities, driven by a unique mind in a unique situation as shaped by a unique point of view. Evolution has put its stamp of approval on that basic scheme.

Dealing with a wide variety of situations because we've had to, we have developed flexibility in dealing with novel predicaments. Just as each of our immune systems is unlike any other, requiring us to deal with infections in different yet very specific ways, so do we assess situations from our individual points of view, and come up with very different plans for how to proceed. Some plans being more appropriate and effective than others, some planners will survive while others may not. If we feel our way carefully while applying full attention, we are more likely to outlast those who are all daring, dash, and flamboyance. The point being to keep going until stopped, then look for another way. There are no rules for dealing with hazardous situations. Survivors are survivors because they make it through while others—perhaps seemingly more qualified—do not. The truth of life is in the living, not the dying. We can only do the best we can with the mind we've got in the time allowed. Which could segue into a promotion for introspection and self-understanding, but I've said enough.

On the theme of snowstorms and altered situations with which I started this riff, two other hiking situations come to mind, both from the same source cited in the example I gave. Both depict winter situations that quickly morphed into entirely new situations. In the first I got lost (March 8, 1996); in the second I scrambled for safety.

I always get excited when I explore new terrain, even if I don't know where I am. I was Charles Darwin making a foray into the jungle from the deck of the *Beagle*. A phrase from my favorite paragraph in *Walden* [came] to my mind: '... not till we are completely lost, or turned around, ... do we appreciate the vastness and strangeness of Nature.' I looked on my surroundings with new eyes, as if I had never seen anything like them before. Snow blowing through the woods made them even vaster and stranger. I was meant to lose the trail so I could experience Nature with a capital N. Thoroughly enjoying myself, not caring that I was lost, I followed the shelf to its far end, where I saw a snow-covered stretch of open ledge above me to my left. Maybe I could get a view from up there to tell me where I was. Scrambling up through loose snow, I found—no, no view, but there was a stone that seemed to float on a drift of snow, which I thought might be the capstone of a cairn. Digging beneath it, I found a three-foot heap of stones. I was somewhere at least, even if I didn't know where. Knowing the way of trail builders, I assumed one cairn was bound to lead to another. Looking in all directions, I found nothing. The terrain gave no hint where a trail might lie. Circling, I inspected every tree, and found one branch that had been cut. Heading in that direction, I came to a rising expanse of snow beyond which, when I had trudged to its summit, I saw the most awesome sight I have seen in all Acadia—a great mountain ridge rising out of a deep gulf across which snow was streaking horizontally, misting and mystifying the air, creating a scene of unanticipated magnificence. Click! I knew exactly where I was: on the south ridge trail of Sargent Mountain overlooking the Amphitheater and, beyond it, the splendid west face of Penobscot Mountain. The transition from being lost to being found was so abrupt, the scene, which I had witnessed under less dramatic circumstances many times, had an aura of spiritual significance (Ibid., p. 148).

A spiritual valence, for me, means feeling connected to the essential order of the universe. I felt it while watching the cartwheel display of aurora borealis (Ch. 1, Incident 17). It certainly came upon me as validation both of my awareness and the universe I was situated in. I have had some variation on that sense almost every day since moving to Maine in 1986. Here's the second episode, from a hike I made around Acadia's St. Sauveur Mountain, February 22, 1996.

From that low point, the trail ascends to the base of Eagle Cliff by a flight of about a hundred steps. In October I had seen falcons from the top of those steps, and thought I would pause there again to give them one more chance to materialize out of the mist. Mounting toward the base of the cliff, counting steps as I went, I had reached step seventy-eight when I heard a sound above me, the faint crack of something letting go. Suddenly a great icicle plunged into the trail at the top of the steps, smashed into a thousand cubes and shards, which hurtled out and down across the talus, spraying the slope with 350 pounds of shattered ice. Here I had been concentrating on danger beneath my feet while an even greater danger lurked out of sight overhead. I had had a rendezvous with that bolt of ice, but missed my appointment because I had taken one picture more than I had intended to. Completing my tally of the steps by eye rather than foot, I examined the range over which the shards had exploded, mapping out a route just beyond its edge. Then I took off across the talus, noting unfamiliar ferns and flying insects and buds big as chickpeas greening before my eyes as I passed without slowing or stopping. The way was steep and slippery across small chunks of granite smashed much as that icicle had been smashed, the entire slope tilted at such an angle it seemed likely to slump if slightly disturbed. There was no way to walk gingerly, so I scrambled across the base of the cliff, soon finding my way blocked by trees and thick shrubs. The way seemed steeper below than above, so I regained the trail—barely a narrow cow path filled with ice and snow at the base of an icy cliff rising into the mist. I tried to gauge the stability of every ice formation I could see, but didn't have the knack. All of it looked like it could fall any instant. I didn't belong there, but that's where I was. The Presence I felt was mad because I had missed my appointment. I did what I had to do. I got out of there (Ibid., p. 141).

In this case, too, the valence I sensed was the universe appearing as a felt apparition in my awareness, not as a bodily thing, but palpable to me nonetheless, made real by the wonder it kindled in my mind. Which is why I get myself into situations such as this last one. There I was reaching for the soul of Acadia, and I was rewarded with a vision of hurtling ice, not a snow-veiled mountain face. Attempting to connect with universal order, that's the kind of danger I run. But the ice missed me by a few seconds. That was my reward for even putting myself in that risky situation. I took it as a warning, knowing it was a one-time offer of grace, unlikely to be repeated. My loop of engagement is ever a loop of vigilance. I've found it works best if I try to anticipate what is coming.

Perhaps the wisdom of dealing with situations is to take them as opportunities, while reserving the right to judge when we are beyond the depth warranted by our level of competence. Knowing when to depart a situation is as much an art as knowing when to take it on. There are the three (suggestive yet arbitrary) stages by which any engagement can be seen to progress: 1) buildup, 2) interaction, 3) re-covery. These stages reside in consciousness, not situations them-selves, which can be thought of as unbounded and multifaceted. It is for consciousness to decide, "*This* is the place, *now* is the time." But typically, engagements can be seen in terms of beginnings, valenced developments, and endings, each stage hosting sub-stages (and sub-stages of sub-stages) of its own. That way we can plan our engage-ment, perform it, and conclude it to see how it goes and what we can learn from that effort. Stage by mental stage, life moves ahead.

On that model, situations are the experiential venues in which we play out our lives on a manageable scale. Some are grand, others trivial, some profound, others airy, but they are our primary tools for making ourselves happen through engagements we can picture and work with on an appropriate level of skill and attention. Going to school is a kind of situation, as is making friends, playing games, finding employment, getting married, having a family, changing jobs, getting divorced, remarrying, going to meetings, voting—in general, rising to the occasions of our lives, whatever happens around us. Preparing and eating meals are situations, as are washing dishes and taking breaks, taking vacations and getting promotions, going on tours of duty and getting laid off, getting sick and growing old, getting saved and going broke, going to prison and being wounded. One situation with or after others, that is the structure of our lives, mapped out in terms of looping engagements in mental space and mental time, the here and the now, the there and the then. The spatial dimension of consciousness is mapped onto provinces, precincts, shires, city blocks, suburbs, farmsteads, rural areas, nations, continents, hemispheres and networks of meaning, while the temporal dimension is mapped onto weeks, terms, innings, rounds, acts, hands, turns, sessions, seasons, years, decades, seconds, minutes, hours, days. Our mental mappings come together in situations partaking of both dimensions. When we say "It is raining," "It is funny," or "It is regretful," that "It" points to the felt situation in awareness both here and now.

The examples I've given illustrate my having to navigate in both spatial and temporal dimensions of my personal consciousness in hiking through a world that changes as I go, leaving me no choice but to adapt to those changes in an effort to keep time and space—perception and action—commensurate with each other in my mind. That is the essential challenge of consciousness in dealing with ever-changing situations. This is the crux of what I have learned through introspection, how I as a moving and changing observer struggle to deal with situations that are developing in unpredictable ways. My personal integrity and survival depend on my mobile consciousness mastering an unsettled and unsettling landscape full of surprises.

Isaac Newton was in a similar quandary in seeing an apple fall from a tree in his garden while watching an apple-sized moon hang above the horizon. (Whether the story is true or not, it illustrates my point.) Why, he asked himself, does the apple fall to the ground while the moon stays aloft? It doesn't make sense in an orderly universe that there is one set of rules for apples, another for moons. What does the moon know that the apple does not? Then he went the crucial next step. What if I refuse to accept such a complex situation, and insist the same rules must apply to both apples and moons—so both are indeed falling, and I hitherto have not recognized that fact? In what way can the moon be falling when it appears to be stationary in the sky? Then he realized that the moon was, in fact, falling toward the Earth while at the same time being propelled by its own inertia along a tangent into space, with the result that it was located precisely at such a distance from Earth that the two forces balanced each other, one drawing the moon toward Earth, the other carrying it away, with the result that the moon must necessarily fall *around* the Earth, its orbit being the predictable track of a body at that distance moving in two directions at once. In addition to the tug of gravity, the apple, too, partakes of Earth's rotation, but, in a fall of only a few feet, its inertia is not readily apparent.

All of us are unwitting Newtonians insofar as we can calculate the goings-on in situations close enough to interact with them while remaining true to ourselves. What consciousness does for us in making that possible is take other factors (such as Newton did the moon's inertia) into account in prefiguring the forces at work in a given situation, and guiding ourselves accordingly. In Rome, do as the Romans do—that is new learning. Newton didn't have the moon just mimic the apple, however, he figured its motion based on its underlying motivation. When in Rome, then, know the mind behind what the Romans do, and you can do the same for a similar reason. That, now, is diplomacy, not mimicry.

In the face of myriad world and personal conflicts, we are often advised to walk in the moccasins of the other if we wish to understand her point of view. Easy to say, hard to do. But not impossible for personal consciousness, which can reset itself by taking other forces and motivations into account. When I went on a hike in Acadia following a snowstorm, I didn't want to remake the world as it was, but took the snow as the determinant of a new reality, so went off looking for animal tracks. When I got lost, I looked to my surroundings so they would tell me where I was. When a giant icicle smashed into the trail ahead of me, I changed course to avoid the base of the cliff. When in Acadia, keep eyes and ears open for new events, and act accordingly.

When I worked in Iowa, I remember being frequently stopped at rail crossings, leading me to pass the time by reading the names of railroad lines painted on the sides of passing freight cars, which seemed to go on for both miles and hours. If I looked with a fixed gaze, the names were only a blur, but when I moved my eyes in a tracking motion following each car, the names were perfectly clear. That is the kind of altered seeing it takes to survive in an untested situation, the kind of seeing it takes to enjoy time spent in Rome.

New situations require new eyes and a new kind of seeing. I once took my children on a tour of the plant where the Boston *Globe* was printed. We ended up on a bridge over the chute ushering printed and folded newspapers from the press to the loading dock. Looking fixedly at the chute, the papers were a blurred river of gray. But when I released my eyes from the chute itself and followed the gushing papers with my eyes, I could read the headlines as if they were standing still. This illustrates the conjoining of time and space in consciousness through the agency of loops of engagement capable of following both actions in space and motions in time. What we see depends on how we set ourselves in advance to act and observe. What we expect to find determines how we reach for new experience. If we engage situations based on fixed attitudes and assumptions, we force everything to fit the mold of our standard perspective—the one we've worked so hard to develop in everyday situations. That way, we assimilate everything to our standard worldview and identity. But when novel situations require accommodation on our part, we may not be up to the job. If our attitudes and expectations are rigidly set, we are apt to lack the agility of mind necessary to act appropriately in situations we are unaccustomed to.

By no accident did the mind that gave us gravity also give us calculus, the mathematics of related changes in time and in space. Consciousness makes use of a similar calculus in dealing with sensory phenomena that, to be seen clearly, are relative to our changing outlook on the world. If we do not account for that changing outlook in dealing with world situations, our impressions are apt to be blurred and indistinct in not accounting for the two-way interaction between our physical selves and our earthly situation. Walking in someone else's moccasins requires empathy with a person who does not share our experience of, or outlook upon, world situations—*as if* we were both speaking of the same thing. If we do not possess that empathy by nature (by growing up, for instance, in a mixed neighborhood, or having a repertory of worldly experiences), then those metaphorical moccasins are not likely to fit our particular feet.

In my experience (as a prelude to sexist remarks), women tend to be more empathic than men, particularly with children and other women. Giving birth creates a bond with the child who has just been given a public life; together, mother and child fulfill each other as essential elements of a complementary duality. I am not speaking abstractly or philosophically here; the well-being of mothers and children depends on establishing both physically and psychically nurturing relationships. This bond embraces all past, present, and potential mothers and children around the world. Though men contribute to conception, after that their role is biologically more indirect in helping (along with grandparents, friends, and community) to provide a more-or-less stable situation for the family to thrive in. When men empathize, it is often to form bonds with other men they identify with as fellow workers, teammates, military buddies, or other colleagues facing challenges similar to their own.

Having grown up in Hamilton, New York, I remember my friend Billy and me tagging along behind his father who was the swimming coach at Colgate. Heading home along dark streets after work, I struggled to keep up with a physically active adult, but my friend did a better job keeping to the pace. I physically tried to accommodate to the situation I was growing into. Determined not to fall behind, I remember what it felt like having to run to catch up with father and son. Another snapshot of me trying to live up to a situation I found myself in. Of me determined to be worthy of that trial, as, later, I was determined to learn how to drive a car so I could take my buddies around Seattle, a hilly town, where examiners would direct novice drivers to the steepest hill in town to test their ability to back into a parking place on a busy city street. Passing that test felt like the greatest accomplishment of my life.

I was nine when the US entered World War II, a situation that, even viewed from a distance, changed my life in many ways. I learned about pilots flying planes, navigators steering those planes over enemy targets, and bombardiers having to gauge the plane's speed and altitude, together with the wind's speed and direction, in figuring when to release a load of bombs so it would hit a target tens of thousands of feet below. It was one thing to hit a stationary target on a bombing run, another to hit a moving target such as an enemy fighter in a dogfight, each trying to gun down the other. Hitting a moving target from a moving viewpoint is an image that has stuck with me ever since. And is now my metaphor for the many challenges my consciousness faces every day in just piloting me through local time and space while walking downtown, say, or driving along village streets packed with summer visitors who don't appear to know where they are or what they are doing. The trick being for me to deduct effects due to my personal motion from the apparent motions of the various goals I am striving to reach, taking visitor perambulations into account so I can visualize in my mind where we all stand in relation to one another moment-by-moment.

In a world where every individual looks out from a unique perspective, it takes a heap of mental calculations to navigate through the myriad situations we encounter so we can work with one another to accomplish what must be done. Just passing the baton in a relay race takes a lot of practice so each team member works smoothly and effectively with the others in achieving their common goal as fast as collectively possible. That simple, linear example suggests how hard it is for larger, looser, more diversified, less trained groups to work to eliminate world hunger, say, to achieve world peace, reduce income disparity, or find ways to resolve tensions between Israelis and Palestinians. Or for families to conduct themselves in such a way that each member is able to engage and contribute to both the local community and larger society.

Yet despite all odds, that is what we expect—that naïve, untutored consciousness is sufficient for us to reach both our collective and personal goals. We grant ourselves all manner of freedoms and rights, but make slight allowances for the training and experience we need to realize them to a satisfactory degree. Declaring them ours is no guarantee they will be delivered to our doorsteps as we have grown used to parcels being delivered these days. I have long entertained an image of tribal elders gathered in a circle around a fire at the center of a wigwam, holding council to decide what to do next. But my assumption in summoning that image is that those elders have lived with one another all their lives, they speak the same language, respect the same cultural values, and are highly skilled in many of the same ways. That is not an accurate picture of any group I have ever belonged to; it is a fantasy image depicting how I wish decisions would get made. It is certainly not a picture of the wigwam inside my head where my personal consciousness resides, determining the course of my life. That course does get determined, but more by serendipity than by any council of tribal elders. It is more a hit or miss affair, made by a random assembly of bits and pieces from my life—as in this chapter of the book I am working on. The discursive, trial and error of the empirical method, risky as it is, is the best I can do under the true circumstances of my daily existence, for no other reason than because that is how my mind seems to work.

The question is: Is that primitive form of native consciousness adequate for me to live the life I aspire to in the situations I actually encounter from one day to the next? Introspection has led me to ask that question. I do not know the answer, but will say I find the world growing ever more complex in my aging experience, and harder to deal with than when I was young and knew little of the world, and the world population was much smaller. I am shocked to remember there were only some two billion people on Earth when I was born; now there are seven billion. Our species has multiplied more than three-fold during my lifetime, yet many of our traditional institutions go on as if nothing had changed. Orthodox Jews are stuck in their understanding of events in the seventh century BCE, conservative Christians are stuck in the first century CE, madrassa-schooled Muslims in the seventh century CE. Clearly, my inner council of elders would have much on its collective mind in days such as these. The discussion would be a far more complex challenge than one held when such councils were state-of-the-art for tribal governance some two or three hundred years ago. I cringe to hear my imaginary councilors saying, "Do you follow me?" "You know what I mean?" "Google it." "Like, what are we waiting for?"

I will close this chapter with an extended tale from personal experience, this time not about myself facing a situation alone, but in company of a great many others joined in Maine's experiment with local bay management, overseen by a group of Taunton Bay Advisors, of which I am a member. The term of that group ended December 31, 2010, having been in place since January 2007. What can I say about that earnest, four-year effort to improve fisheries management in one small bay in Maine? Does it point the way to the future as I had hoped, will it limp forward much curtailed, or perhaps fade from the scene like other forlorn hopes?

The Taunton Bay Advisory Group originally consisted of sixteen members appointed by the Commissioner of Marine Resources. It was led by the head of the Ecology Division of that department, a man dedicated to bringing local experience and expertise to bear on local fishery issues. Early on, we decided that eelgrass meadows—habitat for juvenile members of a great many fish species in the Gulf of Maine—should not be compromised, nor should undue pressure be placed on horseshoe crabs at the northern edge of their global range. Maps were drawn up showing eelgrass beds, horseshoe crab habitats, shorebird habitats, and where different species of interest were harvested. Of the ten fisheries in the bay, we chose to look closely at the four of them involving (or impacted by) drag harvesting: blue mussels, scallops, sea urchins, and kelp. We planned to move on to alewives, eels, sea worms, clams, crabs, and lobsters at an unspecified date in the future—but didn't survive long enough.

We worked up an impressive management plan to guide our effort, and with the advisory group in place, started holding monthly meeting attended by department personnel, and open to harvesters and interested members of the public. Decisions were to be made by consensus, and minutes kept by state personnel were to be the official record of our proceedings as posted on the department Website. Our goal was to achieve a sense of stewardship that would guide every human use of the bay. We worked with harvesters in deciding where the four different species could best be harvested by diving or dragging—while protecting eelgrass and horseshoe crab habitats. We required harvesters to apply in advance to the department for permits allowing them to fish in Taunton Bay, the permits being affixed to their fishing licenses. Harvesters were to take only the quota allotted in each of the four fisheries. Stock assessments of the four species were made, allotments decided, with a requirement that all by-catch (species not sought, but caught nonetheless) was to be reported to the department.

Fast-forward to our meeting of November 2010, at which two advisors showed up, outnumbered by a delegation of four from the department. Attrition had been steady throughout the four years. Local citizens apparently didn't feel a commitment to the project, and harvesters, rugged individuals that they are, evidently don't go to meetings. The plan was comprehensive, the procedure sound—yet the baby died aborning for lack of either commitment or interest, or both. My diagnosis is that coming from very different backgrounds as we did, the advisors lacked training in working together so to complement one another, and independent fishermen did everything they could to block the move to local control (even though they would have a much larger say than they do now under state-controlled management).

After a five year moratorium on dragging, even allowing dragging for blue mussels in two areas approved by the draggers themselves, not one boat has ventured into the two designated areas mapped as mussel dragging sites. My recommendation to the department is that both advisors and fishermen be given free training in group process so we can feel confident that we have the skills necessary to support a local citizens' effort in bay management. The rift between managers and fishermen is so severe as to be a clash between separate cultures that don't share a common language. I further recommend that an anthropologist be named to the advisory group to assist in translating between the two groups.

From my perspective, the situation is dire if not critical. As a pilot project for the entire state, local bay management in Taunton Bay is on the ropes. I see this as an example of an ongoing situation yet to find satisfactory resolution, a more typical example than the adventures I faced while hiking alone. My rule of thumb is that the difficulty of dealing with situations rises with the cube of the number of participants. Certainly situations involving interactions between multiple minds are far more complex than those entertained in the mind of a single introspective investigator. I use this example to demonstrate that personal introspection, productive as it may be, is not the whole story.

Next up, a chapter devoted to speech, the primary medium of social discourse, and its origins in the everyday situations that structure our lives according to the give-and-take engagement of consciousness as thrust into the world by our loops of engagement, and drawn back into ourselves in the form of sensory figures to be enjoyed, interpreted, understood, felt, and further acted upon. O

CHAPTER 9

SPEECH

Awareness arises in the everyday situations that structure our lives according to the dictates of attention as thrust into the world by our actions and drawn back into ourselves in the form of sensory input to be enjoyed, interpreted, understood, felt, and further acted upon. That one sentence is a summary of these pages up to this point. My aim in this chapter is to explicate (from Latin *explicare,* to unfold) what that sentence might mean in regard to speech.

When personal consciousness decides the time has come to act, speech provides a fast and energy-efficient way to make a gesture within a given situation. Winking or lifting an eyebrow would also be fast, but the vocabulary of facial expressions, though powerful, is somewhat limited. The nerve fibers involved in making such gestures are relatively short compared to those involved in moving an arm or a leg. I view speech acts as providing a trial run for bolder actions, allowing something to be ventured quickly with minimum effort, putting all within earshot on notice quickly at very little expense. I think of chickadees, owls, crows, and eagles employing vocalization on that level to stay in touch with those within earshot. Human culture and evolution have elaborated a huge verbal apparatus on that basic foundation of cries, hoots, calls, and distinct auditory gestures sent through the air to all ears within range. Whereas animals apparently rely primarily on innate drives, habits, and instincts in the present moment, humans retain memories of repeated and emotionally-charged events, so our present loops of engagement are informed by felt episodes and concepts formed in the past, giving depth to our awareness, allowing us to interpret the sensory present in terms derived from prior experience. This gives each of us a significant survival advantage, or at least a chance to flexibly reapply lessons learned over the years, freeing us from the dictates of habit and instinct. To begin, I will return to three of the incidents I have been following, probing for insights regarding the role of speech in selected life situations.

In the case of the clip-art cat (Ch. 1, Incident 9), I categorized the sound of a squeaky hinge as the yowl of a hapless cat I had stepped on, so at reflex speed, jumped up to lift my foot from the tail I assumed without thinking was underfoot. That is an example of language at work on the most basic level. The hinge may not have intended to speak, but that's how I took the sound it made—as a command to which I made an instant response. I can't say I did what it told me, but for practical purposes that sound triggered a situation in my mind, and I made what I thought was an appropriate response to that situation. Which clearly illustrates how large a portion of so-called communication is left to the discretion of the recipient of any given message, which in this case was no message at all—just a noise that I happened to interpret as a message within the situation my loop of engagement placed me in at the time.

We talk a lot about definitions and meanings as if they resided in words themselves, but this incident illustrates an instance in which my response was appropriate to the situation I created in my mind upon hearing a sound, even though the message was "sent" by two pieces of metal scraping against each other with not a meaning in mind because there was no mind. I made the whole thing up in the only mind present—namely mine, which was enough for that hinge and me to hold a terse conversation.

On the basis of that first example, I will make the claim that speech acts occur in situations, and the meanings they "convey" are precisely those situations as construed in the minds respectively entertaining them. That is, participants are basically speaking within a situation as they interpret it for themselves, so the meaning of any exchange is more elicited or evoked than "conveyed." This simple yet profound example suggests that speech might be more subjectively created on the spot than is assumed in the conventional model of a message being sent and received. What if there is no message, but only two minds on more-or-less the same track concerning a particular situation? What if the situation itself is the message as construed by those minds respectively? Marshall McCluhan had it almost right: it isn't the medium that counts; *the situation is the message,* opening the way to what we decide to do about it.

That comes pretty close to my model of speech. When a child learns a new word, that word embodies the situation in which that word is learned as construed in her mind. Think of the story of the m-o-o-n, banana I related in Chapter 5 in which the phenomenal

153

image of a crude crescent drawn on the blackboard was categorized by the girl as a banana, so in her mind that is what the pattern of letters "m-o-o-n" meant or spelled. How could she conclude otherwise? That is what she learned and ran home to tell her mother. The story is more about the hunger for mastery and approval than what is specifically learned in one case. At that age we are eager (motivated, driven) to learn; the job of our speech community is to feed that hunger so we grow competent in dealing with life situations as they arise by categorizing them with fluency. If we catch ourselves committing a category error, we don't easily forget it.

The case of the voice in the night (Ch. 1, Incident 12) is another example of the meaning of a sound being the situation in which it is uttered (or heard). The man crying "Fa, Fa" was announcing the import of his situation to the world, including me, lying in bed, deaf to that sound because I didn't recognize or understand it, so it held no meaning. Until I computed the Boston accent and realized the voice was crying "Fire, Fire," a situation I grasped immediately, and responded to as appropriately as I could, checking out the window first to make sure. No squeaky hinge, that was a true cry for help.

The case of the buried remains (Ch. 1, Incident 11) bears out my situation-as-meaning thesis in an example suggesting how two different minds entertained a complex utterance from two points of view representing two different situations. In asking, "Whachagot there, Steve? Looks like some kind of turtle," my supervisor interpreted the scene he came upon with mild surprise and curiosity from a professional point of view, while what I heard in my own ears after brushing particles of soil for two hours was more, "Steve, you jerk, why have you been wasting so much time unearthing a stupid turtle shell!" Here, a simple question is taken as sharp criticism—because that is how I judged myself in my own mind for mistaking (miscategorizing) a turtle carapace as a human skull. We watch our engagements carefully, monitoring how well we perform. It was I who heard a cry of "Fa, Fa" as meaningless nonsense; it was the great doctor (Ch. 1, Incident 18) who could make nothing of my symptoms (of celiac disease, as it turned out thirty-two years later); it was the young student who misinterpreted an intended crescent as the outline of a banana.

My method here is to take category errors as significant mistakes shedding light on the workings of my mind in trying to map consciousness onto the world correctly, yet getting it wrong. In my own case, the disparity between two stages of awareness I construct in my mind is revealing in putting that disparity into the context of the situation—my world as I construe it—at the time, revealing the true nature of the problem. Which I then try to trace back to its roots in my personal experience, or at least interpret as an example of what actually happened so I might avoid making similar mistakes ever again.

Speech acts, I suggest, spring from a situation as a kind of proposition or assertion characterizing some salient aspect of that situation as depicted within a particular loop of engagement—likely to be heard in other minds from a variety of different perspectives. That is, speech flows from our ability to categorize sounds as meaningful in some way. The sounds are interpreted in speakers' and hearers' minds through loops of engagement by which those sounds summon (invoke) conceptual interpretations while, simultaneously, those same interpretations affirm such sounds as making an appropriate fit to the situation at issue as it is construed in particular minds. That sentence fits in no nutshell, but it is what this chapter is about. I am saying, basically, that speech acts announce the essential workings of our minds by drawing attention to events as salient aspects of felt situations. When we speak, we literally speak our minds, and when we hear, we have the words speak to us within our current situation as influenced by prior experience. Listening to speech sounds, that is, we act as a kind of ventriloquist projecting our meanings onto the moving lips of the speaker. Speech is situational in nature, and the relevant situations are invariably internal to the loops of engagement maintained by the particular people involved. Which suggests that in speaking our minds, we can take only one detail at a time, leaving out much that could be said. We speak our minds incrementally and sequentially, making our point, then moving to the next, dealing with our felt situations bit by bit, parsing them into details one after another as we choose to emphasize them and relate them to our overall understanding as we are able to articulate it point by point. Thus we build sentences by predicating (asserting) something about a chosen topic or subject, adding modifiers, details, and emphasis as we go, all in good order (sequence) so we will be understood by members of our speech community, those who taught us to speak in the first place.

How can I put that more clearly? I see loops of engagement as being interactive, reaching in two directions at once: *from* specific sensory patterns *toward* broader interpretations, and at the same time *from* general categories of experience (in memory) *toward* presentations of more explicitly detailed instances of sensory stimulation. When the two processes agree at a given level of discernment that accounts for both an agreeable level of detail *and* generality—that is, the inductive and deductive branches come to agreement—then the situation is grasped (understood) on that level of both sensory being and conceptual meaning. The challenge in any engagement is to find an appropriate level of detail at which speech sounds take on meaning while the overall interpretation recognizes those sounds as appropriate to itself. That is how I explain what happens when I look within my mind and discover category errors of my own making that result in mismatched sensory figures and categorical interpretations such as the eighteen incidents I relate in the first chapter.

In this chapter, my aim is to map my habits of speech onto such mismatchings between sensory patterns and conceptual interpretations in order to write about the role of situated speech in *invoking* a sense of understanding, and in the other direction, about understanding *evoking* appropriate gestures and acts of speech. It is clear to me that loops of engagement proceed in both directions at once, from a store of familiar concepts reaching toward sensory figures, and from such figures reaching toward relevant interpretations within a given situation.

I speak of these mental reachings as coming to agreement at a particular level of discernment that matches sensory details to conceptual inclusiveness at a mutually-agreeable level of understanding. I cannot assign these mutual interactions within my mind to particular neuronal paths in my brain. I leave that to neuroscientists who are knowledgeable about such things. But my reading between the lines of several books by Gerald M. Edelman tells me that the dynamic process of "reentry" via "massively parallel reciprocal fibers," on which so much of his argument depends, might well provide the physiological foundation for what I refer to as "loops of engagement" (*Wider Than The Sky,* Glossary, p. 174).

The fact is, speakers and listeners join in conversations by extending their loops of engagement to one another, *taking turns* speaking and listening, their minds *engaging in complementary ways,* one taking a flow of words *from* the air into sensory awareness as a series of linked sounds, the other sending a flow of words *into* the air as emissaries of a particular understanding, both *united by a situation* centered on a topic of mutual interest. Up till this chapter, I have largely focused on events taking place in my own mind. Speech is far more complex in linking one mind to another, so that events happening in two different minds are to be considered as aspects of a single speech event, which is more accurately an engagement between different minds actively reaching toward one another. Taking turns complementing one another in reaching for meaning and understanding alternately with reaching for being and sensory fulfillment, different minds engage one another in the way humans characteristically do so profoundly (yet often carelessly) in their everyday lives. Done with sufficient care by all partners engaged in a discussion, it is possible to reach shared understanding insofar as the different situations (within which they respectively see themselves as dwelling at the time) overlap, allowing mutual agreement to arise.

Speech is complex because consciousness itself is complex, both speech and consciousness having many different facets which become clear as we turn them in our minds and in our speech. Not that all speech is equally complex, any more than all situations or all minds are equally complex. We each choose the level of detail we feel suits a given occasion—as when speaking to a three-year-old, for instance, or conducting a seminar in textual exegesis of a particular paragraph in a particular chapter of a particular work by a particular author written in a particular place at a particular time. There are levels of discourse, and we adopt the one we feel most likely to be understood by the audience we are addressing. Where do babies come from? Do fanciful storks deliver them, or daddies and mommies make love to each other, or they develop from fertilized eggs by the process of embryogenesis? Which version do you want? What level of detail will you settle for? And even when finished, you'll still have questions because it's a bigger topic with more intricacies and nuances than one mind can entertain in one answer or lifetime.

A mind is a landscape spread in three dimensions, with paths connecting different points, and tunnels leading to hidden caves, and roads disappearing over far horizons. That's an example of a metaphor, which, essentially, is how the mind works, categorizing one sensory figure in terms of those it is familiar with, interpreting for clarity and emphasis, trying to get at feelings which are ineffable and can only be suggested through indirection. That is, categorizations and interpretations are felt approximations that can seldom encompass the complexity of a given occasion. So we settle for standard, dictionary definitions of the words we use, hoping they will fit our use of a term, and then when we speak, largely disregard those standards in trying to convey what we feel at the time—the urgency, the importance, the nuances, the essence of a particular episode of personal understanding.

Words are not adequate to consciousness as a whole, so in portraying the facets of experience we resort to complementary genres of communication such as body postures, hand gestures, facial expressions, music, painting, drawing, sculpture, dance, drama, numbers, videos, moans, groans, mimicry, mumbling, expletives, and all the rest. Y'with me? Y'unnerstan? Y'follow? Y'know what I mean? Y'take my point? In truth, we can never export the full content of awareness to other minds, so are invariably left dissatisfied with the job we've done, hoping to get it right next time. Or perhaps blaming a world that just doesn't understand.

Rational thought is a learned convention made to fit set terms and procedures *as if* they were adequate to describing or dealing with every situation of importance. But one man's discipline shackles another's free thought, so we work our way through a maze of possible procedures for dealing with felt situations, only to find ourselves in a dead end (a so-called fortress of belief or finite province of meaning), unable to say what we want to say, so have to backtrack in order to try another route to where we hope to end up.

The Vienna Circle, a select group of twentieth-century philosophers and mathematicians, committed themselves to finding a scientific language allowing a one-to-one relationship between what they understood logically in their minds and, subsequently, could be understood without distortion by their listeners, only to give up on a job that turned out to be beyond the language they pointedly designed to meet the requirements imposed by a science of reason and scientific convention.

Charles Morris, for instance, came up with a science of language itself in which all meaningful terms were defined through a complex network of mutual cross-references that deliberately cut them off from outside contamination, rendering them sufficiently pure for truly scientific discussions. Seeking "scientific precision," Morris aimed to provide a full accounting for a scientific discipline exclusively in its own terms, as if it existed in a vacuum apart from all other fields of knowledge. But scientific terminology is laden with metaphors from its inception in the figuratively rich minds of the ancients. The upshot being an agonized line of reasoning proclaiming a sign to be a set of conditions such that whatever fulfills it permits the completion of a response-sequence to which an interpreter is disposed because of a sign—that is, a sign functions as a sign because it *is* a sign. If this represents scientific precision, then we had better redefine "precision" to reflect an illusory increase in the order discernable within any particular system of thought. The error here is in pretending that any discipline can exist independently of all others, thereby conserving its internal purity in isolation. No precinct of metaphor can function very long as a closed system (the Inquisition should have taught us this, or, more recently, Nazi Germany and, subsequently, the State of Israel). Any such system of belief will gradually erode in practical use unless periodically renewed by an infusion of fresh insights and perspectives from other minds and realms of understanding (drawn from my *Metaphor to Mythology,* pp. 393f.). For instance, the conflict between Israelis and Palestinians can only be surmounted by their getting together as equals, not by holding themselves apart in isolated enclaves from which they can enjoy the luxury of judging each other from afar.

Which, I believe, is why we need a repertory of languages to choose among if we are even partially to realize the hope of making ourselves happen in the world as we desire. In truth, we are most alive to ourselves in our own minds, and any effort to export the nuances of personal experience to other minds—rationally, say, scientifically, artistically, mathematically, or philosophically—is apt to be only partly successful, leaving us wandering alone in our local branch of the maze where humans desire freedom yet are caught in traps of their own choosing or making. Getting together requires first of all getting physically together in the same space under conditions favoring a free exchange, resulting in honest engagement of each *with* the other. Scrap the protocol and get down to work: taking turns, making music, dancing, sharing a meal—whatever it takes.

Settling for what's possible in a given situation, we deliberately choose a level of discourse suited to our aspiration of being able to explain ourselves clearly and fully to a select group of others. That is, we determine the amount of detail we want to go into, and respond to our situation on that level, knowing we could dig deeper or shallower into our experience, but on the present occasion designate *this* as the level of detail we will strive to get across. In everyday life, usually we choose not to dig very deeply, settling for a kind of general language suited to casual tasks and encounters that will see us through the day with minimal effort. We commonly talk on the level of "things," "items," "goods," "stuff," "commodities," and other broad generalities, for, indeed, that level suffices in most social engagements much of the time. Discussing matters with colleagues, we rely on the specialized terminology of our trade or profession, and when we meet friends, we resort to a more intimate language allowing reference to activities and acquaintances we share in common. Only when we engage those familiar with the finest level of our sensory discernments do we open our souls on that level of our experience. That is, we present different levels of our minds to different people, as we deem appropriate to the relationship we have with them on a need-to-know basis. We express ourselves according to the intimacy or generality of our relationships, engaging other persons at various points across the spread between those extremes.

By setting our discernments at different levels of sensory detail and conceptual generality, we are able to vary our perspectives flexibly from our most general notions ("I see something," "There is an event," "What is that object?") down to a particular degree of fineness consistent with our most demanding and skillful perceptions (as in making medical diagnoses, for example, or forming aesthetic judgments). By anchoring our discernment to a given level on our range of possible interpretations, we preset our expectations to a particular level of resolution so that, in effect, we can scan our surroundings for relevant patterns of stimulation at a meaningful level of complexity and detail. Utterances emerging from those surroundings as phenomena, then, are relative to our expectations on that level, and judgments of novelty or familiarity reflect the degree of acuity made possible by our states of interest and motivation (Ibid, p. 388).

As I said earlier, speech offers us a trial run at making ourselves happen in the world, and now I will add—at a particular level of engagement and discernment. We make a noise or gesture of some sort to see how others will take it, then refine our message and try again, venturing and refining until we get straight in our minds how to proceed in living our lives at our preferred level of concern. In that sense, speech is a precursor to action, one that falls short of a bodily commitment to one course or another. Talking things over is one of the most practical benefits of speech in giving us a chance to sort things out, make trial gestures, and suit ourselves to a given situation in the most effective way. This is particularly useful in planning how we are to engage situations in the future, which is largely the thrust of our education, except for those activities enjoyable or beneficial in themselves, such as playing soccer, dancing, or making music.

Writing this sentence, I am on an anticipatory roll, aiming to make myself happen by putting much of what I have discovered through introspection over the past thirty years into the pages of a book. That is one way I make myself happen using speech as a planning device to help me sort through my life experience and say what is germane to the topic of my personal program of introspection. This places me on the leading edge of my consciousness, applying it toward a goal to be gained in the indefinite future, which is one of my main uses of speech.

This week I took a brief break from working on the book to attend to several other tasks that have been piling up on my to-do list. I sent out four emails dealing with four different projects I am involved with, making suggestions for future actions in each case. After I'd sent them, I realized that, though different, they were very similar in nature in looking ahead to next steps that might be taken regarding complex situations in the near future. "I'd like to have us meet to discuss . . . ." I wrote in one email; "One last recommendation: It strikes me that the best thing that might come from the Taunton Bay experiment . . . ." in another; "I personally think the Executive Committee should visit the house so members can picture the changes it would require in our current operations," in a third; and "I'd like to hear from each of you in an email expressing your support for this agreement, then we can send around a final draft" in the fourth.

Planning ahead seems to be one of my chief uses of speech, whether orally delivered or written. Planning is a huge portion of my conscious concerns, whether in dreams where I am trying to reach a particular goal, but am frustrated in making the attempt, or in my wakeful life where I am not only concerned with making myself happen, but in having a larger body build a future for itself through corporate action. Here is consciousness at work employing prior experience to extrapolate a particular trajectory into days yet to arrive, using speech as a primary tool to bring that about.

Which is an example of interpreting situations in terms of declarative propositions or assertions in the spirit of the Greek word *kategoria,* meaning to predicate, assert, propose. In that sense, speech expresses an intended mental predication, assertion, or proposition, so serves to externalize the inner portion of the loop of engagement in one individual mind. This is how I categorize the situation, how I see things, or how things stand as seen from my point of view. Speech, then, flows directly from the workings of our minds, even when spontaneous and the words are unknown to us before we feel them streaming from our lips.

Where do words come from if not our looping engagement with specific world situations as valenced by personal emotions and concerns? Situations as we categorize and understand them in our subjective, felt experience, expressed in words (and sequences of words) which our language community has taught us to utter as outward and auditory signs of the salient facets of those situations as we construe them on our level of understanding from our limited point of view. That is what introspection reveals to me in countless examples drawn from my everyday experience. Short-term memory does the heavy lifting in formulating speech appropriate to a particular situation. Speech, then, is like the array of shortcuts on the desktop of my computer, conveying me inward to the turning facets of a coherent episode of experience (which comprises feeling, understanding, interpreting, and appreciating sensory patterns) as my attention actively details those facets in a particular situation. The words stream out according to the syntax, rhythm, and intonation of my personal loop of engagement at the time, reflecting how I have been taught to think by members of my most intimate language community. Which is how to categorize and interpret phenomena, how to exemplify concepts, how to take situations apart so I can deal with them in manageable units, putting them together again paragraph-by-paragraph, until I have the whole utterance assembled in words linked together, each in its right place at the right time to bear its share of the load.

Meanings do not inhere in words, they are products of coordinated mental activity. Nor do associations adhere in words. Word lists used in experiments to test associations are essentially meaningless because associations with any given word depend on the situation in which it occurs as viewed from the subject's perspective at the time of presentation. Human subjects are not lab rats, that is obvious. But lab experiments based on word meanings and associations offer a slippery slope every time because so much human variation cannot be controlled for or reduced to a set of parameters.

Where does fiction come from if not a mind's situated loop of engagement imaginatively put into words? Every novel speaks to an author's inner reality where interpreted phenomena course toward deeply felt understanding expressed in words within a mental situation revealed at its most telling level of discernment and remembrance. Every novel is a study in introspection, for where do novels come from if not authors' minds, where they are kindled in two-way, looping engagements between sensory figures and ideas, feelings fanning them into flaming words on muttering lips?

Being a highly visual person, I have never found the English language to be an adequate medium for conveying my experiences to others. What I see is often more important than what I think. My books about Mount Desert Island and Acadia National Park (published 1998–2002) are heavily illustrated with photographs. This present work is an exception, because I have no camera built into my mind. Even so, I can "see" my loop of engagement plunging from sensory receptors to phenomena to interpretations to understandings to meanings to valenced feelings to actions (such as speech). That kind of visualization is a good part of what introspection entails in my case. But with nothing more concrete to show for the effort, written speech, by default, must bear the burden of that inner cascade.

As an example of words being used to suggest a relatively general level of discernment, I offer this paragraph from my picture book, *The Shore Path, Bar Harbor, Maine* (2000):

> In a short distance along the rocky tide line of Frenchman Bay, the path looks onto the five Porcupine Islands (clockwise from the north: Bar, Sheep, Burnt, Long, and Bald), with Ironbound Island farther east. The Bar Harbor Breakwater reaches from Bald Porcupine Island toward Cromwell Cove, leaving a narrow passage for boats on the shoreward end. The barren Thrumcap lies to the south, and Egg Rock with its venerable, red-eyed lighthouse marks the mouth of the bay. Glimpsed between the islands, Schoodic Mountain and the Black Hills stand to the north (p. 1).

Given my fondness for wandering through fields of rich visual stimulation, it is no accident I include photographs in my guides and hiking books. By natural preference, I pay close attention to the phenomena my eyes render in consciousness. Here, I am saying, regard the landscape from my point of view. In the example above, I rely on words alone because they are more general in describing the setting of the Shore Path without going into detailed descriptions. The function of the words here is to serve as a point of departure (for subsequent experience), so I refer to points of the compass, and place names of notable features seen from the path, leading to the photographs themselves, each telling its own story.

In *Acadia's Native Flowers, Fruits, and Wildlife* (2001), the arrangement is not linear along a particular path, but seasonal through the year, starting in April with mayflowers, ending in October (witch hazel), then the fruits and berries of those flowers appearing in July (blueberries) through September (wintergreen), followed by wildlife sustained by those fruits and other sources of food. In the introductory section, "How Acadia Works," I move to a somewhat higher level of detail in summarizing aspects of climate affecting flowers and berries:

> Acadia is powered by sunlight and gravity under the influence of a climate featuring an average of 50 inches of precipitation a year, temperatures ranging between 90° F. and minus 10° F., and winds blowing from the southwest in summer, northwest in winter. Precipitation peaks in November and December with about 6 inches a month, gradually declines through August to a low of some 3 inches, then increases in the fall (p. 3).

Further details are put in captions accompanying each photograph, including flower names, family memberships, habitat characteristics, and months when flowers and berries are likely to be met along the trail. On a finer level of precision, I briefly present details of a fire that ravaged Acadia's landscape on Mount Desert Island (MDI) in 1947 in *Acadia's Trails and Terrain* (2002):

> With only 0.08 inches of rainfall, October 1947 stands as MDI's driest month on record. On October 17th, a fire started at Dolliver's Dump on the Crooked Road near Northeast Creek. The blaze, often fed by strong winds, didn't die out until November 14th after burning 17,280 acres, destroying 17 local residences and 67 vacation cottages, ending the era of stately summer homes in Bar Harbor (p. 10).

Even within that short paragraph, verbal precision ranges from 0.08 inches of rainfall (accurate to the nearest 100th of an inch), to 17,280 acres burned (accurate, perhaps, to within ten acres), to claiming the end of an era (accurate to perhaps the decade of the

1940s, which included Bar Harbor's involvement in World War II). When I wrote that paragraph, I had access to a map depicting the acreage that burned on any particular day, which was too fine a level of detail for my purposes, while I felt that simply referring to the fire in passing would not do justice to an event that changed local history.

What I say or write depends on the degree of discernment I judge appropriate to a given situation on a particular occasion. Lesser discernment requires fewer trips to the library; greater discernment requires more intensive research, better records, and more care in presenting my argument. I have to keep checking on what it is I am trying to do with the resources available, for what audience, within what period of time.

I see these as aesthetic matters, building a coherent whole from an arrangement of individual details in relation one to another, like structures built of bricks or Legos, or a picture based on a palette of colors. How many units I have to work with determines the level of discernment I need to apply to the task. Keeping things simple by limiting the number of units is an effort toward economy—doing the most with the least—requiring each unit to bear a greater share of the load. My mind is useful in making judgments of symmetry, coherence, simplicity, complexity, similarity, and difference, which helps me say the most in few words. But that can lead to very general utterances, which seem to say more than they actually do in leaving details unspecified: Beauty is truth, truth beauty; God is love; Money talks; Ignorance is bliss; among a host of similarly pat aphorisms whose economy is taken to signify wisdom. To be as clear as I can in depicting the link between my loop of engagement and the words it ushers to my lips, I risk giving an excessive amount of detail in trying to be true to my vision. I struggle to pare down the words, but do I go far enough? That is my dilemma in wanting not to be glib, to hit the right balance between saying too little and saying too much.

As I go over these paragraphs to sharpen their meanings, I picture my loop of engagement trading messages both ways—between the words on the page as received in my mind and the interpretations I map upon those sensory patterns—the loop itself enabling me to shape words and phrases to my liking. At 5:46 on the morning of December 16, 2010, these words—the very words you are reading at this instant—are shuttling back and forth along the loop of engagement in my mind, as phenomena that look and feel like words, then to how I interpret them with some dissatisfaction, on to my fingertips typing on the keyboard of my computer, changing the words on the screen, altering the sensory patterns in my mind, refining what I take them to mean, eliciting a valence of good or bad, this will do, or this is not what I want to say. Round and round they go—these phenomenal words—until they say what I intend them to. Then I move to the next station in the loop, the next phrase, next sentence, next paragraph, next episode in the writing of these pages in my mind.

With high unemployment much in the news these days, the word "jobs" is on every newscaster's tongue, where it often seems to be meaningful on a very low level of specificity: white collar or blue, high tech or low, service or manufacturing, healthcare or education, industrial or domestic? Not all jobs are equivalent. What kind of jobs, where, for how long, at what level of skill, for what pay? Whose job, yours or mine? The Dictionary of Occupation Titles lists 28,800 different jobs. Which ones are we talking about: "Fish-liver Sorter, Fish-Machine Feeder, Fish-Net Stringer, Fish Packer, Fish Pickler, Fish Pitcher, Fish Smoker"? In addressing the issue of jobs, newscasters often operate at a low level of discernment in presenting a generalized view of the unemployment situation as if "the economy" were one thing, all jobs and all workers were the same, which it isn't and they're not.

In my mind, this raises the issue of how well we listen when we are addressed. Do we want the whole story, or just a brief summary in general terms? Listening is a high art, which does not get the attention it deserves in our educational system. At least it didn't in my personal education. Beyond "Listen up, people," "Put on your thinking caps," no one ever suggested to me that understanding is something you have to reach for, and listening is a skill that takes concentration, openness, familiarity with the topic on an appropriate level of discernment, and lack of distraction. At best, listening is presented as a passive activity in which you can relax your vigilance and sort of drift along, letting the speaker have his say until it's your turn. For myself, I find I have to put as much effort into listening as into speaking. I have to actively direct my attention toward what is being said, make notes, ask questions, acknowledge doubts, that is *pay* attention, not simply be marked present. I have to engage myself in what is being said in order to keep up with the flow of words and ideas. If I fall behind, I lose the drift and am apt to daydream or attend to personal concerns I brought with me when I came into the room.

Strangely, when I am concentrating on something, a voice in the background catches my attention immediately, whether it drifts into my inner ear from the TV next door, voices in the hall, the lyric of a song—immediately those words command my fullest attention and I quickly succumb to the foreign invaders. Having fought such battles my entire life, I now know when I'm licked and simply move out of earshot if I can. I am particularly vulnerable to distraction in party situations when every conversation in the room babbles in my ear so I can think of nothing to say to the person in front of me. It feels like my mind is preempted by the crowd, so I cease to exist as anything but an audience for white noise, red noise, bright yellow noise. My solution? Absent myself a.s.a.p.

Level of discernment is a characteristic of attention and interpretation, not speech per se. The more specific details we take into account, the better our hearing, the more accurate our interpretation is likely to be. And the larger our vocabulary in keeping with that fineness of attention, making discernment a primary property of our looping interaction with the sensible world we process as phenomena, adding to the complexity of our engagements within a single speech community.

Talking to myself is challenging enough; think how engaging another unique being in conversation compounds that challenge. I fully grasp my side of the discussion—my ears were calibrated at the same time my tongue and lips were. But when other ears are trained to language in different situations by different speakers with different degrees of emphasis and discernment, speakers who interpret those situations using a vocabulary only partially overlapping my own, then the feeling tone may be different, the understanding, the specific sensory patterns—all labeled perhaps by many of the same words I might use, but kindling different experiences, memories, feelings, and interpretations on different levels of discernment. Yet we assume we speak the same language, and both mean what we say, and say what we mean, so when we nod in agreement, we believe we are assenting to the same proposition—except we often aren't because those words are processed differently in one mind than in any other. It is sobering to realize that spontaneous speech acts are often a matter of publically justifying ourselves to ourselves on an ideological level of engagement. Parallel universes of language and understanding, that is where we dwell, not in one universe identical to itself in both our minds. That is our interpersonal conundrum, striving to achieve seeming agreement in terms while our respective understandings actually diverge in many respects.

One thing is clear: passing a check from one hand to another is not a variant form of free speech. Money may serve to enable, compel, or emphasize speech, but it is not speech itself because it is not the product of any such process as I have outlined in the preceding paragraphs. Money does not talk; people talk, asking questions or making assertions. Confounding money with free speech is a category error of the most egregious kind because it deliberately clouds the distinction between linguistic and financial transactions, between the internal-qualitative and external-quantitative domains in which people engage with and relate to one another.

I will leave the topic of speech on that cautionary note. A great deal more can be said, but I am not the one to say it. My interest here is introspection, not the linking of minds. After all, I am the world's leading expert on what goes on in my personal consciousness, and I am definitely not an expert on speech. I move ahead to the topic of the biological values which guide my survival as related to my sense of personhood, my feelings and emotions, and the loop of engagement by which I externalize those values in making myself happen in the world as I do. O

CHAPTER 10

VALUES

Waiting for two new tires for my car to be delivered from Bangor, I used the unexpected delay at my cousin's garage in Hancock as an opportunity to think about the role of biological values in my personal consciousness. The writings of Nobel laureate Gerald M. Edelman had convinced me that the evidence for values must exist in my mind, but I had never recognized it as such. Or if I had, I always assumed that those values were more cultural than innate. I took Edelman's views as a challenge to identify the presence of such values in my own mind through introspection.

Sitting on a wooden bench during my wait at the garage, I made a list of the biological values that came to mind, largely in categorical terms. I thought of *food* right away, including meals, hunting and gathering (now largely replaced in the US by shopping and mall surfing), cooking, nutrition, caloric intake, and so on. *Drink* and other fluids came next; I am some seventy percent water, after all. Followed quickly by *breathing* to fuel my metabolism by inhaling oxygen, exhaling carbon dioxide. Then came *Territory,* a felt need for room or space where I could provide for my needs. *Sex* kept coming to mind, but I wanted to deal with personal life-support issues first, not bodily urges, so I wrote down "sex" as a reminder to get to it later (as if I would forget). *Sleep,* that's a biological value. I'm no good when I'm tired. My best moments are spent rediscovering my mind upon rousing from a dream. *Health* and physical well-being, including all my innards, my sight and my hearing. Related to that, *exercise* and being physically active, which keep me alert. I live in a cluttered apartment, but that doesn't mean I don't value cleanliness and neatness—a general sense of *orderliness* in my personal affairs. Understanding of situations is extremely important to me, so I wrote down "*grasp* of situations." Then I thought of Thoreau's concern for preserving the vital heat in the first chapter of *Walden,* which has always spoken to me, so I noted, "*food, clothing, shelter, fuel.*" Developing *life skills,* is that a value? I wrote it down.

169

Then *companionship* and *community*—two different values. *Belonging* to groups larger than myself, I added that. *Pairing, family, reproduction, children;* finally I got around to *sex, eroticism,* and *sensuality.* Which led to *attachment* and *affiliation. Speech*—I devote a chapter in my book to that—so I added *communication, art, music, dance, etc.*

It was a long wait at the garage, but it gave me a wonderfully stimulating time to explore my own thoughts, so I kept at it, taking a walk in the snow from time to time to stretch my legs. Starting a new page in my steno book under "Values" at the top, I put down *independence, freedom, safety.* Then *dignity, maturity, integrity.* Followed by *respect, playing* or *participating,* and in last place, *making things happen.* Not that I'd covered the primary value categories, but at least I'd made a start. I had enough to work with. I didn't care if all were biological values in Edelman's sense or not, but one way or another they fit my inner review of "values." Culture, too, is biologically mandated, if not predetermined in finest detail, so I treated *cultural values* as variations on biological values.

Then I started thinking about my list, carrying on a conversation with myself. What are values? They seem to be innate drives or motivators, all leading or related to bodily actions. They are more verbs than nouns: eat, drink, provide, do, be, breathe, care, act, join, seek, rest, move, grasp, talk, plan, learn, make myself happen. Yes, definitely motivators. Values seem to have to do with getting things done—putting meals on the table, finding shelter, making babies, staying alive, working with others, getting enough food and sleep to keep going. Values, that is, underwrite consciousness itself.

Then I thought of attention. Values seemed to dictate what I pay attention to on an everyday basis. Attention leads to phenomena in my awareness, to how I interpret them, to feelings and understanding, to planning, to acting, and back to attention. What guides attention? I asked myself. What drives my engagement with my surroundings if not biological values?

I seemed to be talking about the whole of my conscious mind. Well, then, what drives consciousness? If "drives" is not the right word, what shapes or elicits consciousness? Disparity between my actions as intended and the sensory stimulation that confirms or disconfirms them, as I wrote in Chapter 7. Values seem to be the shapers of consciousness through comparison of my inner state with what I feel it actually ought to be. Any discrepancy gets my attention—leading me to adjust my loop of engagement by reaching out for sensory stimulation in ways more pertinent to my goals.

Why am I conscious? Or put differently, without consciousness, what do I lose? Engagement with situations, for one thing. Interactions. Relationships. A sense of purpose and achievement. As I said, values are motivators that get me up and moving about, doing things, working on projects. What do I live and work *for?* What's the point? Why bother? What is worth living for?; dying for?, because that's where my personal values end up—in the trash when I'm dead. What do I want on my headstone? "He made the effort." "He tried." "He did the best he could / With what he had / In the time allowed."

Do values work by driving me through life from behind to avoid what I don't want to happen? Or do they pull me ahead so that situations work out to my advantage? Do they help me avoid hazardous situations, or do they draw me toward more beneficial ones? As a card-carrying empiricist, I have learned that my style is to pitch in, make mistakes, and find my way through trial and error. My built-in error detector keeps me awake and on track. My first take is that values help me avoid pitfalls while, at the same time, heading me toward personal fulfillment and satisfaction.

Satisfaction smacks of sex, like moving ahead to my next liaison—the next time I'll get laid. The next time I'll eat, the next time I'll sleep. Gratification of built-in urges, is that what values are for? After all, we are all sexual beings, all food fanatics, all addicted to sleep. Chemicals build up in our bodies—or else drain away—leaving us out of balance, hungry to satisfy one urge or another. Is "value" a neutral (polite) word for lust and bodily appetites?

I feel like I am asking, "Why do birds fly, fish swim, rivers flow?" Why does Earth turn on its axis? Why does the sun shine? Why am I here? Why am I conscious? "Why" questions are often deceptive, making me feel I can discover answers when, in fact, there are no simple causes behind anything. This is just how it is. Maybe values are illusions, stories we tell ourselves—like Aesop's fables—to "explain" why things are as they are, to make us feel we understand things when we haven't a clue why we do what we do, the world is as it is. Why we are born, why we die, why we live life as we do. From that perspective, values sound like part of the script we are acting out. Who wrote the script? Evolution, that's who. Because organic structure and complexity are cumulative over the eons, and one stage of development leads on to the next. I doubt gravity was a concept in anyone's mind before Newton invented it. He just made it up, a convenient fiction to make us feel we understand more about the universe than we do, or we can from our perspective of relative ignorance. Why should mass attract itself? Saying that gravity is a force of attraction is a description of what we observe, not an explanation. Even when we quantify it, it's still a mystery. But gravity is now part of our conventional wisdom, and as such it got us to the moon and safely back, so there must be something to it. Gravity was standing by, waiting to fell the Twin Towers when conditions were right. We may not understand how it works, but we have the evidence of our eyes that it does. Values are means for explaining ourselves to ourselves, for becoming carnivores that kill and eat other creatures, for attacking those who offend us, for loving those who please us.

I think of my own body as a hostel for roving bands of viruses, bacteria, and mites—which I host in far greater numbers than the cells I am made of. As to survival, the odds are with my billions of microbial guests, not my one puny self. In my lifetime, they reproduce faster and in far greater numbers and mass than "I" do. In practical terms, "my" values favor the survival of those guests making use of my throat, gut, eyes, skin. My values are their values or, more accurately, *their* values are my values. They digest my food, clean up the skin I slough off. If they are to thrive, then it follows that I, too, must thrive in order to serve them, as the tree must grow to serve the birds that nest in its branches, and to serve the bacteria et al. that teem in their feathers. We ignore the life that sustains us at our peril. Without it, I would be dead, and so would you. When we talk with one another, I picture colonies of microbes conducting diplomacy between our separate nations. We humans are the General Assembly for the hordes of microscopic life that make us who we are. Small *is* beautiful, yet we know nothing of our burden of tiny life. We live on a different scale, at a much slower pace. Our explanations of things are crude and coarse-grained, at best half-truths meant to mask the full extent of our ignorance, intended to lull us into compliance with received wisdom, without doubts or further questions.

Introspection opens me to dark reflections such as these in trying to stretch the envelope of my understanding without ripping it to shreds. I need to outrun my goal and pull back in order to set the limits of what I can justly claim to know with any degree of certainty. So far, I have met with no sure signs of an ego, superego, or libido such as Freud made the cornerstones of his self-analysis. Erotic social behavior is one biological value among many, all equally vital to sustaining conscious life. Sexual attraction is like Newton's gravity, a force we recognize when we feel it, but one that defies understanding. Without either one—sex or gravity—we wouldn't be here, that much is certain. They are conditions of life. From conception to death, contending with both is built into our nature. Sexual urges, erect posture, and orientation in space are integral parts of everyday life, along with many other energy-dependent values defining what it means to be one human self among many.

I'm trying to report with some accuracy the stages my quest to identify values within myself has led me to, sitting in Merchant's Automotive, Inc. in Hancock, Maine, waiting for two tires to be delivered by a truck coming from Bangor (by way of Bucksport on the far side of the county). One thing is certain: Having sound tires on my car is one of my values. After seeing that jagged mesh of steel wires worn away in a bald gash on my car's right rear tire, I didn't have to think twice about ordering a replacement, even though that idea was not in my head when I walked in the door concerned about rattles coming from my exhaust line. I invented the value "new tires" on the spot. My values changed instantly to suit a situation I suddenly found myself in. Once I've moved on from that place, I won't think about new tires until the next time they are forced into the spotlight of my attention. Such values are situational, not biological. Or, to the extent situations in my mind are biological, then such values might be construed as biological values once removed. Assuming *personal safety* to be a biological value, then "new tires" comes under that heading.

This riff on values is an example of how my mind actually works. I stumble through the terrain a topic suggests, heading this way then that, briefly exploring an example that comes to mind, then moving on, trying to knit the whole journey into a coherent understanding somewhat as quilters sew scraps of cloth together in making a quilt. In that sense, values are situational, part of the quest to whip chaos (uncertainty) into order by reworking old scraps into a new pattern. The blanket I sleep under is wool, one side made of 3" x 9" strips cut from three different fabrics (light gray, dark gray, green) arranged stepwise into a pattern. The woman who made it put a portion of her life's energy into selecting, cutting, arranging, sewing, binding those strips into a blanket. I now think of her quest for order as being one of her values. Where she didn't find it, she created it. Values, by that view, govern how we apportion our bodily energy in doing what it is we do to make ourselves happen in the world in an orderly way. That is, according to the loops of engagement coursing through us in response to discrepancies in awareness that govern our interactions and relationships by igniting our conscious minds.

Sitting in the garage, that came to me as a new thought. Values govern orderly behavior. Behavior requires energy, so values guide us in putting personal energy into situations so we can resolve them to our advantage. Which is what birds do when they fly, fish when they swim, the sun does when it turns its physical mass into solar radiations including heat and light. Which is what I did in seeking to have my exhaust line repaired, with additional energy (which money represents) directed toward replacing two worn tires. Sex, food, and sleep are energy matters—what we use it for, how we get it, how we restore ourselves at night as a way of getting ready for the tasks we will face the next day. Values must be behind whatever plans we make. Not biological so much as universal. The life force itself, making it essential to burn energy left over from the big bang to keep our portion of universal stuff going as long as we can, creating our allotted share of entropy in the process.

Energy makes us what we are. Values direct the flow of vital energy in doing what has to be done to keep going. A life, once set in motion at conception, uses maternal energy to fuel fetal progress through embryogenesis, the essential rite of passage we all must endure, through which physical matter is turned into a wholly unique instance of life in the universe—namely you or me. Such instances require consumption of energy to support their development, elaboration, and to sustain them in moving ahead into ever-new tomorrows. Eventually, life learns to meet its own energy demands in becoming self-sustaining, taking energy in each day, expending it for repair, maintenance, and new actions appropriate to a lifelong series of situations within which each life makes itself happen according to its own unique stream of consciousness.

Energy propels us on our journey, as heat energy moves molecules in ceaseless Brownian motion, so in that sense, they "have" life, even if it only amounts to a jiggling back and forth within the situations where they are thrown, wandering ("exploring") in that place as long as the energy keeps them throbbing. A molecule's job is to keep moving, jiggling faster when it's hot, slower when it's cold. When the source of heat runs down, molecular life runs down, until, at zero energy, it stands still forever.

Which is also true of human life. We are eminent jigglers and consumers of energy. Without food, drink, shelter, rest, health, we run down and become no good at sustaining ourselves. We wear out, and eventually die because we can no longer live up to our own values, which are biological, cellular, molecular—universal. If we have children, they carry on in our name, not *for* us but *because* we passed our energy hunger and values on to them, which they have to learn to use for sustaining themselves. What is life but a tale of conceiving, birthing, eating, sleeping, growing, learning, working, reproducing, nurturing, wearing out, dying? In short, jiggling as long as we can. The secret is in the overlap between generations so that one endures long enough to train the next in finding and directing its own energy towards meeting the challenges of its place and its time in order to pass the same heritage of values on to its children through genetic inheritance, example, disciplined training, education, and in an existential sense, the course of trial and error that spurs our minds to wakefulness.

Waiting for my new tires to arrive, I found I could relate to the molecules in the arm of the bench I was sitting on, to the dog sleeping in the sun at my feet, to the mechanics who spend much of their life energies repairing cars such as my 1994 Geo Prizm (a Toyota Corolla in disguise) so they can carry on their private lives dispensing personal energy according to the dictates of their personal values. Prove yourself!, that is our mandate. Make it happen! Do it! Be! Or not, as our life situation plays itself out.

Are there essential human values that lead us to direct our personal energies in ways common to all people? Clearly there are: obtaining food and drink, finding protection from the elements, expressing ourselves erotically or sexually, having and raising children, meeting our basic energy needs by controlling one territory or another, sharing life within a tribe or community of people we identify with, staying healthy and productive within that community, living in harmony and integrity with our neighbors, feeling safe, and dying a good death. Without having such values biologically built into our individual selves (as Edelman asserts), we are at the mercy of those around us, who might well use us for *their* purposes, not ours.

Being radically independent, I generally find it better to live for causes I designate as important rather than to have others thrust their causes onto my life as their agent—or victim. When young or weak, we are particularly vulnerable to abuse by others in that sense, reducing us to phenomenal objects in other eyes, interfering with our being persons in our own right according to our personal values. Slavery, begging, deprivation, sexual abuse, child soldiery, forced labor—these and other assaults on the personhood of children in fulfilling their own values for themselves are rampant around the world. Values, that is, do not realize themselves, no matter how forceful or biological they may be. The grand value is survival within situations we find ourselves thrust into, so that we learn to fulfill ourselves by imitating those who are stronger and cannier than we are in that place at that time. It is not surprising that victims of abuse often become abusers themselves—that is the example they have suffered through, never to be forgotten. As we are used, so do we use others. That's how ways of expressing personal values are passed to successive generations. Values control personal identity, but that identity can be taken over by others so that we are forced to fulfill plans in *their* minds, not ours, which is the source of a good deal of abuse and cruelty in this world.

For my argument here, I will claim that we each define ourselves according to the personal spectrum of values that shapes our expectations, attention, and awareness in forming our conscious and unconscious lives. As an example, I will direct my introspective gaze toward a situation I put myself in on the day after getting new tires at the garage. I don't know what I will find, but if I don't make the effort, I will find nothing at all, and be none the wiser about my biological values. Earlier in the week, I had visited my son Ken who, with Linda his wife, runs a glassblowing shop in nearby Ellsworth. I noticed a flyer for an event they were holding billed as a "Fire Gathering" from 10 a.m.–5 p.m. on December 18th. Glassblowers use a lot of fire (in this case fueled by propane and electricity) to heat their glass and keep it fluid so they can blow and shape it. At the gathering, there would be glassblowing, blacksmithing, and music. And in true holiday spirit, blown-glass gift items for sale. Driving to Bar Harbor, it struck me I could take pictures of the event, collect them into a booklet, and give it to Ken and Linda, along with the JPG files. It would be something I could give them (as a solstice gift—I celebrate the beginning of the year when the sun rises farther south than at any other time) that they couldn't give themselves because they're always too busy blowing glass to take pictures of themselves blowing glass. I would loan them a third pair of eyes so they would have a record of the proceedings at this particular event, which they promised would be "heartwarming," a value they highlighted on the flyer.

On the 18th, I showed up at 10:30, took pictures of finished pieces on display in the gallery, then worked my way through the hot shop where the pieces are made, focusing on tools and powdered-glass colors laid out for the day. Linda and her assistant, Emily, were shaping a glass tumbler at the bench where molten glass is blown, worked, and shaped. As people arrived, I photographed them, too, as well as Jeff, the blacksmith, who had set up his forge in the parking lot. By noon, I'd filled the memory card in my camera, so went back to Bar Harbor, downloaded the card, recharged my battery, and returned at 2:30, when many more people had arrived. By then, Adriaan the bladesmith was set up in the parking lot next to Jeff, hammering a steel bar into a sword, alternately heating the steel in a small forge, then literally pounding it into shape, a job I figured would take some ten-thousand blows.

Ken and Linda were the heart of the event, which proved to be a gathering of their personal community, which I thought of as their family. Here were family values in action, each participant doing his or her personal thing as glassblower, assistant, apprentice, student, friend, colleague in the person of blacksmith and bladesmith, potential customer, or interested bystander. And in my case, proud father. All of us rallying around a human passion for making functional and attractive things with fire. The center was the use of energy in making things happen—difficult things requiring great skill to bring about as planned. This, I thought, was the essence of consciousness on display, not so much the finished pieces themselves, but the *making* of the pieces through deliberate attention to detail at every stage of the process. I did my best to follow the various loops of engagement in action, taking pictures stage by stage, blow by blow.

Out front, Jeff and Adriaan were hammering away, shaping hot metal against anvils, delivering each blow with proper force at the right time at the right angle to bring about the results they intended— a wrought hook for hanging plants, or the blade of a sword. At the bench in the hot shop, people took turns working on glass softened by heat in the glory hole where flame meets glass to keep it workable. First Linda worked with Emily to make a glass tumbler, then Ken with Emily, then Alexander the apprentice with Ken, alternately heating the glass, then working it, then reheating it, and working it more, each stage resting on all the stages that had gone before, making it possible to take this particular action at this time in preparation for the next stage, and the one after that. I pictured (literally, took photos of) the event as a series of loops of engagement doing their thing. Until each piece was judged finished, and put in the annealer to cool slowly, when the glass workers turned their attention to the next piece on the schedule, laid out tools and materials for that job, decided who would make it, who assist. Click, click, click, I kept with them as best I could.

The event of the day was Ken and Emily using an iron helix that Jeff had wrought earlier that day (by heating, hammering, bending an iron rod) to blow a vase within that form so that glass and iron interacted in a way they never had before. I photographed Jeff at his forge making the helix, then the glassblowers heating, shaping, blowing hot glass within it, adding a base for stability, and putting it away in the annealer to cool. A universal first, if not in principle, in this particular instance of applied conscious activity guided by the personal values of the artisans who made it happen.

The blowing of a particular piece might take forty-five minutes, blocked off into stages like scenes in a drama or ballet, each worker knowing the part she was to play in relation to what others were doing, conducting herself—her bodily movements in a confined space —with precision toward a purpose. The value I saw enacted before my lens was *purposiveness,* participants conducting themselves to achieve a desired end with an array of tools and materials requiring great skill to master. This, I felt, was powerful stuff because personal values were essential to pulling it off in each case. The crowd gathered to witness and admire difficult feats performed by a team working together in close harmony of motion because they all shared that same value. The gathering was of like-minded people constituting the glassblowing and blacksmithing clan of highly disciplined fire-workers, people who understood the skill, concentration, and judgment it takes to create the contents of the annealer, who appreciate the value of purposiveness required to keep the galleries of the world stocked with artifacts by the current generation of artificers and artists who make galleries happen by making *themselves* happen in keeping with their personal values.

In the parking lot, Adriaan showed me a knife he had made by heating, pounding, shaping a one-inch ball bearing—his personal values personified in a tool of his own making. Imagine the skill and discipline required to hammer out a blade from a sphere of hard steel. Why would anyone want to do that? What value does that knife represent? Yes, it is beautiful; yes, it is difficult to make; and yes, it is useful. Adriaan is not one to shun a difficult challenge; in fact, he deliberately seeks such challenges because he believes he can master them. He puts himself on the line by saying, I think I can do this—I want to give it a try. With a specific purpose in mind, he means to show what he can do in challenging circumstances. Life is a test, and he aims to prove himself worthy at severe levels of difficulty.

There it is, purposive consciousness in action before my eyes, as played out by assembled glassblowers and blacksmiths, witnessed and valued in turn by their fans, friends, and relatives. Photographed by one on the outlook for values being clearly expressed through applied attention and skilled action toward an orderly end as an expression of human engagement and consciousness.

Decorative hooks, sword blades, glass tumblers and vases—what does it mean to express oneself? To admire such expression? To purposefully put life energy into getting something done in orderly fashion? There you have it, biological values on display. Skilled workers turning felt values into handcrafted objects. Objects not only beautiful in themselves, but whose history is beautiful every step of the way—as the biological history of making babies is wondrous at every stage of embryogenesis. Difficult, yes; and energy consumptive; but truly miraculous to those whose biological values lead to such results.

Ken and Linda don't have children, so they have built a community (tribe, family) of friends and co-workers around themselves. The traits (personified values) I saw on display at this particular family gathering included *skillful performance, craftsmanship, harmonious social interaction, cooperation and teamwork, use of available* (in this case commercial) *energy to magnify personal effort, concentration on the task at hand, coordinated loops of engagement, purposiveness, personal dignity, mutual respect, orderliness,* and *self-discipline.* This is some of what it takes to survive year-round in Maine. Here, before my eyes, was life being lived, revealing the underlying values that make it possible for this particular community to survive in the darkest of seasons.

My personal contribution was to do for Ken and Linda something they could not do on their own—be a witness to the complex interactions through which they make themselves happen as individuals within a supportive community. I was there not only to witness the event but to celebrate what they have built over the past fifteen years since moving from San Francisco to Maine—the personal skills, business, and relationships that have attracted a community to form around the nucleus they provide. I took about 400 photographs, which I cut to 300 on the CD I gave them as a winter solstice present, and further reduced to 93 images divided into thirteen sections in "Fire Works," an album of prints. What biological values do those gifts represent? I would say loving and supporting my children as they make their way through this life by letting them know I notice and appreciate what they are doing in being notably courageous, hardworking, and unique in making themselves happen as they do. They will know I mean it by the level of detail I show in my photographs of their activities—intended in a discerning, loving, and admiring sense. My other son, Jesse, is a chef in Boston, and I regret not being able to engage with him as much as I do Ken and Linda. I am a fan of his and am proud of how skillfully he makes himself happen in the kitchen. He brings culinary joy to a great many diners.

What I value, I pay attention to. There is a strong link between biological values and the memories I store as episodes in my personal autobiography. Why are values important if not to guide expectancy, attention, and awareness in the future more surely than in the past? From my introspective session in Merchant's Garage, I now see that values—as gateways to consciousness—set up a cascade in my mind from attention to awareness to new adventures. Learning by trial and error as I do, I eventually get it (my motivated engagement with my surroundings) right, even if I botch up in the beginning because values lack details of how they are to be realized. Values are broad motivators, not blueprints to personal fulfillment. Realizing I am hungry is only the beginning of the story; it is up to me to decide what I want to eat and how to get it into my mouth.

I am apt to remember what I feel strongly (strong emotions build strong synapses). Incidents I frequently recall reveal biological values I live with every day of my life. When I refer to my *self*, that self is built of a variety of personal experiences: what I perceive, what I know, what I understand, what I feel, what I value, what I remember—these are part and parcel of the self that I am. If I couldn't remember such details of my inner life, I wouldn't be this particular person. All of which feeds into my conscious engagement with my surroundings, determining what I seek and what I notice, facilitating how I make myself happen in building a world around myself, a world of my own designing, constructing, maintaining. A world, that is, built inside-out around the personal values at the core of my mind.

How do I—how do you—come by such a world? How else but through learning to be ourselves? Behind all learning, I suspect, lies the wisdom of the geological ages expressed as inherent values selected by myriad situations such as humans have gotten themselves into and lived to tell stories about around campfires with the tribe gathered to review and understand what has happened to each member during the day. If we can only put what happens to us in proper perspective, our actual experience will teach us the essentials of what we need to know to live out our lives. Introspection is the craft I rely on in pursuing that understanding because nobody has the answers I am looking for but me. If I look to others to teach me about life, they can only teach me about their particular lives as lived expressions of *their* values, not mine. My biological values are my personal tutors, with tenure for exactly one lifetime.

The soundest learning of all flows outward from the self of each unique person, not inward from a curriculum set by a complex society that, of necessity, omits the essential details we all must grapple with in coming to understand who we are. If that effort is not at the core of our personal learning, our schooling puts us beside ourselves as if we were someone else—a nameless "student" our would-be teachers know little about. To give an example, just as radio personality Jean Shepherd saw his mother as a "sink creature," I saw my father as a typewriter creature putting in long hours clicking away at his Underwood upright. Through the door of his study, I could hear that muffled clicking every evening from seven till bedtime. I knew *that* he wrote, but had no idea *what* he wrote. All I knew is that's what fathers did. Now, seventy years later, I myself—just like my two brothers—sit for hours on end at a machine, tapping away. Indeed, I have become that prototypical image of my father. Paper, paperclips, pens, pencils, stapler, three-hole punch, and that typewriter—these were the tools of my father's trade, and now of my trade. My loop of engagement was largely set before I entered kindergarten, but no teacher had any idea what my primal homelife was like.

If we don't direct our own learning from the core of our values as we grapple with and experience them, we are bound to miss the point of having a unique existence by mimicking the gestures that others

181

lay upon us, much as a sculptor lays clay on the hollow armature underneath. If the armature is a fixture in other minds as a kind of "knowledge base" supporting a school curriculum, then teaching to that curriculum becomes a matter of laying "knowledge" onto young minds, which is exactly the opposite of what *educate* really means— to draw or lead out, not impose. The armature—the proper structure on which to base education—is within each student's mind when she walks through the door. Treating students as if they were puppets converts them into disciplined mimics, not learners. Memorizing neat facts and formulas is no education. If coming generations learn only what their elders already "know," they will never learn to think for themselves. The challenge every student faces is to outdo her teachers by becoming uniquely herself in fulfilling her personal values. Education for a lifetime is that simple—and that profoundly difficult.

How did I arrive at this point of view? By paying close attention to my personal self through introspection. By thinking about things while sitting in a garage waiting for the tire truck from Bangor to come. By taking pictures of my grown children doing their thing in good company. By remembering errors of expectancy, attention, and awareness I have committed in the past and never forgotten. All this is trying to tell me something about the personal values behind who I am as a person. I am not talking about astrology or reading tea leaves. This is my life, the one I am trying to grasp through introspection so I can make it even better than it already is. There are far too many troubles in the world to settle for living an unexamined life. I think many of us spend too much time conforming to a caricature or cartoon of who others (to whom we surrender our personal authority) tell us we should be, while ignoring what our values, feelings, and memories are clamoring to tell us inside-out. Ignoring these inner voices amounts to selling our souls to the demons around us, those who thrive through a culturally acceptable form of cannibalism by feeding on gullible minds.

The remedy is to keep our respective loops of engagement informed at all times by our personal spectrum of biological values so that we are assured of living our own lives and not lives thrust upon us by meeting others' needs and desires. We cannot deny that those others have different sets of values than we do, so we must live in their midst as a matter of fact; but that doesn't imply that we must become one of them in feeding on our neighbors. Like vibrant molecules, we can run a separate course right through them, leaving them in our wake minding their own appetites.

We may deal with biological urges and appetites in culturally-approved ways, but the drives themselves are unique to ourselves in each case. Tribal customs and ways of doing things reflect common attitudes toward values shared in a particular locality. Given the spread and diversity of ways such motivating urges are expressed in different cultures around the world—burkas on some shores, bikinis on others—we must appreciate the variety of human perspectives on the most basic determinants of human life. I don't hold with theories of so-called normal and abnormal psychology; since each of us is unique at every stage of life, normality is a fiction of convenience. We are who we are in the situation of the moment.

As things play out, however, members of each cultural unit can become trapped in viewing members of other cultures from an ideological point of view, casting their standards abroad, judging strangers and foreigners as if they were deviants, treating them as flaunting different values, not as unique individuals who have learned different lessons from life. Instead of promoting broad acceptance of human diversity, such subjective judgments narrow the field to the "right" and the "wrong," orthodox and heretical, promoting wholly unwarranted animosity and conflict.

Introspection may seem egotistical, but its message is that of humility. My practice informs me that I can be as petty and mean as the next man, which is nothing if not humbling. My learning is based on errors I have made. My personal effort is to understand why I saw things as I did in specific life situations by repeatedly reflecting on them from a variety of personal values and perspectives. If my views of other people are based on personal judgments, it seems only sensible to examine the basis of such judgments in the context of my own life experience. Democrats and Republicans will never work together until they appreciate the underpinnings of their respective points of view—underpinnings in their personal values, not party loyalties. The same is true for Israelis and Palestinians resolving their differences in a one- or two-state solution. Why is it so hard to accept "deviant" behavior as an expression of personal values entertained in minds inhabiting situations we have not experienced or lack the wits to imagine?

Bigotry is a refusal to learn by stretching one's mind around a larger, more complex situation. In truth, identity lies deeper than conventional attitudes. Whether I could see the Rocky Mountains in Colorado or not as I approached them for the first time when I was thirteen and my family was moving across the country to Seattle, I was still the same person both before and after the event. Those clouds were the problem, the very ones I put into place by being true to the grasp I had of my situation. But when I finally saw the Rockies as covered by snow, not clouds, I was still myself—only somehow bigger than I had been up till then. After letting go of the clouds I had put in place, I let the Rockies be their snow-covered selves, as they had been all along when I just couldn't see them because I lacked the life experience of seeing snow at higher altitudes in August. That incident illustrates the power of introspection to include one's own mind in her looping engagement with an external world largely driven by biological values.

Introspection teaches me that perpetual learning is my lot in life. Because I keep venturing into novel circumstances, I have to keep adjusting my thinking and my habits to an endless succession of new situations. Staying in one mindset for too long commits me to a living death. I see that enacted on the news a great deal—the throes of those whose views have outlasted their situational effectiveness. Benjamin Netanyahu, for instance, has outlived his time (really his Zionist father's time, now long out of date, as Hosni Mubarak, Muammar Gaddafi, and Bashar al-Assad outlived theirs). If we get used to having parents or teachers in school telling us what to do, we become dependent on those who supposedly know more than we do. Lifelong learners take responsibility for stretching their minds on their own. Which periodically means having to accommodate to novel (or unappreciated) situations. That is why self-learners keep their legs under them and can move off in different directions without having to follow the one preset course they were headed in when young. I find such adaptability conveys a powerful survival advantage, allowing me to adapt to occasions as I meet them without having to take a detour around anything that blocks my set course. I just keep plunging ahead, learning as I go. Learning, not reasserting views acquired in the far-off days of my youth.

That way, I let my values be my guide in keeping up with my world as it changes instead of insisting the world must remain true to how I saw it in the old days. Introspection teaches me (I learn for myself) that learning trumps knowledge in more cases that I would have thought because knowledge is largely an inert fiction requiring gullible minds to put it into play. I look at each situation from a variety of perspectives, and adopt the one that gives me the clearest view, which may be very different from the one I applied yesterday. Since my values are situationally relevant, and my situation is always in flux, the impact of my values is forever new, and my perspectives change—perhaps making me a different person than I was half an hour ago. If I am the same person after new learning as I was before, I haven't really learned anything. True learning allows me to make myself happen according to the situation I am in rather than having to present the same face to the world out of principle, habit, or because I am stuck in one place.

The topic of the next chapter is the goals we set ourselves to work toward in days ahead. By being flexible, we can work our way into them, allowing us to learn by doing in the process of building a future for ourselves. Putting our values to work in imaginative fashion, we often end up in a very different place than we could have pictured at the outset. Such is life, a learning opportunity, not a set course. ○

CHAPTER 11

GOALS

G oals direct attention to what needs tending to as a means of channeling our vital energies toward a version of the future we prefer over other alternatives. In setting goals for ourselves, we anticipate what might happen, and put our energies into realizing the possibility that appeals to us most, or considering our means, is at least within reach.

In my own mind, I use goals to translate my personal understandings, feelings, and values into strategies that will bring about situations in which I am likely to thrive. I don't just endure events as they happen to me, but (when I can) take an active role in making myself happen in such a way to bring about just those situations that I imagine will promote my survival—that is, the survival of those values that make me who I am or want to become.

In the mid-1980s, when I discovered a subdivision comprising thirty-four vacation-home lots was being built around one of the few active eagle nests on Taunton Bay, I put my energy into promoting the highest and best use of that property as eagle breeding habitat, and, with sustained encouragement from the Maine Department of Inland Fisheries and Wildlife, a pro bono lawyer, and the Maine Chapter of the Nature Conservancy, eventually won my case in Superior Court. My values were affirmed, and that subdivision was never built. Which is remarkable because real-estate speculation was rampant in those days.

I put myself (my bodily energies) into opposing that subdivision. Then, looking ahead, I found I didn't want to go through that experience again, so in 1987, convened a public meeting of citizens interested in founding a land trust to protect wildlife habitat and other wild areas in Maine's (then largely pristine) eastern Hancock County. Twenty-four years later, the resulting land trust, Frenchman Bay Conservancy, is going strong with twenty-nine conservation easements and fifteen preserves under its stewardship covering 5,545 acres (as of November 7, 2011). Again, in phase two, my values were affirmed, my goal achieved.

Three years later, net pens filled with Atlantic salmon appeared without public notice in Taunton Bay (I had developed a reputation as the self-proclaimed king of Taunton Bay for defending the eagles, and the salmon farmer deliberately stayed below my radar to make sure his activities didn't catch my eye). I convened a meeting of concerned citizens at a friend's home to explore the ramifications of a covert aquaculture venture being established on the bay. Those attending thought that a nonprofit organization was called for, so bylaws were written for The Friends of Taunton Bay, which is still in existence twenty years later, with an impressive record of monitoring and research regarding the ecosystems responsible for the bay's natural productivity. A five-year moratorium on dragging for sea urchins, scallops, and blue mussels was proposed as a measure to protect eelgrass meadows in the bay, which was approved and written into state law for five years. This led to an assessment of the influence drag-harvesting had on the local ecosystem. The assessment led to a pilot project in local bay management, drafting of a management plan, and formation of an advisory board of local citizens to work with the Maine Department of Marine Resources in making recommendations for best management practices to put in place. The saga continues, my value of protecting the bay from inadvertent degradation now implemented in a series of ever-more-refined goals, priorities, and actions.

On a particular Sunday in April 1987, I was situated in such a way that I was the only person who could see smoke rising above the trees from, as I discovered, slash piles burning where the road to the proposed subdivision was being run through the woods. Had I not set myself the goal of discovering the import of those plumes of smoke —leading me to row across the bay to investigate—none of the foregoing saga would have taken place. Values have consequences; setting goals in situations reflecting those values have consequences; step-by-step actions to implement such goals have consequences. I could have predicted none of these events beforehand, but by sharpening my attention and discernment over the years, and both expanding and refining my goals as I went, I now find myself sitting at my computer writing these words with the assurance of hindsight *as if* my personal goals, values, and priorities had been fulfilled. But what really took place is I made myself happen in situations as they developed, setting appropriate goals for myself, and as I made myself happen, the situations in which I was a player developed, leading to a great many people getting involved as a consequence of the goals I had set for myself and the actions I had taken in realizing those goals. At the outset, my to-do list was short: Check out what's burning in those woods. But one thing leading to another as it does, that was the beginning of a rapidly expanding and increasingly more ambitious to-do list, which spawned similar lists jotted by others who joined the cause over the years. Together, our loops of engagement got up to speed and changed the climate at the head of Maine's Frenchman Bay.

I don't know anyone who doesn't have a to-do list at hand to jot down all the things that need doing when they come to mind. Mow lawn; Groceries; Haircut; Call X. And if the list isn't on the kitchen counter or held by a magnet to the refrigerator door, it's kept internally: Put condoms in purse (don't get pregnant now); Get gas (avoid what happened last time I ran out); Send Mary a card (she sent *me* one); Balance checkbook (pay bills). To-do lists are how we hold ourselves mid-air by our bootstraps until we do what needs to be done. No one else can do that but each one of us for herself. If we don't set our sights on what needs doing, we risk going under, taking unnecessary chances, falling into debt, etc. To-do lists make life run smoother if not easier. We all know if we put things off, life gets harder. Outside the game of Monopoly, there are no "Get Out of Jail Free" cards. If we are to achieve something in this life, or avoid potholes waiting for us on dark streets, it is up to us to remind ourselves to be vigilant about such things. Others are too busy to be bothered; that's why each of us has a special mind dedicated to putting his values to work through goals and priorities only he can set for himself.

The goals others set for us are very different, full of assumptions, oughts, good advice. Wash face; Brush teeth; Elbows off table; Comb hair; Don't be late; Be polite; Stiff upper lip; Be good. These are matters of routine. We can deal with them by forming good social and personal habits. Setting goals is meant to bring about rare, important, improbable, necessary, or significant events. Like finding a mate with whom to support our mutually agreed-upon dreams, getting into a school that will present sufficient challenge to bring out our best, landing a stimulating job, pushing a career to its limit, becoming the person we aspire to be. Goals emerge from the interaction of personal values with situations full of both peril and opportunity. We make ourselves happen inside-out, acting in such a way to realize the future we are willing to work for, or some reasonable approximation of same. "What needs doing?" we ask: Plant seeds so they will grow into the flowers and veggies we will want later in the season; shovel snow; repair roof; find a cure for cancer or international strife—whatever challenges us sufficiently that we will want to rise to the occasion and, pounding our chests, say, "That's what I want to do with my life!"

Natural disasters provide jobs for anyone wandering around with insufficient challenge to give meaning to each day: earthquakes, hurricanes, tsunamis, floods, volcanic eruptions, avalanches, mudslides, storms at sea, pandemics, droughts, and so on. Add cultural disasters to that short list of natural challenges and there's no need for anyone to live without pursuing a worthy goal defending civilization against: war mongers, revenge seekers, tyrants, the petty and unjust, production of yet-more-devastating weapons of mass destruction, exorbitant concentrations of wealth, corruption, the conceit of corporate personhood, unemployment, big money in politics, human overpopulation, overconsumption, financial speculation (gaming, gambling), spurious opinions delivered as universal truths . . . you name it, there's a need for a lot of us to join in finding some kind of remedy. The goals we set ourselves tell what sorts of persons we are in our own minds.

Life, then, is a projective personality test. The work never ends, so the goals we set ourselves (as expressions of our values) tell who we are at that time. Which kindles the remarkable side effect of instilling hope by working not just for today but for tomorrow and the day after. Setting goals is one of our ways of working to build a future to our liking. Goals bridge the gap between yesterday and tomorrow, providing a sense of continuity and progress toward better days ahead. Without specific goals to work toward, we suffer fits of dread and anxiety: An aimless man is a hopeless man trapped in a dither. The way out is to figure what needs to be done, kindling the hope that things will get better. Then working toward such goals day after day, we tug at our bootstraps, pulling ourselves up and ahead. Goals, that is, are a means of turning our lives into self-fulfilling prophecies. We venture the goal and fulfill ourselves in striving to achieve it. We may not end up where we thought we would, but the adventure has been ours the whole way.

The motto of Seattle's Roosevelt High School in my day (1947–1950) was a saying by Theodore Roosevelt, which I remember as "What I am to be, I am now becoming." Goals are the missing ingredient in that motto, the spice that gives the school adventure its flavor, not as something turned out on an assembly line like so many Twinkies, but which the student contributes on her own by staying true to her personal goals and ideals so she doesn't end up as some uniform standard product labeled "graduate," "worker," "soldier," or "citizen." Are high school students mature enough to set their own goals? Perhaps not, but if they don't practice taking on that responsibility, will they ever sharpen their attention and discernment in developing loops of engagement that serve who they are instead of who others want them to be? If self-knowledge became an integral part of the curriculum, the art of setting personal goals would be out in the open, blooming in clear, sunlit air.

A life filled with hope is better than a life of duty, drudgery, or slavery. Personal commitment is what matters, and setting personal goals is a way of spurring that commitment. I have lived the life, so I know. I couldn't live any other way. Preaching? Certainly. But that's what introspection has taught me. I didn't read it in any book. I firmly believe that the human use of human beings (to quote the title of Norbert Wiener's book published in 1950) requires not automation and communication with machines, but human beings talking openly and honestly about their inner lives so they can be themselves without having to pretend they are someone else. Wiener proclaimed a new day had come based on order and information, freeing humans to indulge in arts and recreations. Trouble is, order in the universe does not declare itself but must be interpreted by one kind of mind or another. Without mind and experience, there is no knowledge, no information, no universe. Wiener's new day has spawned a militant, energy-consumptive, technological society that reduces humans to key and button pushers. I offer these pages as an antidote to that mode of thinking. Better to breathe deeply and go for a walk in the woods than sit in a cubicle confronting digital reality on a monitor all day. I find our engineered selves to be extremely depressing. We have confounded human use with *inhuman* use. Today we can sit at a console in a bunker half-an-hour from home and attempt to bomb the rest of the world into submitting to our will. Is that a fit (human, moral, informed, intelligent, compassionate, orderly) use of human beings? Better to scrap our great leap forward into this technological age, acknowledge our universal fallibility, and set the goal for ourselves to be as human and humane as we can be, not as brutish, selfish, and cruel.

The great adventure is not a matter of controlling the world to our liking but coming to self-understanding through self-exploration and discovery, a topic no era will ever master or exhaust. We all start with one sperm hooking up with one egg, and see how far we can take it from there. Which is pretty far, it turns out. All the way to conceiving, making, and actually using atom bombs, napalm, agent orange, spent-uranium bullets, land mines, biological weapons, and so on. Pretty impressive for a species descended from tree shrews. Such are the results of setting goals in some minds in certain situations. Does that create the world we want for ourselves and our children? For all humanity from now on? Considering that money is to be made by distributing such weapons to those who want them, the global economy has found a place for them in its heart. We are the species that created them by setting goals for ourselves under stress—which is when such goals are set—to improve the moment. But that scenario comes from a particular team playing to win by violent means, not from self-reflection and exploration.

Groups abandon their ethical standards when they become wholly goal oriented in seeking an advantage over other groups and corporate bodies. Winning becomes the standard, not cooperating or merely coexisting. But in modern warfare, all sides are losers. In truth, winning means not losing, and since all are losers, nobody comes out a winner. With, as Wikipedia tells me, some 416,800 service personnel dead and 683,800 wounded, and having dropped atom bombs on Hiroshima and Nagasaki, can the US actually claim to have "won" World War II? Ask any Gold-Star Mother what she would say. Except such mothers are fast fading from the scene. Claiming victory is not the same as winning. Folding all military and civilian deaths into such a claim, along with all harm inflicted on others, is valid only on a very low level of discernment. We won, sort of. But really, we didn't. Who is this "we" who claims victory? It all depends on how you define the goal we set for ourselves in waging that war. Considering all the children who will never be born because of the war, all the maimed and the dead, all the frustrated hopes—can any party to the conflict claim to have "won?" In my view, wars can be fought, but never won.

Again, an example of where my mind takes me when I set a simple goal of writing a chapter on goals and priorities. That's the way with introspection, you have to take it as it comes without fitting it to any theory of what might be acceptable. This book is about introspection, not about me. I happen to be the only subject who volunteered to spend thirty years in the trial. But consider this: if I hadn't set the goal, that line of thought would never have entered my mind. Such is the nature of setting goals. They point in a certain direction, but where you end up is always an open question.

Which brings to mind a discussion I had forty years ago with a math teacher when I taught English and the humanities at Abbott Academy (now folded into Phillips Academy up the street) in Andover, Massachusetts. It was the end of the term, and we were comparing notes about grading exams. He couldn't understand how I could wade through pages and pages of written responses; he simply checked numerical answers against a key, and spent no more than a minute on any given student's exam. I tried to make clear to him that if I was trying to teach students to express themselves verbally, the final exam was the best place for students to exhibit their skills under pressure. Multiple-choice questions would not do the job because there is no right way for individuals to make an appropriate answer in expository form, which is what I was trying to teach. He said something to the effect, "You mean you grade sentence by sentence?" "More by the paragraph," I said, and went on something like this: I want to test language skills I've been trying to teach all this term. This exam gives me a chance to compare results between very different students in answering the same questions in the same amount of time. These guys need all the practice they can get, particularly within real-life time constraints. The exam creates a situation in which they can express themselves in writing. It lets them show what they can do on their own. Or something to that effect. In the math class, the ideal was for each student to arrive at the right answer by performing a specified process correctly. In my class, each student got to defend his own answer. The math teacher taught a *class* to aspire to his goals; I encouraged *individual students* to set goals for themselves, and then to experience what it was like working toward them on their own. Yes, I spent over half an hour grading each paper, but I was dealing with individual minds, not universal right answers. There's a huge difference between learning how to reach someone else's goal and how to set and attain a goal of your own. In one case you need to be methodical and exact; in the other to be able to think for yourself, or as I would say now, to be fully engaged with all aspects of a challenging situation.

I know experientially (through introspection) how my mind runs off in different directions. That's where writing comes from—that turbulent source, with all its flooding into tunnels when I least expect it to. Think of water flowing through the sewers under the streets of London or Paris and you have a rough model of my mind. Writing, for me, is a messy business because my thought processes are a messy business, and order is achieved at the cost of simplifying, clarifying, rethinking, reframing, speaking out loud, and making a fresh start when I get bogged down. If it ever comes together with the right emphasis in the right sequence on the right phrases and ideas, that is only because I am aware of the difficulty and take steps to train the words to my whip by being highly critical of myself without losing my particular free-wheeling touch as the hallmark of everything I write because it is the hallmark of my mind.

For me, the adventure of writing is in discovering what it is I actually think, which my seeming digressions always bring to the fore. My mind is far larger than I can know because I have no way of accessing it at any one time. It's like a network of tunnels (or nerve fibers), as I said. Gerald Edelman points out that the human brain is the most complicated system in the known universe. With such complexity in my head, I keep having similar thoughts at intervals of several years, then I lose them again until they work their way back around the system one more time. I've been chasing those periodic thoughts my whole life. If they're not periodic, then I keep dealing with situations that kindle the same thoughts over and over again. They're so fleeting, I can't remember them one time to the next, when I briefly recognize a familiar idea, only to lose it once more. If I don't write it down in the instant, I can't even recall what it was I wanted to write down. It's like chasing fireflies, usually ending up with a handful of night air. Which is why I've been working on this book for some thirty years. Trying to capture consciousness in action is like trying to carry a sieve full of water for five miles.

Which is why I don't trust statistical analysis as any kind of method for getting at the truth of things. For me, the truth is always rumpled and messy in a particular kind of way. If I present it all ironed and starched, then I am guilty of misrepresenting my own mind. Which I am out to discover as it is, not to dress up in party clothes. In hindsight, I know I transferred from MIT to Columbia in 1952 to give leash to the entirety of my mind, not just the systematic, logical part. The messy, as well as the orderly part. Which let my curiosity out of its kennel because I had questions about everything, not just the topics presented in a particular course. My goal became exercising that curiosity every way I could so it would grow big and strong. It has taken me this long—almost sixty years—to begin to understand my own mind. Not that it's such a splendid mind, but because as an empiricist, I'm an extremely slow learner, having to make every mistake several times until I get a bead on what my mind is trying to tell me in its subterranean kind of way. My mind warns me off with a sign: "Abandon all hope ye who enter here." It was true for Dante and Virgil, and all who seek to discover the order of things within themselves. But they walked right past the sign. As Thoreau writes in his chapter, "The Village," in *Walden,* the best way to discover where you are in this world is to turn yourself around until everything looks strange and you have no idea where you are. In that state, every sign becomes clear and meaningful, and you discover yourself in a new way. That is the story of my life: constantly discovering who I am, each time a new person.

Curiosity is my attitude; trial and error my method; discovery my goal. Which I achieve by giving myself to each situation in order to discover who I am in that setting. When I wrote up sixty hikes I took on trails in Acadia National Park, that's how I did it, simply by not trying to do any more than be who I was in that place on that trail. The book is called, *ACADIA: The Soul of a National Park,* but it was my soul I wrote down, not Acadia's. Acadia gave me the opportunity to jot down my thoughts at various points along those sixty hikes. I didn't *take* those hikes, I *made* them as I went, trying to get the most adventure from my commitment to one route or another. I always saw and heard things I'd never encountered before, expanding my understanding of my mind as well as of the park, the two being coupled as they were at opposite extremes of my loop of engagement. I couldn't write about one without acknowledging the other. Had I tried to give an accurate impression of what the park was like at the time, I'd have edited out all the personal stuff and told a drab little story in terms of generalities I never actually experienced in themselves because they represent a statistical averaging of commonalities, watered down to some kind of impression because the exciting bits had been edited out as atypical or unique. If I had done that, the park would have lost its ability to spark fires within my awareness, and I would have been too bored to take the trouble to write any such bowdlerized version of Acadia.

The sorts of goals we set ourselves determine the kinds of persons we will become. If we insist on right answers, we will become exacting, right-answer people. If we make room for different points of view within ourselves, we will become probing, reflective people. Strongly desiring sensuous or emotional fulfillment, we will lead lives giving prominence to those facets of awareness. Judging by the sorts of goals apparent in the incidents of misinterpretation I provide in Chapter 1, what kind of person do I turn out to be?

Crossing Brattle Square, I was heading for the bookstore on the other side to buy a certain book (I can't recall what it was). In the process of seeking to attain that goal, I found myself sprawled in the path of an oncoming truck. Having placed myself in dangerous situations while writing about my adventures along the trails of Acadia National Park, I came up with the aphorism, *As we live so shall we die.* As a reader, it would have been fitting if I had died reaching for a book, or with the title of a book scrawled on a scrap of paper in my pocket. To some degree, I am a bookish kind of person. One glance at the shelves in my apartment will confirm that characterization.

Chasing after the figure of Fred on Fifth Avenue in New York, my goal was to restore a friendship interrupted by our living on opposite sides of the continent. No such luck, but the incident clearly reveals the goal I set myself on that occasion. Having moved to Seattle from upstate New York, I am the kind of person who misses the few friends he made in high school after having moved on again.

The case of the missing mustard jar reveals me in the throes of making lunch. The goal I had set myself was to make a sandwich, which should have been a matter of routine, but on that day entailed filing a missing mustard report. Unaware I had celiac disease, there I was making a sandwich, probably, if I know myself, on seven-grain bread. But at the time the issue was mustard, not gluten, not wheat. I frequently put mustard on the family shopping list, and often reached for it on the supermarket shelf, so I know it was one of my goals to maintain an adequate supply of mustard for use on just such occasions. There I am, a man embroiled in the fine details of living the domestic life. Between two wives, I've been married for more than thirty years, and have had a partner for seventeen more beyond that. Yes, I am—or I was—a mustard kind of guy.

Not seeing my partner's sunflowers when chasing after my camera bag, I was fulfilling the common goal of taking my camera with me when going for a walk in case I saw something visually interesting. That's me, all right, the walker with the camera slung on his shoulder. I have learned the hard way that the best way to assure seeing a pileated woodpecker is to leave my camera at home. My goal is to be prepared at all times, even on trips to the latrine.

Looking for the Rocky Mountains along the road to Denver across eastern Colorado, I was the intrepid adventurer on yet another voyage of exploration. The same one who later wrote about hiking trails in Acadia as a kind of homage to the spirit of John Muir, and spent years monitoring ecosystems in an estuary in Maine. That feels like me, the one on the outlook for new experience. Not only on the outlook, but always on the outlook for something he'd never seen before. The same person who has been peering into his own mind for thirty years in hopes of discovering what is going on, and how it relates to his behavior in the larger world. Right there, that's me, the one leaning over the front seat in a small car heading west, anticipating seeing the Rockies for the first time. I am still that thirteen-year-old kid, living that same life, setting similar goals.

Carefully scraping soil particles with a toothbrush from a turtle shell while thinking it was a human skull, that seventeen-year-old is also me, deluding himself that he is on the verge of making a significant discovery. Sadder but wiser, he is a true empiricist, committed to a life of trial and error. Here that former youth is today, ever on that same verge, in old age writing a book about introspection. My entire life has been just such an adventure, searching more for what I have missed than for fame and fortune, taking photographs of my discoveries, trying to understand the natural world in which I play an active but very minor walk-on part.

Interrupted by a phone call while transferring files, I lost track of the thumb drive I was using, and found no trace of it after I hung up. In fact, I didn't even remember what I'd been doing when the phone rang, so had to piece the project together from the placement of the two chairs I'd been using. How many days of my life have I spent looking for something I have misplaced or forgotten? Not days but years in the case of lost negatives alone (I worked as a photographer for twelve years). But in each case the goal is clear: to find what I've lost. And retracing my steps is part of my search routine, figuring what I'm looking for must be somewhere along that path. Noise, static, and chaos are a real part of life. My life in particular. To set a goal not to lose anything, ever, is pure fantasy. The truth is, I have no choice but to keep searching for what I've lost or mislaid—glasses, pliers, keys, magazine, toothbrush, pen or pencil, whatever. In a more perfect world, every item would have a proper place, and be in that place when I need it. I've tried to become more systematic in how I handle things, but the fact is I get so engrossed in what I'm doing, I don't pay attention to the details I handle without thinking. I keep having to recreate the scene of the crime, and figuring what went wrong—as I finally pieced together that the reason I couldn't find the thumb drive was because it was a small, black object on a black lanyard that was lying in the shadows under one of my desks against a dark blue rug—where it must have fallen from my lap when I jumped for the phone. Tracing it conceptually, I eventually found it. Elementary, yes, except that such a method works only once in a while. How many items have I permanently lost track of? Let me count them, or better, not. When I was young, family members used to come to me when they'd lost something because I could usually figure out where it was likely to be. That was then. Now I'm a loser in the sense I keep losing sight of things that ought to be at my elbow—but aren't. Putting things in their proper place and finding them when they're not there are two of my life goals to this day.

When I lose something that is important to me, I find it hard to make light of the matter, as when I inadvertently deleted hundreds of photos I had taken of a local granite quarrying operation this past fall. I was fleshing out a presentation I'd been working on for six months about quarrying and stoneworking in Sullivan, Maine, 1830–2010. My goal was to add a selection of photos showing how blocks of granite are cut and then hoisted by crane from the quarry hole. I spent several hours at the quarry getting the right shots, then went back to Bar Harbor to download the files from camera to computer. Admiring the drama of the photos, I got carried away in looking at them on the monitor—which I'd never done at that stage—and then deleted them from my camera before saving them to my hard drive, leaving me without any files to save. On one level, I no longer had the shots I wanted, so had to retake them. But my professional pride was hurt and I didn't want to admit to the quarryman I had bungled the job. After dillydallying for several minutes, I realized I had no choice but to admit my mistake in order to get past it, and retake the shots—assuming that was still possible. It is one thing for me to mislay my glasses or a pencil, another thing entirely to admit making a mistake in my particular area of expertise. In this case, I was crushed. That is, I crushed myself, or made myself feel crushed. I didn't want to admit to myself I had done what I did. On top of that, I didn't want to diminish myself in the eyes of the quarryman who had been so cooperative up till then. But that disappointment in myself gave way to realizing, in light of my goal, I had no choice but to fess up and replace what I had lost the best way I could. Which is what I did, at a cost of taking a big helping of humble pie. My overall goal remained the same—make a presentation I would be proud of.

My goal in going to the university health center was to find out why I felt sick so much of the time. I wanted to stop moping around as was becoming a habit with me since going to at least ten different doctors, all of them dismissing my problem without accounting for it in any way. This was to be my last stand. I worked as a photographer at Harvard College Observatory, so trusted my medical coverage to pay for a full workup at what I assumed was one of the top medical institutions in the country. My goal was clear: get an accurate diagnosis so I could get well. The medical center didn't recommend doctors, so they sent me a list of internists who saw patients there. I went for the one with the most impressive sounding name, and did what he told me to do. I showed up at the medical center Sunday afternoon and the diagnostic work lasted all week, ending with having a Sigmoidoscope (a shiny steel periscope about one meter long) rammed up my innards from the rear. With high hopes, the following Wednesday I went to see the good doctor in his office, as I have related. For the eleventh time, my symptoms were dismissed as if they were my own doing. This time, I gave up on my goal. I didn't know why I felt so awful, and I would never find out. Gloom and doom took over; I became the original aimless man. This was the mid-1960s. In the early 1990s, plagued by a severe skin rash, I went to a dermatologist who did a biopsy, which came back from the lab with a diagnosis of *Dermatitis herpetiformis,* for which he prescribed yet more magical ointments—to no effect whatsoever. In 1997, having access to the Internet for the first time, I did a Webcrawler search on that impressive binomial term, and in the first hit, St. John's University med school told me it was an autoimmune disorder caused by celiac disease. Two weeks later, by my own doing (avoiding gluten in wheat, rye, barley, oats), my symptoms were largely gone and I began rebuilding my ravaged body and my health. My new goal: avoid doctors at all costs. That, now, seen inside-out, is the kind of man I am.

I am stunned by the fact that so much of myself is revealed in those eighteen episodes I not only built the first chapter around, but the rest of the book as well. My criteria for inclusion has been wholly intuitive. I wasn't sure where those incidents would take me, but I knew from blogging about them that they were integral parts of my autobiography, and I suspected that if regarded in the right light, they would share their secrets with my introspective eye.

Ten chapters later, I know I was right. My recipe now is: make a list of ten to twenty episodes in which to catch yourself misinterpreting a variety of sensory figures in a memorable (emotionally tinged or unforgettable) way, then regard those incidents from a variety of perspectives such as I offer in these pages, and see what they tell you about the makeup and workings of your mind.

Talk about self-discovery, I think I am onto a method leading to exciting, potent, and useful results. I start by paying attention to incidents from my own consciousness that present themselves as *attractive* (draw my attention), *memorable* (are persistent and unforgettable), and *mysterious* (I can't readily explain or account for them). Then I work through the stages of the loop of engagement by which I picture my mind interacting with its surroundings (the situation I am in at the time) as I have come to understand it, much as I ask the reader to work through this book chapter by chapter. I picture each stage along the loop as providing a different perspective onto the experiential incidents being considered, opening onto a different dimension of my conscious experience. In these assembled incidents which I find equally attractive, memorable, and mysterious, I recognize the portrayal this effort provides as none other than a significant portion of my inner self, the very object of my introspective search. My method? Learning from memorable mistakes.

Bravo, introspection! Viva, empiricism! A round of applause for phenomena, categorization and interpretation, being and meaning, understanding, feeling and emotion, situations, values, goals, and the loop of engagement itself—with projects, reality, conflicts, and power yet to come. The key is in focusing on incidents in my personal consciousness that have stood as attractive, memorable, and mysterious nuggets of awareness over a period measured in decades, not hours or weeks. To be useful, they really have to have stuck with me so I know they are woven into the fibers of my brain—the synapses and neurons that make me who I am—and are not just passing fancies. That is, the criterion is that each incident be significant in having physiologically changed connections within my brain, making it not only an integral part of my experience but, in the right situation, retrievable from memory as well.

In empirical terms (balancing the perils of error against the rewards of discovery), my method of introspection is to hazard my understanding of how my mind works while, at the same time, trusting my grasp of what is important (attractive, memorable, mysterious) in my mind, along with my intuition as a guide to the various dimensions that such a sense of importance might reveal about my inner self. That is the method I have used in writing this book about my adventures in getting to know my own mind. My goal in this work is essentially to follow my nose to find where it will lead and what it will tell me.

I imagine how crazy and simplistic that must sound to any academically-trained mind. What can I say? In my view, that is how empiricism works. Not by strict adherence to general laws and principles, but by seeking revelations that speak to a particular situation. I am concerned here with how discoveries are made *in* consciousness, *by* consciousness itself. Which in some disciplines is a forbidden topic of investigation because it defies the axioms and rules on which those disciplines are based. But such axioms and rules prevented almost a dozen reputable physicians from diagnosing my case of celiac disease, even though the symptoms I presented were unexceptional.

In the past year I have presented other symptoms to my doctor, who has referred me to the radiology department at the local hospital to have my innards probed by ultrasound—apparently the current rage in diagnostic workups. At significant medical expense, I learned I had no blockage in my aorta that might cause severe pain in my right leg (which was duly accounted for by a different doctor who, with one tap on each knee, told me in less than a minute that a nerve was pinched by my fourth lumbar vertebra, which was likely to heal itself in a few weeks). Gadgetry and technology are replacing the high art of medical diagnosis through applied personal attention. I have heard of a Chinese physician observing a patient from a discrete distance for half an hour, following her pulse and her breathing, and then pinpointing which chamber of her heart was causing her problem. He's the one I want as my personal physician, not the man in the white coat with his battery of expensive and indecipherable tests, and following of ducklings learning to quack just as he does.

Building a high level of discernment through personal experience is the goal of empirical experimentation, which is my kind of adventure. Hiking sixty different loops along the trails of Acadia, I made myself into a local connoisseur of hiking experiences on Mount Desert Island, Maine. By making myself happen in that way, those trails made my mind happen in ways corresponding to the energy I put into moving and watching along the trail. I didn't care where the trails led on the map, it was the experience I had in being alert and attentive in that place that served as the goal of those sixty hikes, all duly noted step-by-step in my earlier book. Much as the experiences I detail here in being alert and attentive to the incidents I relate in the first chapter are the goal of this book, written by the same author some twelve years later. My goal and my method are the same now as they were then. I put myself into both books in equal measure, and take equal challenge, pleasure, and sense of accomplishment from them. I love being myself in this way, doing the things I do, making myself happen by reaching out to aspects of my world, inviting that world into my mind on a level of detail that holds my attention and keeps me engaged doing what I love to do, being the person I am. How could I not enjoy myself doing that, having such adventures, fulfilling my experience in that way? Where Thoreau wrote he was "made to love" Fair Haven Pond and its meadow, "as the wind is made to ripple the water," I would have said, Thoreau *made himself* by applying his loop of experiential engagement to the terrain within a ten-mile radius of his home in Concord—his home turf or homeland—the land he engaged with his mental capabilities, which in turn made him the man he recognized as himself. I identify with Thoreau in that endeavor. We'd both be crazy to devote all that attention to our ramblings if the adventure itself wasn't precisely the reward we were seeking. I don't feel crazy, any more than Thoreau did. For the sake of my argument, I will claim to be of sound mind and body. Further, I attest that everything I have written here makes sense to me in my own mind. As far as I am concerned, I speak the truth of personal experience, as Thoreau did of his. Is any of this replicable by anyone else? Not exactly, because my unique personal adventure is reserved to me, the subject of my own experiment, as Thoreau's was to him, as anyone's must be to herself as subject of her own inward investigation.

The trick in directing the expenditure of one's limited store of life energy, I feel, is in setting a goal appropriate to the adventure one cares to lead. To lead a worldly adventure, it is appropriate to set a goal in that world *as if* it were not translated into phenomena within personal consciousness, with all that transduction entails as I have suggested here. That's how "new" worlds get "discovered," remote peaks climbed, universes explored. On the other hand, if the adventure is to be had in the inward reaches of a particular mind, such as the adventure of composing a piece of music, a poem, or a novel, then attention must be directed toward the proper venue where such things are entertained. I think many would agree with me in making that seemingly logical distinction between outward worlds of action and inward worlds of composition and contemplation. Even so, ultimately, both worlds share the same venue—human consciousness—which, via the respective loops of engagement involved, must be invoked in accounting for the experience of each one in personal terms. All goals, that is, are set and evaluated internally, not in the world. Today is New Year's Day, 2011. Think of the resolutions and good intentions swirling through the air on this day. Clearly, they are figments of the minds that propose them, not entities in the world. If they are to be fulfilled, that is a matter for the proposer in each case to decide by executing a specific projects having that end as a personal goal.

Projects are the tactical means by which we make ourselves happen on the world stage by enacting our hopes and goals into designing and fulfilling our future selves. Projects are the topic of the next chapter concerning the upshot of consciousness. Turn to the following page when you are ready. O

CHAPTER 12

PROJECTS

S etting goals is not an exercise in wishful thinking, as the custom of making New Year's resolutions might imply. More accurately, setting goals is a matter of committing oneself to working within a specific situation to bring about a desired state of affairs. Projects (from Latin *proicere,* to throw forward) are our way of *projecting* ourselves ahead into times yet to come, which I call making ourselves happen in the world. Up to this chapter, these pages have largely been about specific projects or incidents in my conscious life that surprisingly played against my expectations. I find each incident memorable for being somewhat problematic in defying my earnest efforts to make coherent sense within a given situation, sparking consciousness in the process.

For a variety of reasons, these incidents persist in drawing my attention so I can't lay them to rest, but keep reworking them from different perspectives, hoping to understand what they have to tell me in being simultaneously attractive (salient), memorable, and yet mysterious. Why am I so invested in these particular incidents? That is for me to explore through introspection, and if I am persistent, perhaps to claim as self-knowledge through conscious exploration.

I am the kind of person who tends to make a production of everything he does. To be myself, I throw my full concentration into whatever I do. I don't mean I have a flair for dramatics, but projects I apply myself to are apt to become major undertakings. When I don't feel moved to act, then things simply don't get done. I seem to have a motivation threshold that separates tasks I see as opportunities from those that strike me as impositions or irrelevancies. Projects, that is, emerge in my mind within a valence gradient ranging from *Do it now* to *That can wait.* Before I direct my attention to one project or another, I stack each one according to its priority in my scheme of things. A sense of urgency compels me to start at the top of the list and work down. This first-things-first approach is my way of budgeting mental attention and effort to make sure I put my energy into what is important to me. For some reason, the problematic incidents I refer to hover near the top of my list, mentally tagged to receive close attention.

Because of their aura of mystery, I regard these problematic incidents as opportunities for furthering my self-understanding, which is my goal in working on this book in a transparent manner by going public with my investigation. To do that, I try to use everyday language as much as possible to emphasize the fact that much of what we assume in daily life to exist in the real world of material objects is in fact a production of our individual minds projected outward by a trick which obscures the truth that we are personally responsible for directing our attention and constructing our individual lifeworlds as we do. The expressions we use in talking about the outside world all flow from inside our *experience of* that world by way of our personal loops of engagement. The world we see (hear, smell, touch, etc.) is really a world converted from one form of energy into another—from ambient heat, light, and sound energy to nervous energy involving the flow of ions and chemicals in our brains, where they appear as a succession of phenomena in individual consciousness, the true locus, generator, and arbiter of a bioenergetic reality, that is, one based on a biological transfer of energy.

The brain alone is not sufficient to account for consciousness; nor is the brain in its body. It takes an embodied brain in its world—a situated brain—to account for the dynamic engagement we experience as consciousness. Further, we must divide the dynamic flux of consciousness into coherent episodes—projects or relationships—to account for the thematic or narrative character of consciousness in being sequentially focused on one thing at a time.

When talking about a particular topic—the city of Paris, for instance—I can only speak from my personal experience of that city as I can best formulate it, which is different from every other person's experience of what we assume to be the same city, but is a highly personal version in each case. In speaking about Paris, I project my personal, conscious understanding of Paris onto my generalized concept of Paris, using words in a very broad sense to map my inner grasp onto a concept that can be defined in words and shared by other minds—but is very different from my personal experience *of* Paris, which is personally interpreted from my unique point of view in every respect.

Projects are tactical campaigns to translate our inner selves into effective participants in a world we share in common with others. A world we refer to as the *real* world, but is actually far less "real" to each of us than the inner world of sensory figures as meaningfully interpreted by our minds, which is the only world we have immediate access to because it is couched in the neural language of our brains. For each of us the outside world is a second-order derivative of phenomena as we interpret them. In using projects to address the outside world, we translate our inner experiences into outward acts intended to achieve a certain effect. That effect is then translated back into the language of our nervous system by our senses as guided by our expectancy at the moment, to be processed in a neural network that sharpens its features so we are able to compare patterns we hoped to bring about against the patterns which actually appear. Comparison is at the heart not only of consciousness but of the loop of engagement connecting our inner and outer worlds in terms of the situation we picture ourselves being engaged in then and there. If both the expected and actual versions fall within a range of congruity we can accept, we move on to the next stage of the project; if not, we refine our attention and motor control, and try again.

Musicians, dancers, and athletes practice, practice, practice until they master their part in a particular project or performance—or at least do the best they can under prevailing circumstances. But think how different the inside and outside views are on each occasion— how it feels to play the bassoon with discipline, skill, and passion, compared to the experience of listening to someone else play the bassoon, or how it feels to propel oneself down a cinder track as fast as one can for a hundred meters, compared to how it feels as a coach, race official, or spectator to time someone else running that race or that trial. In such cases, inner and outer worlds of experience are almost incomparable, yet we commonly think of them as a single event as if we did not experience it differently. Homework is one thing to the teacher who assigns it, another to each student in the class, yet it is referred to by the same name because it fits the broad envelope of characteristics defining what is generally meant by "homework." Cooking dinner is one kind of project, eating dinner is another, and washing dishes and cleaning up afterwards is a third, all linked to the one general concept labeled "dinner," yet understood differently by each one involved.

Projects are activities we undertake in making what we judge to be fitting responses to situations we find or put ourselves in. Everything depends on how we frame the situation—in the world, yes—

but first in our minds. That is, on how we see the landscape from our point of view within personal experience. For example, "making Obama fail" is a project some see as appropriate to a situation in which President Barack Obama, a Democrat, has the power of an office held formerly by Republican George W. Bush. The goal of that project being for the ousted Republicans to retake the Presidency in 2012. That is only one way to frame the situation, but on a very low level of discernment, iconoclasm (toppling the blocks piled up by, say, your big brother) makes a sort of vindictive sense as repayment for the wrongs he has done you in being older and more capable—more successful—than you are. In the eyes of the adult iconoclast, you are justly seeking to even the score, or at least get equal air time and attention from those who make a difference—such as those who vote one party or the other into office.

To Olson's dictum on landscapes being perspectival, I would add, "in our heads," which is where all of us truly live. The classic example of iconoclasm in our time is the toppling of the Twin Towers by a band of angry little brothers we now call terrorists. Not long before that, it was the smashing of the incised, sixth-century Buddha statues in the Bamyan Valley of Afghanistan by another band of little-brother Taliban armed with rockets and dynamite. There is a lot of free-floating resentment in the minds of little brothers all over the world, which frequently boils over as righteous indignation at those who have offended them in some way. Bullying reverses the dynamic when weaker individuals are pictured as being favored for their cuteness or cleverness over those who feel they deserve respect for being bigger, older, and more powerful. In such minds, beating up on little kids is felt to be an appropriate project to use in a situation in which big kids are unfairly deprived of the respect they deserve and the advantage that goes with it. Bullying, iconoclasm, and terrorism are projects rooted in the minds of their perpetrators, where they seem to make perfect sense in dominating the consciousness of all concerned.

My dreams depict projects I undertake as appropriate responses to situations entertained in my resting mind. In a dream early this morning, for instance, I was staying as a guest in an old house on a fenced and wooded corner lot owned by a housebound widow, to whom my younger brother was returning a box of cherished antiques in a huge eighteen-wheeler. The truck was way too big to fit among the trees around the house, the old road too rooty, winding, and narrow for the big rig to pass. That was the situation. My dream project was to help my brother deliver the box, he in the cab while I walked behind to tell him when the wheels cleared the trunks and the roots. It seemed unlikely the truck could get near the house, but as the dream progressed, each scene depicted one obstacle passed, another ahead. A kind of reunion took place to receive the box, people streaming out of the house to greet us as members of the family. I woke up, leaving the truck stuck beneath the branches of a tree as it climbed a rise toward the field behind the house. The dream was vivid, and made perfect sense as it progressed from one predicament to the next within the larger situation. Without sensible input or an ability to act, my loop of engagement was stymied, but the dream went on nonetheless, the sequence of images flowing from one scene to the next.

Such detailed dreams suggest to me that, yes, my mind alone is capable of sustaining the burden of a seemingly real world. Add the ability to perceive and to act when I am awake, and I envision my mind fitting itself to evolving situations through a constant give and take through my loop of engagement, not just the random movements of my eyes behind closed lids as during dreamtime. To create consciousness, equip our dreamselves with loops of engagement so we become capable of acting and sensing—voilá, we recognize our everyday selves.

We take situations and projects so for granted as items in the real world, it is difficult to imagine them as creations of our sleeping or wakeful minds alone. But consider the writing of fiction, a project that fleshes out situations conceived in the mind, providing locales, characters, plotlines, dialogue, tension, release, and all the rest—simulating a real world but not becoming real to other minds until the narrative is internalized by reading a book of several hundred pages. Watching dramas play out in TV, film, or stage performances, we get hooked by tensions flowing through the plot, and forget that none of what we are following is in any way real, which is beside the point in that we are convinced because our loop of engagement is rushing ahead to keep up with the story as it unfolds. The scenarios play out by activating personal memories, feelings, and values, which combine to give a tinge of reality to the whole show, making it *our* show because it only comes to life in our mind. If we close the book or turn off the TV, the loop is broken, our attention flags, and consciousness itself fades away.

Think about it. If the locus of dreams and phenomena is particular human minds, and the locus of values, feelings, emotions, memories, interpretations, and understanding is the same, along with the locus of planning and execution of motor programs, being and meaning, time and space—what does that leave to the real world? That is the question of all questions, which I will get to in the next chapter. Here I will stay with projects as a way of dealing with situations in which we are invested, allowing us to make ourselves happen in those situations according to our understanding of the challenges they present to our attention, discernment, experience, and motivation.

Loops of engagement allow us to work cooperatively on projects, not only with other people (who operate through loops of their own), but with features of the objective world that radiate, reflect, or modulate energy affecting our sensory receptors. These receptors translate that energy into the chemical-ionic language of the brain, to be processed as phenomena—that which appears in awareness. The neuroprocessing itself focuses and sharpens the images we form, in cooperation with our effort to account for the resulting pattern by categorizing it in the very act of reaching out to it as an episode of felt and meaningful experience. Introspection has made this process so self-evident to me, I can actually watch myself reaching out, interpreting, achieving understanding, and moving on to the next round—just as I participate in my dreams as they unfold scene-by-scene without my having to do anything but show up and play the part I am assigned.

In *The Poetic Unfolding of the Human Spirit* (Essays on Exploring a Global Dream, Fetzer Institute, 2011, *not for sale*), John Paul Lederach undertakes the project of explicating the concept of *internally displaced persons* (IDPs) on three levels of meaning—physical, social, and personal. He points out that it is one thing to be forced to flee your homeland, another to be socially displaced so that you do not belong where you are as a homeless person, and a third thing to be lost to oneself so that you have no identity and can't recognize who you are. On all three levels, these are devastating dimensions of experience, suffered by 26 million displaced persons in the past ten years, mostly as casualties of war (pages 33f.). Lederach cites Tom Cauuray, a poet from Sierra Leone, as an example in all three senses of an internally displaced person whose experience of having no homeland, no home, and no family to return to shattered his identity, leading to his death by suicide in September 2009.

In Lederach's presentation of Tom Cauuray's plight, I saw life itself as a project dependent on maintenance of a functional loop of engagement on all levels of existence. Once interrupted, the circuit broken, the meaning of life itself is destroyed, and the human mind, with nothing to work with, unable to take on new projects to restore meaning, declines into unconscious oblivion.

Projects, as I present them here, are our personal, social, and physical salvation in keeping our minds toned and active so that we are as effective in making ourselves happen as we can be within the constraints imposed by our situation on those three levels of engagement. The natural and cultural disasters I mentioned in the last chapter to suggest areas of challenge that, if approached in a positive spirit to see what we can make of them, provide exactly the opportunities we need to be consciously engaged in living our lives to good purpose. But as Paul Lederach points out, such challenges can be—and often are—overwhelming. Well-intended projects meant to prove and redeem ourselves in meeting disastrous situations can, instead, do us in because we are not strong or skillful enough to do the work that needs to be done, as our dreams keep reminding us.

The unexpected death of a loved one can destroy the orderly universe we've spent years building around ourselves. Getting through a divorce by admitting earlier mistakes and trying to carry on nonetheless can tax our understanding, acceptance, and energy beyond anything we have experienced in aiming for a lasting relationship without success. Returning from a war zone, we can find ourselves so adjusted to battlefield chaos as to be unfit for the civilized reality we've been dreaming of for months and years in giving us something to look forward to. We are all likely to get into situations we can't work our way out of for one reason or another. Beyond our accustomed depth, we become lost to the selves we once were. What do we do? When lost, a lot of us devote ourselves to busywork by watching television, playing checkers, doing picture puzzles, reading romances or adventure stories, playing computer games, eating snacks without end, swigging gallons of soda, getting drunk, taking drugs, complaining about stressful symptoms—anything to distract ourselves from being victims of a dysfunctional loop of engagement, leaving us cut off from involvement in a larger, more stable society because consciousness itself is unbearable.

I've been in several of those hopeless places in my life, resorting to routines to get me through days, weeks, and months on end. At one stage of my life, holidays were particularly hard to get through because they broke the daily work routine, leaving me not knowing what to do, so I'd stand at the window looking into the rain, vowing to do something different, but in the end going on as before out of desperation. That is my old self, the one I left behind in moving to Maine. Where I reinvented myself to fit my new situation, and have not stopped compiling lists of projects for making the new person I have become happen in ever more challenging, engaging, and satisfying ways. Now, I never run out of ideas for new projects to work on. What needs doing? I ask myself, and several suggestions are there in my mind, clamoring to receive full attention.

What made this transition possible was my changing my identity from a job holder to being my own man. Dependent on an employer, I always did what was asked of me, sometimes with flair, but always wondering if this was what I should be doing with my limited store of life energy. It was easy to explain having to make ends meet, but I knew there was far more to holding a job than the income. But working my way into life without much guidance, I got married while still in college, held several simultaneous jobs to cover food and rent, did my military service, had children, always realizing myself in the moment, but giving little thought to any sort of career trajectory. Once I got a job, I always put myself into it—that is, until the work became routine and boring to me, when my interest would shift to personal projects in concrete poetry or photography, which I never ran short of. Winning a fellowship to teach photography at Phillips Academy got me into teaching one subject after another on the high school level—photography, art, humanities, poetry, reading to students with learning disabilities, English—and then, leaving family behind, I chucked it all and moved to Maine, my mother's homeland, a place I'd visited most years since I was four. And became myself in the transition, living up to my personal expectations from the day I arrived. Since then, I've kept track of the projects I've worked on by collecting related materials in loose-leaf binders, 159 of them at latest count, number 160 being added today for yet another committee I have become a member of, all related to projects I've worked on, or aspects of projects.

Think of it, twenty-five years spent compiling notebooks nobody can understand but me. Jottings and images from life, all to be thrown on a bonfire when I die to celebrate my having lived somewhat as Doctor Reefy lived in Sherwood Anderson's *Winesburg, Ohio,* slowly rolling along country lanes in his horse-drawn buggy, thinking grand thoughts as he went from patient to patient, jotting them on scraps of paper, which he dropped into his pocket, and rolled between restless fingers, to flick after a time onto the roadside, moving on in making his rounds, moving on in his thoughts, inventing himself as he went.

All the projects detailed in my notebooks are of my own doing. Since coming to Maine, I have largely invented myself according to the dictates of my personal consciousness. That is what Maine now represents in my mind, a place to be who I am by steering my own course and choosing projects to work on that make a difference solely to me. In that sense, yes, Maine is a state of mind, notably, an independent one. But we are all unique in genetic heritage, rearing, schooling, training, and experience in order that we fit ourselves to the unique situations within which we emerge on our own as competent human beings. To be born to our times is to be born to the situations that dominate those times, leaving us a choice of projects by which to make a fitting response. Avoid military duty in Iraq at all cost, or pitch in and be part of the action—which is it to be? Love the new digital media, or hate them, preferring hands-on participation?

I left Massachusetts not only to take charge of myself, but to avoid having my life commandeered by jobs and an economy run by people with no interest in my person other than how I could advance their projects, not my own. I choose to believe that humans evolved as free wanderers navigating on their own under their personal recognizance. Remember the five-thousand-year-old Ice Man found frozen in the Italian Alps? I am his kin. A free wanderer. I for one am not made to have overlords. Humans, I feel, are best suited to a life spent seeking whatever is important and challenging to them at the time—that is the most taxing and rewarding life I can picture for myself—or anyone else. What are we but Bedouin shepherds, nomads following our flocks from valleys in winter to mountain meadows in summer, always on the go, making ourselves happen every day of our lives? As Polonius advised Laertes: "This above all: to thine own self be true, and it must follow, as the night the day, thou canst not then be false to any man." In moving from field to city, we have traded our independence in nature for a life of paid labor on behalf of corporate business and industry. At least when we lived on the land, we celebrated the round of the stars and the seasons. In stores and factories, we celebrate corporate profits for others, every day the same, lights on at all hours. Get into the rhythm: every day the same, the same, the same. Such a life is an oxymoron because no two days can be experienced alike. But if that's how they seem in everyday life, then we're in a rut. If the rut is deep enough, we are not truly alive.

By exercising our loops of engagement within projects and relationships addressing specific life situations, we raise ourselves to consciousness. We play in a band, join Alcoholics anonymous, become political or environmental activists, get married, raise a family, change jobs, get a divorce, move to Spain, build a collection of jazz CDs, get re-married, take classes, keep a dream journal, work on yet another great American novel, or otherwise structure our days and awareness by projecting ourselves ahead, building a life and a future for ourselves out of the scrap materials we find lying around our conscious minds. At least, that's how I think of projects working, but they can have a dark side as well. Sometimes the scraps don't add up to a life.

My son Michael committed suicide when he was twenty-two years old because he could not convert his life experience into projects that would propel him further into life. He was stuck in his own time, and found solace only in escape through drugs, eventually heroin. Inadvertently, I was largely responsible for his fall, because I had left home when he was young, and for the rest of his days he yearned for the relationship we had built together, which he couldn't replace or sustain on his own. His loop of engagement had been broken. He took it that by divorcing his mother, I meant to divorce him, which had not been my intention. In fact, on a night walk in Cambridge, Massachusetts, looking up at trees lit by streetlamps, I vowed that is exactly what I would never do. I saw him every weekend for years, and we kept doing things together, but because those visits came to an end every Sunday afternoon, things were not the same as before. Mike's mother remarried, and eventually moved to the West Coast, then to Italy. Mike was not happy in a foreign high school, and eventually returned to the US, but in the meantime he'd met up with a friendly man on a park bench in Milan, who'd introduced him to drugs as a means of easing his pain. That intervention may have given Mike temporary relief from his sorrow, but it stopped him in his tracks, leaving him incapable of maintaining stable engagements or relationships. Back in the States, Mike connected with old friends, and was in and out of detox centers around Boston several times, which only entrenched him in the drug culture. He and a group of his buddies drove a van to Maine on a weekend jaunt to the island in Taunton Bay, taking along their guns. Aiming at great blue herons in their nests, they shot up the island, leaving spent and scattered cartridges to mark their trail. A few weeks later, falling out of the back of a pickup truck landed Mike in the hospital, where, battered and bruised, he seemed to sense he'd lost control of his life. He called me one night, telling me, "Papa, I know what I have to do." Knowing what he meant, I said, "Don't do anything drastic." He wouldn't tell me where he was. I checked with his friends, who had all seen him, but they wouldn't tell me where he was. I asked the police to be on the watch for a suicidal kid with a shotgun. They called me at eight the next morning—it was Mike's twenty-second birthday—to tell me they'd found him. He'd put his shotgun in his mouth and killed himself on a park bench in the rain on the night of full moon, his blood draining into the duck pond. That was his last project, and it worked just as he intended it to.

Shall I call Mike's death "Incident 19" and study its effects on my innermost mind? That was five years before I moved to Maine and took up new ways of making myself happen in the world. Yes, there is a strong connection between that death and that move. And, no, I am not going to explore that connection in these pages. Or, rather, everything I have written here points to that connection in one way or another. Mike's death marks a complete break with my old self leading my old life. Everything changed after that. I built myself into a new person, the person I've been writing about in these pages. New in being alive while my son was dead. New in carrying his memory everywhere I went, unable to add anything to it. With Mike in my heart, I had the foolish conceit I could live for him as well as for myself. But that defied the fact of his death, which I could not alter. No one can live for another. Each is stuck in leading the life he makes for himself. At least I have learned that. Death is a powerful teacher. Mike died thirty years ago, and I still remember that day as if it was this morning.

Obviously, I cannot project myself into Mike's mind, but can only imagine his felt situation through empathy, never knowing how close I come to the mark. My eldest son has become unknown to me, someone I can never know. I did that to him; I did that to myself.

The only way I can be true to Mike's memory is by being true to my own person. That way, I keep him somewhat alive in my conscious mind by cherishing the cluster of personal memories I build around him, as his mother keeps him alive through her cluster of memories, his brother, his girlfriend, and all others who knew him.

Consider how Mike added a new word to my vocabulary when he was two years old. Living in Billerica, Massachusetts, I was looking for photographic work in the Boston area, and had two prospects, but nothing definite. At Christmas, I took a break and pretty much stayed home. My then wife undertook a project with Mike to make Christmas cookies. They made the dough together, rolled it out, cut it into shapes, baked it, frosted the warm shapes, and decorated them with many-colored sprinkles. The next day, Mike kept wanting "geckyracies, geckyracies," but we couldn't understand what he meant. I picked him up and carried him room-to-room, but we couldn't find geckyracies anywhere. Evidently he didn't know where they were, but knew they must be somewhere. We ate lunch, and when a plate of cookies appeared for dessert, "Geckyracies!" Mike beamed. Finally I got it. In his own way, he was saying "decorations," his name for the project he'd worked on with his mother in baking Christmas cookies. I'll say more about Michael in the next chapter.

We all know what projects are, but seldom appreciate the fact that they are an expression of a remarkable set of mental abilities for turning disciplined imaginings into plans into done deeds. Growing up, we acquire the necessary skills and dexterity to do just that. Learning to crawl, walk, and talk are three major projects by which we become humans instead of feral animals. Then we move on to learning how to hop, skip, color, count, spell, read, draw, and play all manner of games. We learn about taking turns, obeying rules, sharing, working hard. What we see or hear others doing, we want to do for ourselves. First we learn to recognize the urge to "do" something, then gather equipment and materials, find a workspace, decide where to start, get help if we need it, and off we go, making mistakes, but getting the gist of the idea, the process, and how to succeed in the project. Eventually, we write term papers, master's theses, doctoral dissertations, symphonies, string quartets, poetry, code for computer games, and inventories of everything needed to stock a battleship, to mention only a few projects of a more complex nature. Our minds can do this for us if we put in the hours necessary to sharpen our project skills so we can make ourselves happen according to our personal aspirations, more or less.

In 1953, Edmund Hillary and Tenzing Norgay made a project of climbing Mount Everest, as in 1867, John Muir had made a project of walking from Indiana to Florida. Discovering a westward route to India from Spain was a project for many early explorers, backed by a Doctrine of Discovery granting them the right and obligation to subdue pagan peoples and seize their lands for Christian purposes. Making an incandescent lamp became a project in the late nineteenth century, then a flying machine, a submarine boat, and a rocket that would take men on a two-way trip to the moon. At the same time, women and children in much of the world made (and still make) projects of gathering firewood, finding and lugging clean water from miles away, and growing, gathering, and cooking food for their families. Everywhere, cleansing and burying the dead is a project by which the living show respect for those they love (while safely removing the threat of decaying flesh). And everywhere, too, arms merchants and military forces collude to make projects of war, and not incidentally, profits from the trade in expensive weapons which destroy themselves once deployed, assuring their makers of great wealth by promoting modern warfare. The US invasion of Iraq was a project founded on our new get-them-before-they-get-us national security strategy—even if we had to trump up weapons of mass destruction to justify the "preemptive" strike, *as if* Iraq was about to strike us. There was much talk in those heady days of our troops being put "in harm's way," but since we were the aggressor, our troops were harm personified, so it struck me we were disingenuous in claiming to be victimized by our own attack. Rallying support for our invasion of Iraq became a huge project internationally as well as at home, showing how maintaining an ill-conceived war takes on a life of its own, no matter how shoddy its beginnings, turning citizens into sacrificial pawns as if war were only a game.

Projects highlight our common humanity, because through our similar undertakings, we can identify with those in other places and other eras. Food, water, shelter, warmth, health, and travel are always challenging issues, so we can connect with hunter-gatherer tribes in adopting projects to meet our survival needs. Our humanity is told by the essential projects through which we devote our lives to the common good. Now that we have settled into homelands supporting agriculture, we put a lot of energy into defending our turf from foreign aggressors. All people claim a right to national defense, which has become the defining project of nationhood. Some three-fourths of our national budget goes for national defense. As soon as we bond, we circle, and watch for suspicious movements along the perimeter indicating another wave of invaders (or immigrants) is coming through.

Projects depend on remembering from one day to the next what we are working on. Memory is essential to our extending our loops of engagement into the physical world. And essential to understanding the significance of the feedback we receive by way of the world's response to our motivated actions. Without our ability to remember what we were doing yesterday, there would be no day-to-day continuity, no projects, no long-term undertakings, no great achievements. Picture the old man wandering into the kitchen, asking himself, "Now, what did I come in here for?" Life lived strictly in the now would be a reactive life without projects. Projects require proactive effort, thinking before we make the big leap ahead. Museums are mausoleums for old projects (paintings, steam engines, costumes, technology). Projects brought to fulfillment on this Earth comprise the record of our consciousness as a people. Here, before our eyes, are our mental processes writ large in durable materials. The Pyramids, Stonehenge, Great Wall of China, Chartres Cathedral, Machu Picchu, Trinity test site at White Sands Proving Ground, the 9/11 Memorial—these are monuments to past projects in particular human minds, artifacts of what it means to be human. Here, for all to see, is the ageless reality we have built around our mortal selves, true expression of humanity's undauntable aspirations. Or if not that, then at least a record of extravagant and prideful mistakes made that we may learn from them how to do better.

What we call "ego" might well be a manifestation of conscious enthusiasm for one project or another in fulfillment of a particular goal a person is pursuing at the moment. Introspection gives me a strong sense that I work primarily through projects, so the energy I put into those projects is highly structured in being personally meaningful to me. I have built no cathedrals, but I have made numerous PowerPoint presentations, and I have been heavily invested in making each one. That is who I am at the time, a maker of presentations. If I meet my personal standards, then I derive a great deal of satisfaction from pulling off what I set out to do, which is not that easy in any disciplined human activity. Pride is a demonstration that our loop of engagement is working as we want it to. No potter ever threw a bowl without pride in the achievement, no writer ever settled for a paragraph without feeling it carried its burden as desired. Pride is a badge of craftsmanship in having projects work out as planned. I find no seat of ego in my mind, but I do find oversight of how my loop of engagement is progressing, and take satisfaction in its running well.

Projects lead naturally to a discussion of human reality, topic of the next chapter, not in terms of great works, but in an introspective view of where one man's life has actually been lived. When you feel ready to enter the real world, proceed at your own risk. O

CHAPTER 13

REALITY

The word "reality" refers to (or labels) a concept in the human mind, a concept which is apt to be somewhat different in each mind, and in each instance of use in each mind. Concepts serve as broad mental categories for classifying episodes or incidents of sensory awareness. Carabiners, for instance, together with key rings, shackles, handcuffs, padlocks, bicycle chains, and in a metaphorical sense, wedding bands, are members of a conceptual class of *rings or connectors* used to hold things together in secure fashion. Taken collectively as members of a group, their common feature is the security they provide in keeping things from coming apart under pressure. Concepts work similarly to hold things together in our minds, things that in each specific case might perform that function in very different ways. As a concept, *reality* refers to a class of situations known by their common features in awareness, namely, their demonstrable existence or perceptibility.

As that which cannot be directly experienced, *death* defines the bounds of human awareness and sense of reality. Denying us sensibility itself, it is that place we cannot go in our minds. Death is the place of emptiness and nothingness, a foil to everything we entertain in being conscious. Death is not-consciousness. End of discussion; we have no words or concepts we can use to describe it. Instead, we can talk about what death is not. In death, the capacity for self-renewal is over and done with. Cells can no longer repair, replace, or reproduce themselves, as we take it for granted they do while we are alive. A few years ago I was a different person because the cells making up my body were different in those days. To be alive is to remain undead through repair, replacement, or removal of damaged cells and cell parts. Living requires energy and constant bodily maintenance. Without sufficient energy, or when the repair process fails, then cells fail, organs fail, systems fail, life fails. We enter the forbidden realm of the concept of death.

Introspection is my way of checking my personal consciousness to see how it's doing. So far, every day, every second, I find something new and specific to the moment in which I direct my attention inward. Neuroscientists these days look to the brain as providing the neural substrate—the biological underpinnings—of consciousness as being not only responsible for mental activity, but for the emergence of awareness itself. I see the relation between brain and mind somewhat differently. I would say the brain develops a *capacity* for mental life, but that capacity is fulfilled differently in each case because its specific form and character depend on an additional substrate as well, the one provided by an energy-rich, physical and social environment within which each nervous system develops into a unique mind hosting an idiosyncratic flow of experience. That is, develops a particular way of being undead. Our personal experience is enabled by our respective brains, that is true, but it takes an energetic environment to stimulate the phenomenal precursor on which that experience is based. Individual consciousness is grounded on the complex engagement between each brain and the energy it receives and transduces from its physical surroundings.

Which is where the loop of engagement enters the picture as the dynamic link between our inner and outer substrates (worlds or milieus) in allowing the complex exchange of energies from both inside and outside our minds that characterizes bioenergetic mental life. The loop of engagement is another member of the class of secure connectors referred to above. When we die, we are no longer able to sustain our end of that connection. We come unmoored from the energetic substrate around us, which from that point becomes moot or conjectural—opening the way to wishful thinking about such paranormal topics as eternal souls, spiritual rebirth, resurrection, afterlives in heaven or hell, and other yearnings in other minds having difficulty releasing the deceased from her engagement with both substrates at once, more or less on an analogy with seasonal rebirth in the plant kingdom when sunlight and water combine in bringing forth new crops as a seeming matter of course. But consciousness in every instance springs from an organism's interaction with its environment by way of a loop of engagement requiring not only stimulation but a great deal of mental energy as well. When that personal energy source—the physical body and brain—no longer functions, consciousness dies of starvation. End of story. End of life. End of reality as a conceptual facet of life.

Consciousness, then, depends on a working mind finding itself in a stimulating, energy-rich surrounding situation, both self and situation engaging in an ongoing exchange that can endure for one human lifetime. That exchange itself constitutes the reality of the two taken together as what we call consciousness. Reality resides neither in the person nor in her surroundings, but in the bioenergetic interaction between the two operating in tandem through the looping engagement they establish with each other. That, in essence, is the upshot of my introspective research. Reality comes down to our forming a secure relationship with our surrounding milieu—our niche in the universe—whether it is composed of significant others, work opportunities, energy sources, or situations in which we can make ourselves happen in the face of difficulty or opposition. Essentially ecological, reality is our term for the dynamic exchange of energy between inner and outer substrates that keeps us undead.

And it is the disparity between those inner and outer states of energy—as revealed by our ability to compare them via our looping engagement—that gives rise to consciousness as an error signal waking us to our current reality. It is the bite of that error signal that alerts us to a discrepancy in our understanding of our situation, rousing us to consciousness so we can investigate the source of that signal which runs counter to our expectations. Widespread through the ancient world was an image of a serpent circled upon itself so it could grasp its own tail in its mouth—*Uroborus* (pronounced something like ur·ah′bur·es or uh′rob·ur·es, from Greek *oura,* meaning tail, and *boros,* biting or eating, the two roots combining to produce "the tail-eating one"). The image stands for cycles in nature that periodically return to nearly the same state or location, such as successive sunrises at nearly the same point on the horizon, or the zodiacal constellations returning to approximately the same yearly beginning. (Check Uroborus or Ouroboros on Wikipedia for details.) The punch to the idea behind the image is that cyclical events are similar each time around, but never exactly the same—as tail and mouth may be part of the one snake, but with different characteristics. Too, the serpent can be seen as giving birth to itself—and destroying itself at the same time—themes conveyed by the phoenix and Russian babushka dolls as well, and the cry, "The king is dead; long live the king!" Events emerge from both change and continuity. Which is the essential message of what William James called the stream of consciousness. We expect continuity, and pay special attention to the changes. If events flowed in endless repetition, a steel ring would be a more fitting emblem than a snake. But old Uroborus reminds us not to take cycles for granted. If events were ever the same, there'd be no need for consciousness, and mindless zombies would do better at less cost. But given the vagaries of worldly events, our survival depends on coping with variations, novelties, and surprises, so the wilder the swing of events, the sharper the bite that rouses us to consciousness.

Thirty years ago, during my last telephone conversation with my son Michael, he told me he knew what he had to do. That was the last I heard from him—ever. The next thing I knew, I was looking at his body on a slab, his skin yellow from loss of blood, his skull misshapen. It wasn't that he was somewhere else; he had ceased to exist as the person he'd been. His last project was to put a shotgun in his mouth and pull the trigger. His life energy simply was no longer there. I could tell that by looking at him. It was like I'd been hit by an arrow between my eyes. Except he was the one who'd been hit, not me. I was alive; he was dead. The difference struck me full force. He was gone. I had lost him, his mother had lost him, his brother had lost him, his girlfriend had lost him—forever. I had had my chance, and I blew it. The king was dead; there was no successor.

From that moment, I began to appreciate what it is to bear the spark of life, no matter how briefly. I think mothers have that appreciation upon sensing life within themselves. Giving birth certainly brings it home. For mother and child, the loop of engagement is well under way. Women are born with all the egg cells they will ever carry; they know what they are about. Men, once mature, create a constant flow of sperm cells without having much of a sense what they are for, which on occasion seems almost irrelevant. The urge is all; the consequences will be revealed later. Or there might not be any consequences. Mike was the direct consequence of my sexual activity with the girl who became his mother, but I didn't have much of a sense of the drama unfolding at the time. Once I saw baby Mike and began to interact with him, I think I was fairly quick to catch on. Watching him learn to hold his head up was a big revelation. Followed soon after by his crawling, toddling, walking, jumping, skipping. One day he was babbling initial consonants in his crib, then he was saying multisyllabic words in appropriate situations—such as geckyracies at Christmas.

I think I began to waken from my stupor somewhat, with an inkling, at least, of what conscious life entailed, but I remained pretty staunch in promoting my brilliant career in photography, and that, clearly, was my highest priority. Babies were for women, while jobs and careers were for men. That had been the dynamic in my family, my father having kept my mother from pursuing her doctorate in geology, though his career as a teacher of English was sacrosanct. That's how the world was in those days: men were men, women were women, and there wasn't much overlap in their family duties. A lot has changed since then, mainly for the better, but it's been a big job just keeping up. I was playing a role I'd learned in the old school of supposed "reality" when the new school had already begun.

Looking back at my father's controlling influence on my mother's career, I see now that he basically retooled the loop of engagement by which she made herself into a geologist through the influence of her father, who worked for a granite company in North Sullivan, Maine. At the time, the granite industry was booming in turning out paving blocks for city streets all along the East Coast, shipped by the tens of thousands from local wharves not far from where my mother grew up. She spent the summer of 1923 working as a geologist for Acadia National Park, but when she got married in 1926, the axe fell, and she had to stop being a geologist and become the dutiful wife of a college professor.

In my judgment concerning the way realities evolve, the part of my childhood best left behind was John B. Watson's method of child rearing, which he introduced in 1928 in his book, *Psychological Care of Infant and Child,* as well as in Nursing Service pamphlets distributed by the US Department of Agriculture. Watson had been the first graduate of John Dewey's new psychology department at the University of Chicago. He became famous as the father of behaviorism. I give the flavor of the child-rearing theories he promoted according to his behaviorist theory of reality in the following three excerpts:

> Mothers just don't know, when they kiss their children and pick them up and rock them, caress them and jiggle them upon their knee, that they are slowly building up a human being totally unable to cope with the world *it* must later live in (p. 44; the emphasis is mine).

> There is a sensible way of treating children. Treat them as though they were young adults. Dress them, bathe them with care and circumspection. Let your behavior always be objective and kindly firm. Never hug and kiss them, never let them

sit in your lap. If you must, kiss them once on the forehead when they say good night. Shake hands with them in the morning. Give them a pat on the head if they have made an extraordinarily good job of a difficult task. Try it out. In a week's time you will find how easy it is to be perfectly objective with your child and at the same time kindly. You will be utterly ashamed of the mawkish, sentimental way you have been handling it (pp. 81f.).

In conclusion won't you then remember when you are tempted to pet your child that mother love is a dangerous instrument? An instrument which may inflict a never healing wound, a wound which may make infancy unhappy, adolescence a nightmare, an instrument which may wreck your adult son or daughter's vocational future and their chances for marital happiness (p. 87).

Watson's book had an appeal among those who respected academic research and opinion. That is, those likely to be academics themselves. Raising children as if they were lab rats may not have seemed outlandish to them at the time. Both my parents were academics, and one distinctive characteristic of my childhood was the shaking of hands. I recall sitting in my father's lap only once—and being aware how unusual that was. Watson issued his book in 1928, the year Anne Sexton was born. I was born four years later. Sylvia Plath was born 23 days after I was, to an academic family. I have often wondered about how we were raised as children. My mother once told me some people didn't approve of how she raised her three sons, but I never understood what she meant. Sexton and Plath were both poets. Both had unhappy lives and died by suicide—Plath by putting her head in a gas oven in 1963, Sexton by carbon monoxide poisoning in a closed garage in 1974.

It is fitting that at the end of my life I am writing about introspection, a topic which John B. Watson would have decried as a waste of time because mind was not a concept in his thinking, human behavior as he viewed it resulting from putting subjects (including children) through their paces by a course of external manipulation, instilling desirable habits they would retain for a lifetime.

As shown by the excerpts above, the behaviorist program is an authoritarian affair that goes against the grain of what I have been claiming, in the case of humans, for the loop of engagement. It makes a huge difference if consciousness is seen linearly in terms of a stimulus eliciting a response, as opposed to a looping give-and-take with energetic surroundings (such as children provide). I picture consciousness as passing through a sort of permeable membrane or outer boundary surrounding the sensory mind, reaching out to the world through active gestures, taking in the world's response through its sensory receptivity, constantly feeding forward to the next stage in the process, pulling itself ahead stage-by-stage, creating a bioenergetic reality from concrete phenomena informed by the ambient flow of energy impinging on the senses, contributing interpretations received from memory at an apt level of discernment to create meaningful episodes of understanding and experience as a basis for action—and round and round—comparing sensory input against muscular output the whole time, the whole way. Old Uroborus is alive and well in each of us, symbol of our giving birth to our own awareness through our loops of engagement.

Reality, then, is a participatory venture by which one puts oneself out there, and sees what happens next. Reality belongs neither to the world alone, nor to the mind alone, but to both in a cooperative venture to which each contributes on its side of the membrane between inner and outer worlds. When we no longer have the strength to contribute, we withdraw from our side of the engagement, and are dead to the world, leaving it to continue without us.

Applying this view of bioenergetic reality to the incidents in Chapter 1—the idea of reality as a continuous looping engagement between two essential substrates—I find those incidents fall into two classes: 1) those in which each substrate contributes its share to my sense of reality, and 2) those in which I miss part of what the outer world is contributing, largely because I am stuck in a state of expectancy dictated by my earlier experience. In seeing cows along the Bar Harbor Road, the black raingear with white stripes contributed its bit, the raindrops on the windshield softened their outlines, and my mind converted flicking, blurry raingear into large spotted animals—which I took to be cows. Additionally, 3) a third class of reality is evident in dreams, which largely rely on memories cued by random eye movements during REM sleep, together with sexual arousal, pressure of blankets, alarm clocks, and penetrating noises coming through the window, etc.

The dying crow I encountered fit the same reality as the cows on the road to Bar Harbor. A roadside trash bag did its part by flapping against the wind. I put the roadside context, that motion (which looked intentional to me), and the size and blackness of the flapping shape together—and came up with a dying crow, not wafting trash bag, as the interpretation that best accounted for the phenomenon I saw. I felt I was working *with* that phenomenon, not against it. But as I got closer, I saw I was wrong.

The down-gliding jet about to crash over the rooftops of Bar Harbor embodied input from both sides of my mental membrane in one image, but on second look it resolved into a shiny, sweptback TV antenna that fit the same sensory pattern even better because I had never seen a big jet in that location, whereas I had seen a great many rooftop antennas. My level of discernment was off—which mine often is in quick glances—so I came up with a hasty explanation on the basis of very little sensory evidence.

In the case of my friend Fred's alleged stroll up Fifth Avenue, the figure I saw certainly looked like Fred, enough so to convince me it really *was* Fred, but several minutes later when I caught a quick glimpse of the stroller's profile—oh, oh, I realized I was chasing an imposter of my own making. All the other phenomenal clues added up to Fred, but that one was sufficient to disprove my assumption. Leaving me standing on the sidewalk feeling empty, making me realize how the anticipation I had contributed to my loop of engagement had led me astray.

Much the same dynamic produced the opposite effect in the case of the missing mustard jar. It was the stereotypical image I had in mind that blinded me to the atypical round, red top on the refrigerator shelf so I didn't see it from two feet away. The gestalt I had in mind trumped the image that was there, rendering me sightless. I can't blame the jar for lying on its side, presenting its top. I was a victim of my own haste and carelessness. Advantage to the far side of my loop of engagement.

Again, I was blinded by the image I had in mind when I missed my partner's bouquet of sunflowers. The flowers were there to be seen; but my eyes were looking only for the black camera case I had come upstairs to retrieve from the nook where I usually put it. Again, I was blinded by my own haste, expectancy, and low level of discernment, which amounted to no discernment at all for anything but that case.

Such incidents have huge implications. In my case, *the more determined I am that I am right* in viewing the world as I do, the

225

more probable it is I am out-and-out wrong. I have to take pains to maintain a reasonable balance between the two sides of the membrane separating my personal consciousness from my surrounding situation. Wrong assumptions, strong emotions, carelessness, over-purposiveness, hasty judgment—these can tip the balance, throwing my discernment off kilter, making me prone to error, which I am apt to strongly deny if confronted in the heat of the moment.

Those who act hastily are likely to make mistakes. We all know that from firing off email replies without due consideration, shooting from the hip, thinking we are being efficient when in fact we are foolish. There's a lot of that going around these days—in almost any circle you can name. Pressure to invest in haste, pass legislation in haste, make war in haste, do business in haste, eat dinner in haste—all lower our discernment unto blindness, leaving us blaming others for what are truly our misjudgments and mistakes. We should all make a pen stroke on the back of our hands every time we catch ourselves or anyone else getting carried away by incautious zeal, then tally the results. By that scheme, our tattoos would reveal just how flakey our witness to reality has become.

I, after all, am the man who looked at a cedar blowing in the wind and, midwinter, made a man scraping paint out of it. How discerning is that? Where did that man come from? If I hadn't looked again some minutes later, I would have sworn my neighbor was out in the cold working on his house. Tree outside the membrane, man inside; which side is real? That is why it is always a good idea for us to check the status of our engagements more than once to avoid being misled by first impressions. Reality might prove harder to pin down than we think. Make that, *is* harder.

The episode of the clip-art cat still has me buffaloed. The yeowl was clearly in my mind, as was the alleged cat, and even the lasting image of the alleged cat. All the outer world had to supply was a squeaky hinge, and I jumped wholeheartedly into my response-to-an-indignant-cat routine, a routine I hadn't practiced in more than twenty years. It all seemed so real at the time—as my actions demonstrated—yet it was in my head and nowhere else. My loop of engagement apparently has a secret routine I never knew about, and when it runs, I have no control over it. It required only a few hundredths of a second to play out, but in that time, it was unquestionably real to me. My loop was left to mop up in determining there was no cat for me to step on, there had been no yowl, the image in my head was of no cat I'd ever known, and what *was* there was a hinge that had never once squeaked in twelve years. I was caught by surprise, which got my heart really pounding. Physiologically speaking, that cat was as real as thunder and lightning, even though I made it up. But who is this "I" who makes my heart surge? Some sort of sentinel who lives in my skin and keeps watch for trouble. The one who abruptly yanks my head over to investigate when I spot something flitting out of the corner of my eye, probably the same one who shoots expletives between my teeth when I am thwarted by a sudden turn of events. Pleased to meet you, Mr. Sentinel, glad you're at your early warning post, even if your discernment isn't always as sharp as I'd like it to be. I now view that incident as an example of a physical reflex built up over years of my living with cats, together with its mental accoutrements. Caught unawares by a squeaky hinge while I was putting dishes away, I abandoned my current engagement—with astonishing consequences. My mental caribiner broke open and I fell into an altogether different reality.

The snow fields that would be clouds were clearly in my head as my family drove across eastern Colorado in August 1947, masking the snowcapped peaks of the Rockies which were hiding behind them. I kept coaxing my loop of engagement, trying to get it to show me what I knew must be there, but all it brought back was clouds, clouds, an endless line of clouds running north and south parallel to the most famous mountain ridge in the country. In that case I was forcing the issue to fit the facts as I knew them, not the facts that were in full view waiting to be recognized. I was inflicting summer clouds on winter snow because that was an expectation based on personal experience in upstate New York where snow fell in November, not August. It was August, I knew it was August, so those had to be clouds. My calibration was not appropriate to Colorado, but never having been there before, I didn't realize it. Leaving my consciousness unable to adjust to the new zone of reality I was entering for the first time in my life. My past just wasn't ready to let the future move in and take over. That reluctance is an inherent part of my consciousness, a kind of inertia to see how far I can push what I already know.

Countering the ubiquitous pressure to act quickly, there's a lot of resistance to having to keep up with rapidly changing times. That resistance seems to be in the air as part of our *Zeitgeist*, which shows up as a yearning for the good old days when men were men, women were women, marriage was for keeps, and things ran as they should.

Which of course is the great myth of a sheltered, middleclass child-hood that unwittingly sets personal expectations for many years to come. The current so-called Tea-Party mentality puts a halo around the founding fathers and mothers of this nation as the standard by which modern events are to be judged. Back to the future is the rallying cry, back to certainty, truth, justice, personal safety, and liberty. Which never existed except through the eyes of children who took in the world at a very low and uncritical level of discernment. Do you notice how many animated films are playing at the local movie theater, made-up confections in the tradition of *The Wizard of Oz?* Which I loved when I saw it in 1938 in living Kodachrome (except for the Kansas part, which was in homely sepia). The move-ment now is back to the days of that sepia Kansas, when Auntie Em was all sweetness and light, workers were your chums, and the old lady down the street would never think of making off with your dog. *Avatar* is the *Wizard* updated for a new (more violent) generation. The Tea-Party agenda is the agenda of children who don't want to face up to the reality of today's world. We want luminous and ethereal spirits to alight on us to show how special we are, how de-serving of a better life than the stressful one we've grown into. We want that stress-free life, and we want it now! Exactly as I insisted within myself that there be clouds over the Rockies in August, not snow, because in my childhood the powers made snow hold off until its proper time in November.

Where is reality? That depends on what we have grown used to as the basis of the expectancy we cast on the world. There is a time warp across our loop of engagement, the outside running in the now, the inside running on the remembrance of things past as they were in the days our formative concepts and memories were laid down—the very concepts and memories our security depends on. On the outside, times change: hurricanes happen, along with earthquakes, tsunamis, volcanic eruptions, wars, and cross-border migrations. While on the inside we look out as if such events were temporary distractions tempting attention away from the world as we know it should be. People who put resources into dealing with current events are steal-ing energy away from our efforts to maintain our habitual outlook and expectations so we can recognize ourselves and not have to accommodate to a world that no longer resembles the one we grew up in. If the world is not the same, we feel threatened because we no longer know who we are. So we fight for our right to defend our childhood selves. If we don't, we might as well be dead. That is what the National Rifle Association is all about, the Tea-Party movement, Fox News, the conservative side of politics.

That is also the essence of the cross-boundary dilemma consciousness finds itself in because of the inherent nature of the loop of engagement by which it maintains and updates itself. The updating is not automatic if we feel like dragging our feet to remain true to our more youthful, inner selves. If we entrench ourselves in our minds, current events become missiles aimed at our homeland in personal memory. The words making up the US Constitution no longer mean what they did when set down on paper; the entire document has become a morass of competing interpretations. To survive, originalists claim the old meanings are the true meanings; all the rest being new-fangled distortions of the truth as the founders intended it. Once again, back to the future! Except, language, like all human endeavors, is a living, breathing, changing creation in keeping with our nature as organic beings. In the United States we no longer speak Anglo-Saxon, or Shakespearean English, or colonial English for that matter, or even the stilted (to our ears) language of Melville and Emerson. Our experience has changed, and the idiom we use in describing it has changed. Modern minds are not capable of understanding the language in which the Constitution was composed because we no longer have the kinds of minds possessed by those who debated and framed it. In those days, property, which the judiciary is much about, included slaves as personal possessions. To base law on words written in 1787 requires a continuous effort to translate those words for modern ears. Earth has rounded the sun 225 times since those days, and American English has evolved in keeping with the times. Colonial English is not up to the job of regulating behavior of people who have grown up with high speed transportation, the Internet, nuclear arms, the holocaust, global war, television, evolution, genetic engineering, or microbiology. The words and concepts of today simply didn't exist in those days. We are no longer the same people as those who wrote the Constitution. The only proof we need is to hear jurists claim the old words are sufficient to the task of describing and delimiting the nation as it is today.

But I am getting ahead of myself. Back to the incidents at the heart of this book. Unearthing a turtle shell on the Nespelum Indian Reservation on the banks of the Columbia River in 1950, I was carefully following the contours of a human skull in my mind as I did so. Turtle on the far side of my loop of engagement, human remains on the inside, a chasm of taxonomic proportions from one side of my loop to the other in mistaking a reptile for a mammal of the primate order. That it could have been a turtle never entered my mind. It was the sutures that led me to believe I was uncovering a braincase, even though adjacent bones were smaller than I thought they might have been. I was heavily invested in mapping the concept of a human skull onto the sensory reality presented by a turtle shell, so to me, that's what it was. As I saw clouds when I might have seen snow in eastern Colorado, in Nespelum I saw a skull where my supervisor saw a turtle. I was digging out a skull, not a turtle shell. Under such conditions, reality is as reality does. Perhaps it is as simple as that. I hadn't yet caught on to the disparity, and because glory came with the one and insignificance with the other, I was biased toward finding a skull. Apprehended *flagrante delicto,* what could I mutter but something along the line, "Yeah, I thought some Indian kid might have played with it"?

It makes little sense to me now that I could have thought the voice calling "Fa, Fa" on the street outside my window was talking nonsense. I think of myself as being particularly woodenheaded on that occasion, which, roused from sleep, I probably was. Nonsense on the inside of my loop, fire on the outside, I couldn't bridge the gap, so went back to sleep. Which is perhaps understandable, but could have led to tragic results. As a phenomenon, I took "Fa" at face value when I might have probed deeper by asking not what it meant to me but what the man was so intent on declaring to the night world. It was his persistence that got me up to look out the window, when I saw flames and finally got his message. How many times have I dismissed what someone was saying as nonsense, when instead I could have asked him to say it in other words? Dialogue takes effort on both sides, an effort to be clear, and an effort to listen and understand. Settling for garbled communication isn't good enough. Particularly if the mouths and ears involved are used to different dialects or languages.

I haven't spent much time on my hearing, humming, then forgetting a tune while standing at the sink washing dishes, but it tells a lot about my preferred mode of communication, which is visual, not auditory. In college, I took voluminous notes because, if I didn't write down what the instructor was saying, I wouldn't remember what I'd heard. If I wrote it in my class notes, I could go over it later, increasing chances I would remember it. Particularly if I connected one thought to another by drawing lines between them to direct my review, or by underlining them, or drawing boxes around related ideas. Also, taking notes gave me a chance to doodle as I listened, creating visual images to go with what I was hearing. Smells don't play much of a role in my mind, with a few exceptions in the case of balsam fir sap, sweet fern oil, and lilacs in the spring. Even the taste of food isn't much of a draw for me. Part of that is the tantalizing aroma of pizza wafting through the air of downtown Bar Harbor on summer nights, which I have deliberately desensitized myself to since learning I have celiac disease, making pizza dough strictly taboo. As doodler, concrete poet, and photographer, I emphasize the visual aspect of my loop of engagement, at the price of underutilizing my auditory synapses, making it difficult to remember music, songs, poetry, jokes, stories, and gossip. Forgetting songs is nothing new with me. What *was* new in the particular episode I recount was actually recalling a song twenty-four hours after hearing it on the radio while washing dishes, a haunting experience. I think it was being in that particular location that brought it back—facing my reflection in the darkened window, sight of faucets and stainless steel sink. The next night, even that tune was gone.

Finding my memory stick meant recovering it by giving it a place in my visual reality so I could reach down and pick it up. As a black shape on a dark blue rug in the shadows under my desk, that was a tall order. When I found it, I felt it by brushing my fingertips across the rug more than by peering into the gloom. For my eyes, it didn't exist until I held it against the palm of my left hand where I could see it clearly.

Deleting the quarry photos in my camera after looking at them on my computer, but before copying them to my hard drive, I saw them as real because I had just looked at each one of them, even though the JPG files no longer existed. I had sent them to digital heaven without thinking, and was shocked to discover I couldn't bring them back. Conceptually, I held them in my mind, while in reality they no longer existed. While touch typing, I often not only select text inadvertently, but hit Control-X in the process and cut that selection in the heat of typing away. I can retrieve it by undoing the cut, but it is always unnerving to find myself working so close to the edge of disaster. I remember in the early 1980s (when I got my first computer) being told that no matter what I did, I couldn't do any permanent damage. But computers have gotten so (unnecessarily) complicated, that is no longer true. In trying to have them do all jobs for all people, programmers have made them so cluttered that the interface users confront is a nightmare of possibilities. Digital reality is not my kind of reality, which is slower paced, and better managed by a give-and-take exchange rather than a set of authoritarian commands.

Clearly, my reality and the speaker's reality were not in agreement in my being an audience of one. She was projecting the familiarity of her son's face onto me, when I didn't even know she had a son, or that she wanted a familiar face to ease her tensions while speaking to an audience of strangers, of which I was but one. While calming herself, she raised my anxiety level in wondering what she knew that I didn't. She was speaking to an aspect of herself, not to me, which I found extremely unsettling in not being in on the joke.

In the case of the cartwheel aurora, a show I have witnessed only once in my lifetime, I felt I was closer in harmony with the universe than ever before. I was fully present to the display, as it was to me, and I was hooked for several hours of devoted attention. On the far side of my loop of engagement with the universe, there were moving swatches of flickering light passing upward from the horizon to the zenith along the "spokes" of the "cartwheel." On the near side as phenomena realized in my mind, there was an endless procession of identifiable forms—mostly of animate life—floating upward along several spokes to mingle in a gyre directly over my head. The outer reality may have been radiant energy from solar flares interacting with Earth's magnetic field, but my inner reality ascribed sensory figures derived from that energy to motivated locomotion on the part of individual creatures floating upward into the sky, which is what my conscious mind made of the display. My seeing was essentially metaphorical in that I projected or mapped my categorized life forms onto the light show as if they were actually in the sky overhead, all the while knowing it was an exercise in my imagination, producing a kind of double seeing in which I suspended disbelief and went with the parade of animals, even though I knew it to be a full-blown illusion.

Where is reality in all this? It seemed so real at the time, yet only the flowing patterns of light were actually before me; the animated forms I "saw" were all in my head. The categorized phenomena in my mind could be treated as one man's rendition of reality, as true or valid as anyone else's. That's one option. What you see in the inkblot is what's there for you, a different reality for each one. Another option is equally conceptual, but focuses more on the cause of the phenomena as radiant energy interacting with Earth's magnetic field, based on an intellectual understanding of the physical mechanism behind the phenomena more than on the characteristics of the figures themselves. That's a rational, more scientific approach of mapping phenomena onto the conditions responsible for their generation in perception. Such an approach removes reality from being in my mind and puts it out there in the physical world. But you have to understand things in that conceptual, intellectual (opposed to immediately experiential) way to feel comfortable in claiming such roundabout thinking as real.

A third option would be to seek the big picture incorporating all such apparitions in awareness, the cartwheel display being but one instance. By this view, seeing is spurred by radiant energy impinging on the retina of the eye, energy which rods and cones convert to electrical potentials pulsing along nerve fibers and crossing from one fiber to others via neurotransmitters flowing across synapses between fibers, resulting in spatial mappings of qualities displayed by the radiant energy onto areas of the brain, the several maps of qualities producing the phenomena as perceived and interpreted by a particular individual. Which only sounds complicated because it *is* complicated—far more so than we realize. This is the neuroscientific approach to understanding conscious reality, and you would have to pore over several texts based on recent research to get anywhere near a smattering of an understanding of what happens when you "see" anything at all (Among other works, I have referred to Eric R. Kandel, et al., editors, *Principles of Neural Science,* McGraw Hill, 2000; Michael S. Gazzaniga, Editor-in-Chief., *The New Cognitive Neurosciences,* MIT Press, 2000; Joseph LeDoux, *Synaptic Self,* Viking, 2002; Christof Koch, *The Quest for Consciousness: A Neurobiological Approach,* Roberts & Co., 2004; Gerald M. Edelman and Giulio Tononi, *A Universe of Consciousness: How Matter Becomes Imagination,* Basic Books, 2000; and Gerald M. Edelman, *Wider than the Sky,* Yale University Press, 2004).

Our general aim in approaching reality seems to be to identify a single reality that applies to all cases of perception for all persons so that we can decide whether any one person is engaging the "real world" on a particular occasion or not. But because of the dynamic and elusive nature of what we mean by reality, such a claim is extremely difficult to support with demonstrable facts. We all believe (or want to believe) such a reality can be known to immediate experience, and that those who do not recognize such a reality when they meet it are inferior in some way to those who know it when they come across it. To think there might be *schools of reality* reduces reality to a matter of belief, which many people would dismiss offhand as untenable, while others would insist it provides them with a privileged outlook onto the one reality that is actual, true, and real in itself.

Which leaves me where? Standing in a meadow looking skyward at night, ogling a cartwheel display of aurora borealis, having the time of my life being at one with my situation in the universe. That, now, is reality. Which I can only explain by visualizing my inner sense of interpreted, phenomenal reality as being joined to whatever is taking place in the sky by a continuous loop of engagement. I extend my attention outward toward something moving overhead, and then entertain sensory phenomena based on the energy my surroundings share with me on that occasion. The visual part of my brain sorts and sharpens radiant energy into familiar figures I am able to categorize in trying to grasp what is happening in terms I can readily understand. That is, terms I can make sense of as who I am in order to participate in the event as a coherent episode of personal experience. And participate I do, in my own way, for several hours on end. If reality accounts for the interpreted phenomena I entertain, then reality worked for me then, was made memorable by a sense of beauty backed by strong feelings, and is still available to recall many years later. Which suggests that attention and memory are the gatekeepers of reality. We should trust whatever they configure in awareness as being relevant to our personal values and feelings—and for that reason profoundly real.

As my diagnostic workup in the university health center is still profoundly real forty-six years later, even though it bears a strong negative valence in my experience. I was disheartened at the time, and I have not changed my mind. That was one of the lowest weeks of my life because I went in with such high hopes of finding out at last what was wrong with me, only to have the doctor tell me that all the poking and prodding and peering and quacking had been to no purpose, and he had no idea how to interpret the symptoms I presented. That was my new reality—not that nothing was wrong with me—but even the best internists couldn't categorize it, so it must be something truly rare and unusual. I was a medical curiosity. That was the take-home message of my stay in the hospital.

Well, so be it, then. Failure is as much a part of life as success. The earth moved under my feet; a new reality set in, a new landscape came into view, a new situation emerged. I was licked, but so what? I had no choice but to keep going as before, as ignorant as ever. Yes, I did become cynical about doctors who took an oath to do no harm. But if they hadn't helped me, at least they hadn't killed me. All they had done is dash my hopes, which were under my care, not theirs. I went into a kind of mental tailspin, an aimless, messy time in my life. I turned more and more to photography as an outlet for my inner vision, taking many very gloomy pictures, which I now see as a portrait of my inner state at the time.

All the inner turmoil eventually led me to take an interest in how people (namely, me) interpret their personal situations. I enlisted in several sensitivity training workshops, took up jogging and tai chi, read books by Fritz Pearls about gestalt therapy, and started keeping track of my dreams. On the outside I looked much the same, but on the inside I was changing into a new person. I began to think about going back to school for an advanced degree in something or other, which eventually led me to the humanistic education program (if that's not its true name, that's how I thought of it) at Boston University School of Education, where I wrote a doctoral dissertation that was my first go at writing this book. It has taken me thirty years to overcome the academic bent (depending on the words of others) I had picked up in writing my dissertation, as well as to internalize what I had learned from browsing through the stacks of the university library.

In the face of that diagnostic fiasco, I rethought my inner reality because I finally realized that the outside world wasn't going to solve my problems for me. And I wasn't about to blame the world for not helping, because my problems were *my* problems, that was clear. Michael Polanyi's book, *Personal Knowledge,* which I read in a seminar led by Sigmund Koch in grad school, was the first book I'd found that took inner life seriously after an incident of being summarily dismissed by the intellectual masters of the real world. Marcel Merleau-Ponty's *Phenomenology of Perception* was also extremely helpful in providing a terminology based on inner experience. I found these books difficult to read, but in giving myself to them, taking my time to probe what they were saying, I began to rise to their level of discourse, so slowly began to make sense of my own inner life. This was no so-called talking cure but an experiential cure based on personal commitment and engagement. It is no accident my shelves are still lined with books that I have marked up in the course of my search for self-understanding.

One last point. The incidents I assembled in Chapter 1 represent problematic cases drawn from my personal reality, which embraces their affective, sensory, and cognitive dimensions. I included each of them among other incidents I felt had much to tell me if I could only look at them in the right light. I began these pages with that hunch, along with a list of the several perspectives I wanted to run those incidents through in a sequence that made intuitive sense to me. That sequence turns out to provide a rough outline of the stages along the loop of engagement by which I build my inner reality. The text you've been reading is the protocol of my working out of those incidents in light of the perspectives I've use to examine them. No, it wasn't some angel whispering in my ear that is responsible for this flow of words; it is me trying to understand my particular world through application of my personal resources. Introspection is as easy—and every bit as difficult—as that.

I am heading into the final two chapters in my sequence. The next one looks at conflicts with other realities in other minds, and the clash of actions based on those respective realities. I've experience a great many conflicts with others who do not share my views on one thing or another. Since so much of life is spent coping with such strife in the world, it is important to see if loops of engagement between different realities can suggest how we might work better *with* one another, while respecting our differences. The final chapter is about power, by which I mean taking control of one's own consciousness—or delegating that control to others who aggressively claim it, in the process elevating aggression as America's national virtue. This is a big part of the competitive spirit driving so much of our national culture, and needs to be looked at if we are to achieve a better understanding of ourselves as individuals maintaining our personal integrity, coherence, and inner harmony while working on common tasks within larger groups. O

CHAPTER 14

CONFLICT

My reflections on the subjective nature of reality have convinced me that once a belief becomes fixed on whatever grounds, the human mind is apt to become set in regard to that matter. There is no need for error signals—the bite of Uroboros—because error is no longer thought possible. I then see the duty of the loop of engagement becoming enforcement, not exploration or heightened discernment. A portion of the mind is dedicated from then on to making itself happen in a particular way in prescribed situations. As a result, pledges are recited, vows taken, contracts signed. Any restless quest for reality (topic of the preceding chapter) no longer applies. Once the loop of engagement becomes staid, certainty is all; little remains to be doubted, questioned, explored, discovered, or learned. The search is over, the story ends.

Such a turn of mind accords with one of the basic tenets of human civilization that holds truth to be not only real but recognizable upon sight and graspable upon reaching out. But truth, is always partial, temporary, situational, and perspectival. It is a way station, not the end of the line. That is the nature of my dreams and personal experience: always in transit, never arriving at a final destination. If I lock up my mind in one belief or another, I close myself off from living a life of adventure and discovery. Smugness is apt to set in, unto self-righteousness and intolerance for other views in other minds, creating fear of those who hold deviant views, perhaps hostility toward them, even mounting to hatred, anger, and aggression— ironically leading to conflict in defense of the "truth," *as if* truth ever justified violence. That kind of truth is not beauty, as the good poet claimed, but mental rigor mortis, a true deadening of the mind.

I can identify in myself several human qualities that are likely to cause conflict with other minds. If I take my mind to represent the norm—which is easy for me to do since it's the most vivid example of consciousness available to me—then I am apt to alienate those on either side of me who are norms unto themselves in being more auditory, say, or tactile in their sensory preference than I am. In claiming each mind to be unique, I step on the toes of those who claim that humankind is one creation, as many do, and each member possesses the same rights as all others. The concept of "universal human rights" has no meaning to me, but it is much in the air these days as an ideal that people around the Earth strive to claim for themselves. As I see it, rights are earned, much as understanding is earned—not inherited, not simply granted. My view of rights is that they are claims people make such that, once made, the state will back them up. That is, rights are political, not natural, and are hardly universal. Rights are earned, not given. They are yours when you put your body where your values are and do the work necessary to defend them. In my experience, states generally protect the rights of the wealthy and powerful, not the people at large—no matter what lofty thoughts are undersigned by their founders and rulers.

These days, I feel people are much too busy in hopping out of bed, grabbing a bite to eat, and rushing off to school or work before consulting their own minds to see how they are predisposed on any particular day. In taking that point of view, I conflict with those who prefer the hustle and bustle of such a life to a slower, more reflective way of making themselves happen. I am sure the self-reflective nature of this book irritates some in appearing to be narcissistic in the extreme, the very essence of what writing teachers might warn students away from in personal exposition to avoid appearing self-centered. In some circles, first-person singular is the kiss of death, and here I am offering it as the road to personal study, understanding, and fulfillment. My college advisor at Columbia called me a "prima donna" for wanting to take a General Studies class in color woodblock printing with Hans Mueller, a craftsman from old Europe. I took the class and still remember it, where many of the more "intellectually challenging" ones seem to have slipped from my grasp. I was out for adventure then, as I still am today, and I went in the direction of what I recognized as difficult territory, the only kind I could learn from.

Certainty is a stranger to the empirical mind, a limiting case never likely to be met in practice. The empirical method has more in common with mucking-about than certitude. Anathema to true believers, empiricism is regarded as a dangerous philosophy, a game for doubters and skeptics. But in my case, I am an empiricist by choice and through convincement by my own experience after years of restless searching for and discovering that there are no ready answers to any question humans can frame in their minds. The struggle for under-standing is all, the endpoint largely irrelevant in leading to the next round of engagement. Certainty, I find, is invariably a wishful as-sumption at the beginning of a search, not a warranted conclusion at the end. The preferred answer predetermines the question, so comes as no surprise to anyone. But naming the host of uncertainties in our minds—the spirits, gremlins, poltergeists, ghosts, demons, elves, an-gels, gods, monsters, witches, et al.—does nothing to explain them. It merely acknowledges those uncertainties as features of experience, and tenders their reality as topically acceptable. Empiricism is a venture of high peril, and those who believe in fundamental truths or principles decry it at every turn, leading to fundamental conflicts re-garding the nature of consciousness itself, that by which everything is doubted, known, or experienced.

The hallowed field of education is based on assumptions concern-ing the nature of learning, teaching, knowing, truth, inquiry, experi-ment, language, and other fundamental matters of great importance. In some quarters, questions are regarded as tokens of heresy, so education is reduced to rote memorization of orthodox texts, accu-rate recitation being taken as proof of wisdom and understanding. With a quotation at hand for every issue, the truth becomes self-evident to all who have undergone proper indoctrination. Again, an-swers are known before any questions are asked. Reciting the words of ancient masters, pupils build a future for themselves that is meant to be a replica of the distant past. Back to the future; as it was in the beginning, is now, and ever shall be, world without end. Amen.

Though I didn't start out with this view, through my life experi-ence I have come to believe that, no matter what culture we live in, each one of our minds is unique. Certainly each genome governing the synthesis of proteins in our separate bodies is unique, our early childhood experiences are unique, even compared to our siblings or an "identical" twin. Our educational experiences are unique, our work experiences, our social lives, our family lives, our most inti-mate love lives. Our individual immune systems are unique and, in being governed by conditions beyond genetic control, the detailed connectivity of neurons within our own brains. Because our bodies, brains, and experiences are unique and ever-changing, the life of our minds—our very consciousness at every moment of existence—is unique.

I am one of a kind, and so are you. We are made to deal with whatever situations may arise during our lifetimes—on our own, or with whatever help we can enlist. Evolution is not up to the job of crafting a standardized mind capable of dealing with the myriad unforeseeable situations we collectively must deal with. Instead, it has allowed us a mind to deal with the specific difficulties we face in making ourselves happen as only each of us must confront such troubles on his or her own.

So here we are, single-mindedly leading our lives while rubbing shoulders with seven billion others doing exactly the same, all doing our best to engage the situations we respectively face, all hating to be thwarted in reaching goals we set for ourselves within those situations. Both cooperation and conflict are potentially built into every human interaction and relationship. Conflict (from Latin *conflictus,* collision, from *confligere,* to come to blows) should be taken as the norm, not the exception. Which sounds like the view of a hardened pessimist, but taken as a word to the wise, I mean it more as precautionary advice to be on the lookout for probable sources of strife rather than wishing such sources would go away or not exist. Before lashing out, we must credit our opponents with strengths and convictions of their own in order to learn what they have to teach us. That is, it is better to look for icebergs in the North Atlantic than trust the steel hull of our vessel to get us through dangerous waters, no matter what. In an enlightened era, we would respect the uniqueness of everyone we meet, including spouses, children, relatives, friends, co-workers, students, public servants, criminals, and the public at large.

Taken en masse, "humanity" is a myth because each person is unique and must be accounted for individually, not as a statistical fiction of convenience. The mass media, too, are fictions in purporting to address an audience as if members were all the same when, in fact, each is demonstrably different from the others. Playing to a studio audience that claps and laughs on cue merely heightens the absurdity of the mass-audience gambit. All generalizations referring to individuals by their various group memberships—students, classes, sexes, unions, corporations, religions, races, teams, and so on—are convenient fictions that ignore the fact that each individual mind is distinctive in being different from all others. To claim that all members of a group "look the same to me" is an admission of just how low a level of discernment is acceptable in lumping individuals together into larger units for the sake of convenience. Taking a sample from the center of the pack is another ruse meant to suggest that the one is a model effectively standing for all the rest, which cannot be true no matter how convenient it may be as a shortcut.

In reporting the news, compiling governmental statistics, conducting polls and surveys, and all other efforts to sample groups in order to characterize their members, we do a disservice not only to those singled out but to ourselves, the gullible public. Gullibility is a pose we assume in order to deal with things in the mass, not as individual entities, which we know them to be. The people we fool in such endeavors are none other than ourselves as individuals. We willingly let the wool be pulled over our eyes, as it is over the eyes of the child who strikes and lunges to find the piñata while everyone else laughs at how wide of the mark he is.

In writing these pages, my aim is not to concoct generalities true for all minds, but more to discover what my one mind can tell me about itself and how it works in order to suggest to others that they do the same to see what light their respective minds can shed on themselves. Then we can compare notes and see what aspects of consciousness we hold in common, and where we are likely to differ. This chapter is not about the similarities we share but the differences between our mental engagements, leading to such collisions as are told hourly in news bulletins and reported in newspapers, magazines, and on the Web.

What's *right* with the world is not nearly as salient as what's *wrong* because it does not demand any such urgent preparation or response as calamity calls for. The issue comes down to "What am I going to do in regard to this new situation?" In doing more of the same, consciousness rests on its laurels. In adopting new behaviors, it has to adjust to novel situations, which is far more taxing. The news, by definition, is always "breaking" or forcing its way into awareness, alerting us to an altered state of affairs. It is an endless variation on Vesuvius spewing ash on Pompeii; mudslides in the suburbs of Los Angeles; wildfires in Texas; earthquakes in Haiti, China, and Iran; tsunamis in the Bay of Bengal and the Pacific off Japan; Alaric storming the gates of Rome; floods in Pakistan and Queensland; and bands of militant young adults raping mothers and girls in central African villages. This is exactly what consciousness is made for, building a future from the ruins of the past.

I spent the month of July 2006 at a seminar conducted by the Quaker Institute for the Future. Each member worked on a research projects meant to improve some aspect of the world situation. I had experienced conflict between fishermen in Maine and fishery managers bent on achieving sustainable levels of harvesting by protecting marine ecosystems from inevitable degradation. That statewide conflict was at the heart of my personal project, which was to promote intercultural understanding and stewardship as a basis for sustaining not only the marine food supply, but the ecosystems that produce it. I saw fishery managers as composing a culture made up of highly trained biologists, while fishermen composed a very different culture dedicated to the practical matter of catching and selling food taken from the sea. My goal was to have members of both cultures join together in protecting the state's public trust resources—in this case, its estuarine and marine ecosystems—by jointly sharing stewardship responsibilities as their first priority, while enjoying a sustainable catch as their second.

I made an ambitious (detailed) PowerPoint presentation meant to encourage the two cultures to combine their respective skill sets and understandings of the marine world. What I didn't see at the time was that I was effectively declaring the fisheries biologists as the winning team, stewardship being *their* goal, not the fishermen's. Biologists viewed my show as presenting a self-evident truth, while fishermen saw it as an attack on their traditional (pre-stewardship) way of life. So I undertook a number of revisions, stressing the need for community forums up and down the coast, where all marine-resource users could interact from their deeply held, personal perspectives, with the aim of highlighting coastal sustainability as a goal held in common. That goal could only be attained through stewardship by all parties, where competition (business as usual) would inevitably destroy both the fisheries and the ecosystems sustaining them for all users of the coast.

After receiving mixed reviews of my efforts, which continued long after the seminar was over, I realized that part of the problem was that most people had little idea what ecosystems are, how they work, and how vulnerable they are to overuse and abuse. I then focused on making PowerPoints depicting how marine and estuarine ecosystems respond to changing conditions through the years, horseshoe crab populations, say, shifting their locations with the seasons, while eelgrass would thrive in years of high rainfall, and decline in years of drought, with juvenile fish populations falling and rising accordingly. But these presentations drew only audiences predisposed to such topics, that is, those already familiar with the issues I was dealing with—which did not include the fishermen and their supporters who I had hoped would make up half of my audience. Leaving me once again preaching to the choir, not reaching across the divide between cultures so common understanding might become possible.

Everybody knows that fishermen don't go to meetings and slide shows. They prefer to engage one-on-one with other fishermen whenever they find themselves within hailing distance of one another, which is more likely to be when unloading their catch, or hoisting gear into their pickup trucks—the everyday occasions of their lives. Too, they talk all day on their marine radios, keeping in touch with those who share the dangers and responsibilities of their chosen way of life, always watching out for the other guy. They're not a group that readily makes up an audience of chair sitters while some guy projects slides on the wall. I took that as a sign of the fierce independence which fishermen are known for. I undertook a blog on consciousness, because that's where the source of our conflicts must lie, inside our minds and not on the pages of books.

What is conflict? In my case, a painful jab telling me my world is out of joint. My loop of engagement is breaking down. I am thwarted, as in my latest dream: I'm late leaving for the airport. I missed the bus. The others left without me. I don't have the money for a ticket. My neighbor is stealing my doorknobs. My gear is stuffed in plastic bags headed for the dump. The kids are crying because they don't understand. I am crying because *I* don't understand. That's what conflict feels like, that dream. The world is against me.

In the blog I wrote from 2008–2010 (Consciousness: The Inside Story, onmymynd.wordpress.com), I tackled the conflict between harvesters who view cutting rockweed on an industrial scale (particularly in Cobscook Bay, Maine) as a source of personal income, and those who regard rockweed as a source of food and habitat for wildlife and marine species all along the coast. In the interest of full disclosure, this was a conflict in which I was personally engaged (as I shall explain below), so I had strong motivation to add my piece to the debate. To give an example of how I dealt with that conflict, I quote "Reflection 187: Rockweed Perspectives," as posted to my blog on March 8, 2010:

There is more to rockweed than meets the eye. This is because we regard it, for the sake of clarity, from highly selective perspectives. To see anything at all clearly, we screen out much of everything else that gets in the way of what we're trying to see from our point of view.

In the case of rockweed harvesting along the Maine coast, the two chief perspectives look at rockweed from opposite sides, from the economic-industrial side, and the research-ecological side. From a management perspective, the challenge is to find a sustainable balance between the two sides.

You can tell immediately which side people are on by the terms they use to discuss rockweed. If you hear "biomass," "wet tons," "weed," "standing crop," or "jobs," you know you are listening to the industrial side of the discussion. On the other hand, words such as "habitat," "primary producer," "refuge," "ecosystem," or *Ascophyllum nodosum* (the Latin binomial by which the desirable species of rockweed is known), you are hearing the ecological side.

Rockweed harvesters dwell in the space where the two perspectives meet. Their motive for being there is primarily economic—to make a living—but to do so in that particular way they also must develop a professional understanding of what it is they are converting from a nurturing and protective habitat (as seen by one side) to so many wet tons of biomass (as seen by the other). Generally not scientists themselves, [harvesters] pick up enough ecosystem talk to carry on a conversation with landowners and anyone else who engages them. But they fall short of acquiring an informed ecological perspective; their allegiance is to the industry, not the ecosystem. By way of compromise, they develop a rationale for taking so much from a given bed of rockweed—often cited as 17% of the "standing crop," deliberately leaving the rest to carry on its ecological function. Their ultimate goal, however, is to deliver so many wet tons of biomass to a dealer at dockside.

The lobster industry in Maine is a notable example of harvesters regulating themselves to assure the sustainability of their fishery. They gave up dragging for lobsters in the 1940s, and now V-notch [the tails of] egg-bearing females, impose upper and lower size limits on the allowable catch, put escape vents in their parlors for undersize lobsters, limit their strings of traps, set up an apprenticeship system for those wanting to learn the craft, and generally conduct themselves in a responsible and professional manner for the sake of long-term job security. That is, beyond being harvesters, they have trained themselves to be stewards as well. Even to the point of feeding their catch by reliably filling their bait bags, which brings the wild fishery to the verge of being an aquaculture operation.

The question faced by the rockweed industry and ecologists alike include: 1) how much rockweed can be taken without disrupting the long-term structure and productivity of the ecosystems within which it functions?; 2) where can it be so taken?; 3) by what methods?; 4) at what intervals?; and 5) by harvesters with what experience and training? The challenge I see in such questions is that of asking rockweed harvesters to act as good stewards of the resource they depend on for a living. Which comes down to the issue of whose standards are they to meet—those set by the industry, or by impartial ecologists?

Harvest standards set by ecologists consider not only the biomass of the rockweed taken, but the function of that biomass if left in place. As a primary food producer—along with kelp, eelgrass, low marsh grass, and phytoplankton, among others—on which marine ecosystems depend, rockweed supports the survival of the living coast that complements upland forests in giving Maine its character and identity as a human habitat.

How does that work? Rockweed constantly feeds energy derived from photosynthesis into coastal waters from branches breaking off through wear and tear from constant motion imparted by tides and waves. As free-floating wrack, that organic material rides up and down on local currents, providing a surface habitat for amphipods and other life forms, which in turn attracts birds like Bonaparte's gulls and various species of terns—direct beneficiaries of the energy stored in bits and pieces of rockweed. That wrack either exits the bay to feed a variety of species farther along the coast or out in the Gulf of Maine. Or is perhaps deposited at the high-tide line along the shore, where it provides habitat and food for shoreline scavengers—sandpipers, song sparrows, thrushes, gulls, crows, and schools of small fish, among other wildlife species.

Broken into ever-smaller particles, rockweed eventually decays, becomes colonized by protein-rich bacteria, and assumes a new identity as energy-rich detritus, food for filter-feeding mussels, scallops, oysters, barnacles, juvenile lobsters, and early life stages of a great many marine creatures both vertebrate and invertebrate. Detritus is a variant form of the rockweed and other primary food producers from which it derives. In supporting entire marine and estuarine ecosystems, a ton of rockweed in the form of detritus is worth far more than the $40 the rockweed harvester gets paid by the ton. In fact its value is inestimable. What is the going price of a breath of fresh air, a glimpse of sunlight, or a raindrop falling from the sky? Coastal Maine and its gulf run largely on detritus. What is that worth to a fox, eagle, harbor seal, or to you? What is the value of Cobscook Bay, Taunton Bay, or the Gulf of Maine?

The history of Maine fisheries is a tale of descent lower and lower on the food web, until now even primary producers such as rockweed and kelp have a certain market price—not as value-added detritus, but as materials in the raw. Which is the highest and best use of rockweed—detritus to feed the entire coast, or a commodity sold as fertilizer or an additive for commercial foods and cosmetics? Perspectives have implications and ramifications which, like by-catch, often go unrecognized.

To end up, I will shift from the food-web to the habitat aspect of rockweed. Whether providing shelter; opportunity for grazing, foraging, reproducing; refuge from predation; or otherwise essential habitat, rockweed invites life to the intertidal zone, a hardscrabble habitat of extremes if ever there was one. Yet by expanding and collapsing as driven by its highly variable circumstances, rockweed offers its services to all comers with great efficiency, tide after tide, season after season, year after year. Again, what are those services worth to alewives, eels, periwinkles, crabs, copepods, amphipods, crangon shrimp, eiders, black ducks, loons, herons, kingfishers, and the likes whose lives depend on them? What are they worth to you in comparison to having a tub of industrial-grade ice cream in the freezer, or a creamy cosmetic on your lips?

The essential question is: At what harvest level do the ecological and industrial values of rockweed come into conflict so that opting for one penalizes the other? The rockweed industry aims to convert 17% of selected beds of rockweed to biomass.

That figure assumes a great deal about the continued functioning of local ecosystems after those beds are cut, their structure radically altered, their biomass removed.

Since the energy stored in rockweed fuels much of the Maine coast, it strikes me that removal of even 17% of select areas is excessive. Given that 100% of rockweed energy turns over every two years, distributing its wealth as wrack and detritus among species such as I have mentioned, a 17% cut on top of 50% annual turnover sounds to me more like a 34% reduction of the "standing crop" on which that natural distribution of food energy depends in the following year. In light of the habitat and energy reductions implied by that level of rockweed harvest, I propose that a 5% cut seems eminently more reasonable,

At the February 10 [2010] Rockweed Research Priorities Symposium at the University of Maine in Orono, Sea Grant joined with the Department of Marine Resources in initiating a process of discovery to find out what gaps still exist in our understanding of the ecological consequences of rockweed harvesting. On February 17 [2010], current findings were relayed to the Joint Legislative Committee on Marine Resources, which considers last year's legislation regarding the harvest level in Cobscook Bay a done deal. That is, the state sides with industry recommendations. Which makes it all the more likely that the 17% level of harvest will spread to the rest of the coast.

It is up to resource managers in Maine to decide whether to take a short-term view for the sake of feeding biomass to the industry, or a long-term view including habitat considerations and the gradual distribution of rockweed energy as viewed from an ecological perspective. Stakes are high: Nothing less than the continued productivity and viability of the Maine coast is at issue. I have testified before the Marine Resources Committee that I consider a 17% rockweed cut to be unsustainable. From my perspective, a less risky harvest might be as high as 5% every third year in the same bed if closely monitored.

It is clear which side of the fence I am on regarding rockweed harvesting in Maine. I had the issue thrust upon me by a seaweed harvester I know who was setting up a rockweed biomass assessment workshop on land I am a part owner of—without telling me what she was up to. The state was to pay the consultant who would conduct the workshop. I had a file of aerial photos of the property, which the harvester wanted copies of. I took it from her interest in the photos that she was planning to have the assessment conducted on land that she didn't own, but I did, land with a conservation easement on it prohibiting all commercial activity. I told the harvester I wouldn't allow the workshop to take place. When she didn't listen to me, insisting on her right to have the workshop held wherever she wanted, I called the Department of Marine Resources, which moved it to a different location. From that point, the conflict grew hotter by the day, my acquaintance claiming I had betrayed privileged information about the workshop, which I said wasn't privileged at all since the affair was paid for with state money, so was essentially in the public domain. With the upshot that I had my attorney notify her by mail that I would regard her harvesting of rockweed on my land as a willful act of trespassing. Which she fought with surprising fury as if she were the one trespassed against. Which is how conflicts play out, each party claiming injury, for which the other is at fault, and the whole affair winding up like a tornado hurling across the landscape, driving straws like so many darts into solid telephone poles.

Which might seem a far cry from my theme of introspection, but it is that destructive release of energy in overt conflicts that I am trying to get at, whether aired in courts of law, or otherwise. The same energy that turns Tutsis and Hutus against each other, Israelis and Palestinians, Shiites and Sunnis, Muslims and Hindus, and other factions and parties of all sorts, so that nuanced, affective valences in the human mind play out in acts of anger or violence aimed at members of opposing mental persuasions. Even as I try to be reasonable in depicting some of the complexity of rockweed harvesting in Maine, my bias shows through in the amount of detail I give regarding the side I favor in the dispute. Am I being a propagandist by promoting the wider role of rockweed in supporting marine life in the Gulf of Maine? That is, am I propagating an environmental point of view? Yes, I am. I am an agent of the Earth as a natural system supporting all life on the sole planet in the universe where we know life exists. My duty is to life itself, not the manufacturers of ice cream and cosmetics whose executives make millions of dollars for themselves on the backs of harvesters selling rockweed they don't own for forty dollars a ton, which comes down to two cents a pound of natural habitat reduced to biomass suited to industrial purposes.

While devoting a significant share of my limited mental energy to this issue, I know that the matter cannot be resolved without the sides shifting from taking opposite positions to seeking to complement each other so their strengths can be fairly acknowledged and balanced, their weaknesses overcome through mutual agreement and support. My post on rockweed harvesting is based on internal evidence provided by my personal experience. If not common knowledge yet, it is certainly knowledge in my mind through participation in the life I have lived as driven by personal feelings, values, and attention to details. That knowledge is available to me by looking within my own mind, checking the sources, then assembling the various segments together in coherent form.

I do not believe the human mind is committed by evolution to be better at competition than cooperation. It is true we are subjective and independent by nature, but also true that we can be broadminded, trusting, compassionate, and more-or-less objective when we feel secure within ourselves and aren't threatened with bodily harm. Once bricks and bullets start flying, we lose it and go into battle mode, from which neither side can emerge victorious.

I trace the difficulty in letting the world change around us to its roots in the sheltered world we experienced as children. If not protected at that vulnerable age, we would never have survived. Without realizing it at the time, each of us acquires a perspective on events reflecting our youthful naiveté and inexperience. The world comes across in bold, simple terms belying the true complexity of events. Memories are built from the synapses we establish in our brains at the time, and we know that to build lasting brain connections requires strong, clear, unambiguous signals made possible by suppression of contradictory indications. Our version of the world is a cartoon, a quick sketch in bold strokes made salient by lack of any alternatives, strokes which are good for a lifetime. Our perspectives are nurtured by the ambient family attitudes of our early years, which we internalize, and subsequently project in good faith onto the phenomena underlying our sense of the real world, without realizing the attitude is our doing, and may not be entirely appropriate. Just as childhood language serves a lifetime of usage in unanticipated situations, so does the early perspective we acquire become the parent of our perspective as adults in a wholly different world incorporating issues we never dreamt of. Like so many rolling stones, we stick to our early paths until stopped by insurmountable obstacles, which we can either adapt to through accommodation, or try to shove aside with brute inertia.

I think of my forcing clouds onto the snowcapped Rocky Mountains as an example of just such childhood inertia, along with my willful insistence that a mustard jar should look like a mustard jar, and that whatever yowls must be a cat, or whoever cries "Fa" at night must either be speaking in tongues or batty in not speaking my childhood brand of English. The plan that events are supposed to stick to is the plan inferred from my earliest memorable experiences. Any deviation from that plan is heresy in denying me the right to be who I am—the one whose mind is set according to that plan.

The roots of conflict, that is, can often be traced to violations of assumptions laid down in childhood for lack of any prominent alternatives. That, I propose, is the true source of a lot of the anger we thrust onto the insurmountable arguments our opponents throw back at us from the plans they enact from *their* childhood days. Conflicts, by that view, become battles between different sets of childhood expectations, each as staunch, deserving, and innocent as the other. Fishermen and rockweed harvesters are often carrying on traditional family ways of making a living, as natural resource managers may be products of childhoods spent learning the ways of nature through firsthand experience. When I was a kid, I sided with muskrats against those who would trap them in winter, so would follow trappers' footprints in the snow along the local creek, and spring each trap with a stick. One of my strongest memories is of watching a mother robin swoop low to the ground beneath her nest, back and forth, diving again and again. I figured a nestling had fallen to the ground, so determined to rescue it. I went to the spot where I'd seen the robin diving—and she kept at it, strafing the top of my head. I looked and looked, but couldn't find her lost nestling—until I lifted my right shoe and found its flattened, featherless form in the grass underneath. The gist of the memory is that being well-intentioned didn't mean I would be effective in giving the aid that was in my heart. That was a hard lesson, and it's still with me today. Yes, I'm still that same little kid, now with an Ed.D. in humanistic education.

Conflict emerges when we dig in our heels and try to stop the world from turning on its axis, or are determined to make it turn to our personal advantage, even at others' expense. Personal advantage is gauged by standards set in childhood, that is, by how events in those days calibrated our attention and expectancy. Or if not strictly in those bygone days, through subsequent hard knocks that balked our personal efforts to get ahead. Such experiences (opposed to what we are taught in school) provide the true curriculum by which lifelong learning moves ahead.

"Heaven has no rage like love to hatred turned, / Nor hell a fury, like a woman scorned" (Congreve, *The Mourning Bride*)—unless it be a rockweed harvestress prevented from cutting where she has a mind to, that is, on territory she considers "hers." Such turns of events stir deep feelings because they thwart expectations regarded as just deserts. For myself, I hate being thwarted, in any way, anywhere, anytime. Outrage can be my response, or righteous indignation. On bad days, within a few hundredths of a second, I can be counted on to rise up in fury at the affront to my personal dignity. When the spike of transient emotion subsides, I calm down and think about ways of dealing with the problem. But in the heat of the moment, I am apt to swear, shout, or throw things around to vent my anger. Picture me at my computer when a meaningless error message flashes on my monitor, telling me that such-and-such is impossible just now. Stupid machine! That message is not in my plan. Send it back to wherever it came from. But the message just sits there, waiting for me to give it the OK. Which means approving something I neither want to hear nor can understand, which makes me feel dumb, so I really get fuming—to no purpose whatever.

That interface between me and my computer is an example of the interface between my mind and the substrate which serves as the basis of my world once it has been translated and reshaped as sensory patterns in my mind. It is my loop of engagement that is disturbed, the primary link between me and my world, by which I cast expectancy outward to find how the world substrate will respond. That loop is the fundamental basis of my reality at the time, a dynamic state of affairs that tells me things are progressing as they should, or not, as the case may be. My sense of how that loop should progress is rooted deep within the substrate of my mind, in the brain that keeps humming along like the engine of my car, doing its job without my knowing how it works or what it is doing. So my fury at being balked is properly directed at myself for not understanding or accepting what is happening, very similar to the anger I directed at myself for killing the baby robin in wanting to help ease the mother's distress upon losing her nestling.

Owning the fury directed at such inherently personal causes is extremely difficult. It is far easier to point at some external source as being the problem, which, if eliminated, would put events back on their normal course. Fear is internal. Hatred is internal. Anger is internal. Fury is internal. The source of conflict itself is internal as a disruption between essential parts of our minds—the past as we carry it forward as expectancy, and the present moment that drives the phenomena we are currently aware of as the basis of our understanding of ourselves in relation to our world. Is it possible to intervene in such conflicts to any positive effect? If so, then I would say the only suitable route would be introspection, because no other mind would be likely to understand either the problem or its causes. And if, when thwarted, we are rash in hitting out at others, then we ourselves are already beyond help because our loop of engagement has moved beyond the point where our motives would have been accessible to ourselves. I view the Israelis as being beyond themselves in regard to the Palestinians they threw into turmoil in invading Palestine following World War II and the Holocaust, and the Palestinians being beyond themselves in having endured the situation for more than sixty dreadful years of displacement and internment.

Many of the people of the world seem to be more infatuated with celebrities and the lives they lead than with the inner workings of their own minds where the real action takes place. This feasting on superficiality keeps us from recognizing our own strengths and weaknesses, and from developing the one and doing what we can to remedy the other. Through stubbornness, we cling to our proclivities, knowing what we know, not knowing what we don't, allowing us to march in place without either moving ahead or helping the world meet the myriad challenges it faces. That is, in not facing up to our childhood selves, we expect the world to cater to our needs for the kind of stimulation we want, in the process holding the world back from what we could make of it if we put ourselves into the job. Introspection taught me that lesson in allowing me to see how I hold myself back in trying to be true to my past when I have moved well beyond the point where that would be at all useful to me in living my own life. Putting energy into keeping things familiar is self-defeating in the extreme, because that prevents me from working on what needs to be done to keep up with a world that changes every day of my life. If I am still the same person when I go to bed at night that I was when I got up, I have failed to keep up with the day's challenge. Complaining about the rapid rate of change is self-defeating because as an Earthling, it is my job to keep up with the world, not to hold the world back to a rate of change I can readily assimilate. Looking outward, I see the world racing ahead; looking inward, I see where I need to grow if I am to keep pace with events.

To avoid unnecessary conflict with our former selves, we need to keep up with the times in which we live. If we fall behind, we become dependent on others helping us along. The only way to really keep up is to face into the changes taking place. Denying those changes only leaves us dragging further behind the times, blaming events instead of doing our best to keep abreast of them.

The turn against multi-culturalism in England, Germany, and France is a current example. The demise of colonialism led to a kind of domestic colonialism in the home country where guest workers were welcomed as long as they abided by local conventions. But when immigrants brought their own traditions and beliefs with them, and didn't meekly give them up, the bloom faded from the ideal of diverse cultures living side-by-side without borders between them. If ever there was a universal principle, diversity is it. The trick is in finding ways different cultures can complement one another, adding to a larger understanding on all sides. Accommodation is the way of the future, requiring new learning on the part of all involved.

Rather than facing each new day with a fretful groan, we do better to sit up in bed and ask ourselves, "What's new?"; and then ask the first ten people we meet the same question, followed by, "How can I help?" And they would do the same for us, knitting us together as a community of complementary skills and interests based inside-out on mutual concerns, not concerns laid upon us from above, such as political maneuverings and using natural resources in other lands as justification for waging war. Instead of deliberately colliding with self-seeking others, we can accomplish a good deal more with our limited ration of personal energy by complementing our neighbors in common endeavor, and by cooperating with individuals such as ourselves, not corporate or national interests furthering private motives and objectives of their own.

Our entire legal apparatus is dedicated to conflict resolution. The problem being that paying attorneys and bringing suits is more draining on the limited resources available to the relatively poor than the relatively rich, with the consequence that the wealthy have readier access to justice than do the poor, leading to the conclusion that justice can be bought if you have the right legal team and enough money. Too, courts are set up to deal with situations in which one party claims to be wronged by the other, the positions of the plaintiff and the accused being far from equal, one side having to demonstrate the truth of its accusation, the other to defend itself against spurious or wrongful prosecution. Juries are selected by attorneys for both sides trying to approve those apt to entertain a hidden bias favoring their side of the case. In the end, justice is a judgment determined in the minds of judges and juries, who being human, are prone to all manner of influences and opinions bearing on the case, such as posture, appearance, or tone of voice. Whether rightly or wrongly, justice is as justice is delivered. Next case.

Which supports my contention that, since all people are unique, conflict between persons is inevitable, and will be forever. My thought is that we are wise to become as familiar as we can with the traffic through our own minds so we can recognize which issues are ours and which can be traced to other sources. There are always two sides to our loops of engagement, internal and external, leading each of us to live in a complex, multidimensional reality largely, but not wholly, of our own making. We bring more conflicts on ourselves than we commonly realize. Some of us are drawn to conflictive situations in order to feel alive, others attract conflict as a way of life because that is what we are used to. Since conflict is ever present in our lives, from earliest childhood to old age, our minds and loops of engagement are geared to it, often in reflexive or habitual ways we do well to recognize at first bite, the better to avoid slipping into the same old conflictive routines again and again. Just resolution of conflict, that is, starts within us, not when we seek it in court.

Too, it is good to remember that more laws are written to benefit the interests of the powerful than the meek. In introspection, we discover that whoever we are, justice begins by our becoming familiar with our own minds. From that realization, we can carry the benefits of self-knowledge as far as we have the energy to bear them. In cooperation with others, we don't have to settle for any limits on how great a distance we will be permitted to go. Which brings me to the verge of my last topic, the use and abuse of our mental powers, which I deal with in the next—and last—chapter. O

CHAPTER 15

POWER

The raw power of the human mind is to seize new experience in terms it is already familiar with. Awareness is a matter of seeing (hearing, touching, etc.) sensory patterns as examples of concepts it has formed in the past. Every instance of seeing is an instance of *seeing as*—of seeing one thing as another, the concrete *now* in terms of the abstract, conceptual *then*. This primary mental power is essentially metaphorical in nature. We reach out to the unknown world in full expectancy that it will conform to the world we have already assembled from bits and pieces gleaned on earlier occasions, creating the illusion that we are prepared for every eventuality. Which we truly aren't and can't be because every situation is unique in itself—as each person is unique, each day is unique—and we risk distorting events by dressing novelty in worn meanings and treating the new as a violation of the old.

This is astounding news—that metaphorical seeing is not the rare exception but the common procedure. The mind is a metaphor generator, an apparatus for turning out mental metaphors one after another as a matter of course. *Seeing as* is metaphorical seeing, reaching for one thing as if it were another. Consider the incidents of what I have called miscategorization that have brought me this far. Each one is an example of *seeing as,* of confounding one state of affairs with another. I assumed it was safe to cross Brattle Street when it was not; I saw flicking raingear *as* cows, a trash bag *as* a dying crow, a rooftop antenna *as* a crashing jet, a stranger on the sidewalk ahead of me *as* my friend Fred, a mustard jar presenting its top *as* not even a mustard jar, sunflowers *as* so irrelevant to my errand that they didn't exist, a swaying cedar tree *as* a man scraping paint, snowfields in the Rockies *as* a line of low clouds, a buried turtle shell *as* a human skull, a thumb drive *as* disappeared, quarry photos *as* safe on my hard drive when they weren't, and wavering lights in the sky *as* animal shapes morphing one into another. I heard a squeaky hinge *as* a yowling cat, a man crying "Fire" in his own language *as* talking nonsense. And in incidents involving other minds, the speaker told me afterwards she saw me *as* her son, and the internist told me he read my symptoms *as* signs of cystic fibrosis. All of these are examples of reaching for the world metaphorically *as* some kind of alternate reality.

Under less-than-perfect conditions that may be understandable, but to claim the mind works as a metaphor generator seems to be a far stretch. My claim, to take one example, is that the quintessence of a turtle shell resides not in the shell itself, but in the concept-laden mind of its observer. The day was clear and dry, conditions were perfect for unearthing what I saw *as* a human skull. That was no nonce miscategorization. I took pains to unearth a skull, not a turtle shell. When he came along, my supervisor saw it differently. Right away, I knew he was right and I was wrong. But for the duration of my concentrated effort, to me it *was* a skull. To sustain a metaphor for that long is no fluke. Out-and-out, my reality that day was largely metaphorical. In light of my felt understanding, I reached out for a skull as the best fit to the sensory pattern in my untrained mind. The business of the mind is to grasp the world in terms of the most appropriate concepts in its repertory. I was fully familiar with conceptual turtle shells and human skulls. I mapped the wrong one onto the shape I was uncovering—that is, in hindsight, my mind mapped the wrong one. It is the mind's business to wrap concrete sensory phenomena in abstract conceptual categories in order to see them as clearly as possible. My mind was not separate from me in any way. It determined my outlook, I did its bidding. My mind made me do it. That's how it was.

OK, so I was mistaken. The mind part of me was mistaken. It mistook a turtle shell for a human skull. At the time, my mind was operating metaphorically, doing its job when subject to compelling excitement and motivation—also aspects of mind. In making me who I am, my mind always does its best to sort things out in light of the situation it fashions from the sensory figures it is presented with. The turtleness of a turtle, the skullness of a skull, is not in the object itself but in the mind construing the object. Without a mind to interpret it as such, a spade is not a spade, a rose is not a rose, a skull is not a skull in itself. The label, the category, the schema, the concept—these are features of mind, not of any self-labeled, self-categorized, self-schematized, self-conceptualized universe. If the world comes across as pre-labeled and pre-categorized, that is the work of other minds that have come before us, not of the world itself. I took my supervisor's words as referring to a more accurate interpretation in his mind than the fanciful one I'd come up with on my own. I immediately knew he was right. That is, my mind recognized its own category error at last. Self-correction or self-improvement is also a facet of mind. If I engage a scene long enough, I tend to get it right eventually through a series of successive approximations.

Never underestimate the power of metaphor, particularly if inadvertent, for that is the power of mind itself. That is my message. The mind doesn't *know* what anything is; it relies on the closest fit it has in its repertory under the circumstances determining a given situation. In writing my doctoral dissertation, I concluded that perception on a small scale is fundamentally metaphorical because that's how the mind goes about its business in seizing novel phenomena in terms of conceptual categories it is familiar with. On a grand scale, the mind tends to the mythological. For ancient Greeks who were in love, Aphrodite was not a pretty face laid upon the facts—Aphrodite herself was there *in* those facts from the beginning. Mythology was raw truth, not a fanciful comparison. From the petty to the grand, metaphor is the boldest way of reaching for novel phenomena in terms of the known and familiar. Roadside crows are stock, familiar characters in my mind, as are jet aircraft, my friend Fred, and to a lesser extent, men scraping paint. I readily cast them onto striking phenomena because in the heat of the moment, stock concepts are sufficiently detailed to carry the burden of blunt awareness, feeling, and intentionality on their own.

Consider the power of religious thought revealed in its endurance through ages of criticism against rival systems of belief. It is the metaphorical truth that survives, not the literal, which has been discredited many times over. Spiritual belief is metaphorical belief, belief that convinces the mind without being demonstrably "true." Our word *spirit* comes from Latin *spirare,* to breathe, which is a biophysical matter, not spiritual. But in crediting an unseen *causative agent* with the bestowal of life at birth, and with its withdrawal at death, the giving and taking of life became understandable in metaphorical terms appropriate to the level of human understanding at the time. I go so far as to say scientific truth itself is largely metaphorical, because that is how the mind works—by seeing novel phenomena in terms of the known and familiar. It is no accident that scientific terminology is highly metaphorical in the guise of terms so ancient that their figurative nature is no longer recognized. But when we analyze key Greek and Latin terms still in use by tracing their ancestry, their literal quality dissolves in shimmering metaphors of old. Our words *divine* and *divinity* stem from reference to ancient ways of seeing heavenly bodies (that is, planets) described as radiant or shining angels, *aggelos* being the ancient Greek word for messenger, which is how bright planets were understood—as messengers sent by the heavenly host to apprise mortals of the will of the gods (who to this day form the basis of many of our constellations). Our word *atom* stems from a root meaning uncuttable or indivisible (even though now we believe atoms to be highly divisible into subatomic particles). *Matter* stems from the Indo-European root *mater* meaning mother, and *proof* stems from Latin *probus* meaning upright, good, or virtuous. Scientific terminology is largely based on forgotten metaphors, but metaphors nonetheless.

Not verbal metaphor per se but *the experience of metaphor* is the basis of meaning in the human mind, whether that mind be trained in theology, say, or science, politics, economics, or the art of war. It sounds better to say such minds indulge in metaphor than that they perpetrate the illusion we know what we are talking about, but both are true. Employing terminology we are *comfortable with* is no guarantee we are speaking the truth. Without minds, there can be no truth, no expressiveness, no reaching out on the basis of prior experience. The mind itself stems from a flow of charged particles across cellular membranes and of chemicals across gaps between neurons—that is the language of the brain which gives rise to perception, interpretation, understanding, emotion, and the language of the mind, which is a matter of comfort and familiarity, not neuroscience.

Metaphor is the language of so-called reality, of the seemingly real world. Which is why different cultures use different sounds and different terms in describing what they believe to be of fundamental importance in the experience of their members. A good deal is lost in the process of mapping one metaphorical language system onto another, as in creating topographic maps of selected landscapes. Think of the life forms that do not show up on any map—the ants, elephants, serpents, trees, shrubs, herbs, birds, and fish that go missing from our atlases, no matter how detailed. Cities and roads are there, but not living beings. Similar omissions occur in using words to reach from one mind to another, even within the same language group. We should celebrate the fact that at least we have mental metaphors to use in keeping track of such things; without them we ourselves would have no minds to speak of.

In serving as the basis of thought, metaphor is a powerful neurological agent that makes possible everything the mind can entertain. But, too, it is not as systematic as the rational processes we'd like to believe are fundamental features of the mind. It doesn't make any sense to see TV antennas as crashing planes, or trash bags as dying crows—yet that's what I saw at first glance. There is a haphazard quality to the mind that doesn't fit the rational model we profess to believe in, just as terrorism and religious extremism exist as aberrations in a world we wish would come to its senses and extinguish both. But if every mind is unique, that means no two operate alike, so a seeming randomness is built into us as part of the supposed "plan," as terrorism, rape, drug trafficking, and criminal habits are not aberrations but integral parts of human culture. I do not mean to excuse such practices, but they certainly demand recognition as attributes of human civilization along with art and music, making culture far more complicated than we commonly acknowledge. Think how much time, effort, and money we expend in dealing with issues we wish would go away—but become more entrenched. Criminalizing a good portion of human behavior is an effective way to make matters worse. One alternative would be to accept our nature for the concoction it is, such as it is, and deal with that reality rather than attempt to deny or suppress it.

I regard the restless or haphazard quality of mental events as trying to tell me something about how my mind works. I attribute that seeming randomness to a hunger in my own mind for an understanding of novel phenomena to be achieved through creative interpretation of my personal experience. After all, I have become highly vigilant in keeping track of novel incidents as I do, so I am far more alert than I would be if such incidents never took place. That may not be the law-and-order way to proceed, but it is the creative and adventurous way to deal with whatever comes to mind, even if it means going where no man has gone before. As always, for the empirical mind, life is an ongoing experiment entailing some peril.

What if we made allowances for a certain amount of noise in the system—any system we feel is important to an organized life or society? Is terrorism just so much white noise in the background of the culture we have built around ourselves? No one would categorize the felling of the Twin Towers as background noise, nor could anyone predict that crashing two planes into them would trigger such a catastrophe. The terrorist attack on that day was extremely violent, but not as disorderly as it seemed at the time. It got our attention, so we had a chance to take a closer look at the message the hijackers sent, which was: "We take offense at your flaunting your obscene Western ways in our Islamic homeland!" Instead of dealing with that message, we initiated two preemptive wars, which compounded the damage to ourselves and millions of innocent parties, bringing us to the verge of moral and financial bankruptcy because such wars are unwinnable in being sinks that will absorb whatever we throw into them by way of personnel, arms, money, allies, outrage, or good intentions.

We fought those wars in Afghanistan and Iraq on metaphorical grounds, grounds that focused on our pain and desire for revenge instead of what really happened in New York on September 11, 2001. But we have found that there is no winning a fight against glorious-martyr wannabes. Here we are, playing *Hamlet* on a stage a thousand miles wide, building to a final scene with bodies of the good and the innocent lying among a sprinkling of bad actors, everyone stressed and angry, no one understanding *what* has happened, or *why* it has happened. What we do know, however, is that we made it happen the way it did by putting ourselves into the fight the way we did, as we put ourselves into the Spanish-American War, Korean War, Vietnam War, the war against drugs, war against crime, war against indecency, war against abortion, and all other challenges we structure in terms of militant metaphors.

Categorizing and interpreting phenomena more-or-less metaphorically as we do, we can turn an event or situation into anything that serves our private agenda at the time. That agenda might well be to make ourselves look good in bad times, such as Exxon and BP tried to do with public relations campaigns during their respective oil spills. Propaganda in wartime is meant to play up defenders of the homeland as heroic gods, demean enemy forces as vermin or some kind of noxious disease. Political campaigns bring out the same partisan fervor, distorting an opponent's record to demonstrate his lack of stature, canonizing the party favorite as statesman of the people. The fact that political parties can get away with such bald tactics as often as they do is proof that voters themselves play the metaphor game in their own heads, manipulating their proclaimed reality in conformity with preconceived notions expressed as metaphors. It takes one metaphorical mind to appreciate another. That's just how the game of democracy is played. As the games of advertising and public relations are played, tongue-in-cheek to some extent, but self-righteously and ruthlessly all the way. Political campaigns have become exercises in public relations that drape the home candidate in flattering metaphors, his or her opponent in slanderous conceits. Increasingly, character assassination is the name of the game. Aggressive and unethical candidates can win by smearing their opponents to make them seem unelectable. It costs a bundle to fund such campaigns, so the spoils of office tend to accrue to the candidate with the wealthiest backers, who expect to be repaid a thousand-fold for their good-faith investment.

Based on metaphors of one's choosing, the real power of the mind becomes apparent in campaigns to influence or control other minds. Politicians do it, college professors do it, grade school teachers do it, entertainers do it, writers do it, film directors do it, businessmen do it, corporations do it, parents do it, advertisers do it—all people do it every day of their lives. To hold someone's attention is to captivate his mind. We are all out to change other people's minds to our liking. Figuratively, we want them to see the world through our eyes, hear it through our ears, touch it with our fingers, so when they act, they act *as if* they were us—to our advantage, as it were, always for our own good. As Aram Roston remarks in "How Bloomberg Does Business," "'Mind share' is the current term of art for brand awareness in the marketplace" (*The Nation,* Feb. 28, 2011, p. 12). Our minds are for sale to the highest bidder, or that's how we appear to be viewed. Teachers get paid to influence young minds as society directs them to, so education has become politicized on federal, state, and local levels. Throughout most of history, people have been illiterate; now we say success in life depends on literacy. But literacy is tricky business because it can put metaphors into our minds for reasons that others decide, reasons which are more for their good than ours. Metaphors are frequently used to propagate one faith or another, in such cases the business of words being to assert a certain power over impressionable minds.

Education is big business, and everyone in that business is a practitioner of mind control by one system or another. Politicians want people to express a mental preference for themselves above all other candidates for office. Businessmen want people to buy the products they make or offer for sale, and buying, like voting, is an expression of mental preference. Parents raise their children to do as they are told, a dictum resisted by independent young minds subject to a wide range of influences, so a good share of parenthood is devoted to tactics of mental domination.

Cooperation (as opposed to control) is based on a meeting of different minds based on synchrony between those minds' respective loops of engagement concerning a common issue or project. Teaming up is a major part of conscious life. It does not require full agreement on every part of a project, but it does take coordination and interaction between people to get a job done. Complementarity between cooperators is the key to such projects, each contributing in his or her own way to the success of the whole, even though each cooperator is unique and may not fully agree with the others. Specialization, that is, is key to the smooth running of any group or society. Personal differences need not gum up the works if they are acknowledged, and more importantly, respected or even affirmed. That way, each contributes to the common cause as she is able while retaining her personal sense of identity and integrity. In place of "don't ask, don't tell," I prefer the more transparent approach of "acknowledge, affirm, and respect."

Things go wrong when one mind among the cooperators dictates to other minds how they should do their jobs. It makes sense at the outset of a project to sign up people who are fully capable of doing what is expected of them, leaving the finer details of how that might be done to each individual. Sharing of mutual respect is key to all cooperative ventures. When respect is withdrawn because of differences in personal style or belief, then rivalry or resentment is apt to emerge, leading to conflict, hurt feelings, fear, and perhaps anger. The project is disrupted, cooperation gives way to factions, and common cause is stalled in its tracks.

As I see it from my individual perspective, the drive to dominate others' minds for personal advantage is at the heart of entrepreneurship and our capitalist version of democracy, including the notions of corporate personhood and the spending of money as a variant of free speech. Capitalism sets up two classes of people: owners and workers. Because owners have wealth, workers have jobs—we take that as the desirable state of affairs. Getting a job means working for somebody else. Owners, on the other hand, are seen as public benefactors in keeping workers off the streets and public dole. This formula gives all power and all virtue to owners, to whom workers owe the duty of arriving on time, working hard, not complaining, and being grateful for regular paychecks. But as company men, workers lose the right to exercise their own minds, which is more than any man or woman should bargain away for the sake of employment. The powerful have always depended on the labor of others—spouses, children, servants, minions, slaves, laborers, stewards, consultants, staff, hands, and all the rest. Bodily control depends ultimately on mind control, so workers are expected to devote their lives to the welfare of those they have the privilege of serving (from Latin *servus*, slave). The economy is designed to justify such a situation as being true to the reality of how life really works—as if individuals were born to one class or the other as children of the owning or of the laboring class—an idea whose time should have come and gone long ago.

Adopting a particular currency as an agreed-upon medium of exchange has unintended consequences far beyond the demise of the barter system, and the accrual of personal and national wealth. Money becomes the great enabler, the cultural equivalent of potential energy. With it, you can do anything you want. You can buy a toothbrush with money, a loaf of bread, a Glock 19 9mm semiautomatic pistol, a stash of heroin. Money comes to mean all things to all people. It has become not only one value among many, but the *prime* value of all values. As such, money preempts the mind, shoving all lesser values aside. Money is now what land (territory) used to be. It is Earth liquefied for easy acquisition. As our capitalistic economy reveals, money has become the most powerful force on Earth. Without it, you not only lose your dignity—you cease to exist. Bill Clinton's embrace of the coded expression, "It's the economy, stupid," tells the whole story about our modern state of mind.

All of us are victims of other minds thinking they know what is good for us, minds backed by wealth or power of office that can drive *their* thoughts into *our* heads through legislation, speeches, news stories, books, articles, public relations campaigns, advertisements, social networks, tweets and text messages, films, recorded voices, billboards, editorials, paychecks, bribes, and every other weapon of mind control ever devised. It is no accident that the masterminds of electronic media make billions of dollars by enabling and peddling means for others to influence our minds and behavior. As I have written, the media exist to direct our attention to whatever messages the powerful want to insert in our heads. That is where abusive power lies, in controlling the public mind, which includes both you, me, and everyone we love.

Introspection is our best defense in helping us to know our own minds before alien forces take them over. Imagine a state outlawing independent thought. Stifling a free press is one thing in foreign lands, but inserting ideas directly into gullible minds is with us to-day. I don't have to single out Muammar Qaddafi's suppression of his own people, the US midterm election of 2010 is all the proof I need to back up that statement, followed by the most lucrative movies at the box office, and by the ranks of arch-extremists already among us. The best defense is for us to manage our own minds on a high level of discernment that the powers cannot reach because they are no match for that amount of specific detail and conviction. The takeover has begun with the naïve and gullible as the first target be-cause they are the easiest to reach and cheapest to persuade. Their minds are already predisposed to the ultra-orthodox metaphors they want to hear. Those who strive to engage their worlds on the finest level of detail they can manage will be the last to surrender.

If I sound peevish or cranky in delivering these words, that's an apt description of the persona I fall prone to in thinking about the corrupting influence of free enterprise on the American mind. I find our national progress stymied, our so-called democracy balked.

My message in writing this book is that my loop of engagement is *my* loop of engagement. I am responsible both for how I see the world and for how I act in that world. Not that I created myself as I am, but as the end result of the complex series of events and count-less interactions that have led to my being the person I am, I bear responsibility for how I make myself happen in my world. The most essential part of my education has been the games I played as a child, which taught me to follow the rules of play, to be transparent and aboveboard, to take turns with others as equals, to specialize on what I do best, to team up, and above all to have fun. All cultures play games, just as all cultures make music. We have much to learn by paying attention to what we already know without realizing it.

I see treating fellow citizens as a mass market to be tapped for personal benefit as antithetical to what I regard as the true nature of each person as an experiment in individuality and self-determination. As such, our goal is to complement, not compete with or dominate one another. Our dignity as persons stems directly from our uniqueness, not our naïve gullibility, which may have a certain innocent charm, but leaves us vulnerable to hostile takeovers by other minds.

The general welfare is best improved by each of us having equal opportunity to conduct her own affairs without falling prey to those who would use us for selfish purposes. Introspection shows me that individual opportunity is not only possible, but is the desirable state of affairs in which we thrive on the basis of our mental skills and effort, not our vulnerability or submission. In a democracy, it is an oxymoron to conduct our affairs by seeking to take advantage of our peers. True power is the power of the individual to lead her own life as her unique self, not as who others tell her she should be. Self-determination, in my book (which this is), is the source of individual personal power. It requires not only empathy and compassion, but agreement that our uniqueness is our gift and our strength.

Through introspection, I find in myself the power to engage the world and make myself happen on my terms, not those dictated by others—without infringing on others' ability to do the same. If conflicts occur (as they do), we need to find ways to complement one another, not dominate or subdue those who differ from us. My personal fulfillment comes from dealing with values radiating from my core self, not those imposed upon me from the outside. The story of my life is told by the engagements I have achieved with situations I have really cared about at the time. I always move on from there, but in the heat of the moment, I know how I feel, what my values are, what I care about, and what I have to do to be fully myself. No one else knows me from the inside as I know myself. If that inside work is to be done, I am the only one qualified to do it. Or if I don't feel up to the job, then I need to qualify myself by doing the work I have to do to get ready, and accrue the experience I need to get ahead in my own life. Ahead in an internal, not an external sense. Which is my judgment call, not anyone else's. Personal judgment is our greatest treasure, which I see aggressive powers trying to influence, suppress, or deny us.

True power comes from keeping myself on track to becoming the person I am determined to be, which I realize by working on the projects I have set myself for achieving that end. Such power is not the power of contentment but the power to engage my situation as I am able. Not ten years from now, but in the coming minute, then the minute after that. Grand plans for the future are hard to realize, so effort has to go toward taking next steps. This is done by engaging the world *where* I am, *when* I am there, so my actions are concrete and specific, not diffuse and abstract. True power is now, right here, not sometime later, somewhere else. That's what I mean by putting my body where my values are in making myself happen as I do.

Seize the moment, I say; do it!—that is the power of the loop of engagement. That puts me on the leading edge of my own life, where even if I fail, I gain the most learning, equipping me for doing better the next time around. Staying on the leading edge of experience is the key to every engagement, which is precisely where assertive others don't want me to be because they want me to further *their* cause, not my own. But whose life am I leading if not mine? What's the point of following someone else in leading *their* life as they desire me to? No, introspection tells me I have to do the heavy lifting for myself. If I don't try, how will I learn to make myself happen through my own powers, not good fortune, not someone else's beneficence?

Uprisings such as the Arab Spring and Occupy Wall Street movement announce the time has come for excluded peoples around the world to stand against oppressive elites by making themselves happen in new ways. Confrontation, like novelty, spurs consciousness. On a national scale, it can prompt not only sports mania but protests and revolutions. The American Dream is more a yearning for personal liberty, justice, and equality than for comfort and prosperity.

I can easily take a detour through a landscape featuring all the wrong ways to lead a life. My thoughts have headed me on that path several times in these pages. Look, there's the economy asking me to become a consumer of goods and services provided by others; there's a political system dunning me into becoming a party member to support a platform written by people whose motives I can't know and have no reason to trust; there's an educational system that instead of helping students become themselves, spouts high rhetoric about our civic duty to support the economy, meet industry's needs, and cram for standardized tests; there's a legal system claiming corporations have the rights of individuals, and even worse, that money is a form of free speech!; and over there is a religious enclave devoted to perpetuating beliefs from the distant past in far-away places.

The one thing these landscapes have in common is omitting the facts of your and my personal existence and experience, so since they are directed toward the public at large, they leave you and me out of their plans by default. I have no choice but to find my way on my own as directed by the personal pursuit of discovery and understanding, for by following the conventional way, I find I am turned into someone I don't recognize as myself. That is, myself as introspection shows me to be, the one person on Earth I am intimately acquainted with, the one having the power to make myself happen as I choose—again, as long as I don't impair anyone else's power to do the same. From my philosophical days, I recall what existential philosopher Nicola Abbagnano called an *authentic* possibility in allowing choices to be made without curtailing future options. With seven billion minds making choices for themselves, the only power that will work for us all must work on that authentic or complementary level of choice. In living for ourselves, we must live in equal degree for our brothers and sisters. Or as the Hippocratic oath puts it, we must strive to "do no harm" to others.

The power of personal engagement is the power of constructive mental life. Without it, we become droids serving other minds in other bodies and other places. The point of active engagement is not to increase our levels of wealth, comfort, and power, but to push on to a level of discernment providing a grasp of our current reality based on personal values, feelings, and judgments. If we can keep up such engagement long enough, we maintain a balance between our inner and outer worlds, allowing us to fit ourselves to our current situations as effectively as possible. I see introspection as a means of getting us into that position through insights we can achieve in no other way than by overseeing our own personal efforts.

The most telling feature I have discovered in my mind through introspection is the level of discernment I will settle for in interpreting complex and kinetic phenomena over a period of time. Many of the incidents I have examined in these pages reveal hasty judgments based on first impressions. Upon further investigation, the metaphorical nature of my assumed reality is revealed. It takes a while for the full power of my mind to kick in through continued engagement with particular situations. If I am to act appropriately, I have to give myself time to form an adequate judgment concerning the makeup of that situation—which is always more complicated than I assume at first take.

Compare that finding with mobs responding in fervor to bumper-sticker slogans chanted over and over again, arms linked, fists raised in the air, eager to storm the Bastille. Or, again, with families passively watching TV shows in the comfort of their homes, taking in every word and gesture without being able to do anything but eat chips and drink soda, watching the passing scene while being unable to participate in any meaningful way, which is precisely the point of mass entertainment—to sell particular brands of chips and soda. To remove Mubarak from the scene, Egyptians of all persuasions had to gather in Cairo's Tahrir Square and speak for themselves individually, not as a mob. Every protester I heard interviewed on BBC said her piece in her own voice; together they sang the chorus of personal freedom, as America, arms merchant to Mubarak, looked on from a safe distance.

The coursing of our loops of engagement tells us who we are. If we think we live in the real world without our minds interceding for us, we leave our own uniqueness out of the picture, which I believe to be the greatest yet most common error we can make in living our lives, leaving us unprotected from manipulation by those who would control us for their profit. Which is how fads spread by our buying things we think we have to have in a show of belonging to the current rage. Fads are campaigns by others wanting to sell us things we don't like and don't need. If we follow the trend, then we become creatures of those who perpetrate the new style or latest gadget, essentially submitting to their campaigns to dominate our minds and actions for their benefit. People camp out in store parking lots to be first on the scene when the doors open, wanting more to belong than to be themselves, or thinking they can only become themselves by belonging to others. "Had to have it" is admission of a severe habit or addiction of mind, which is precisely the point our controllers would bring us to in getting us to meet *their* needs, not our own. There's always a nice man ready to sell us a new supply of drugs, a new car, a new home we don't need and can't afford.

America has become a nation feeding on itself, and through global entrepreneurship, feeding on the people of other nations, and on Earth itself. That realization is the upshot of my little experiment in introspection, for by following the exploits of my personal loop of engagement, I have developed a perspective from which to observe others engaged in the process of leading their lives as they do. What I discover is a rage for using other people for personal advantage, which seems to have become the American way of seizing power and wealth through declaring war on other minds in the modern version of colonial rule through aggression and economic might. How many times do we have to learn that colonial rule and mind control are disasters requiring centuries to overcome—when we aren't sure we have that much time left to us?

We appear to be a nation of slow learners. Just as those who put their faith in rote recital of ancient texts are apt to be slow learners. As are ultra-orthodox traditionalists, authoritarians, bigots, opinionated pundits, self-proclaimed experts, and the horde of those dependent on other minds to tell them what to do.

For me, writing this book is an adventure in exploring what it means to be different from everyone else on Earth, and in recognizing that difference as the basis of the true, personal, mental power by which I lead the life that I do. I now appreciate the folly of belief in corporate personhood; money as a form of free speech; the notion that anyone can truly represent the interests of anyone else; the existence of a universal reality; the appearance of humanity in the mass as anything but an illusion; and strength residing in our sameness, not our diversity. If we are equal, it is in our uniqueness, and in sharing the equivalent challenge of fulfilling ourselves, which each must do for herself.

We all begin in the same way, summoned by a man and a woman who for reasons of their own initiate the process of embryogenesis, usually in her womb, from which we emerge some nine moons later as unique beings consisting of a small body and an outlook upon a certain time and place on this Earth. We find ourselves in circumstances we engage as best we can through a series of successive approximations that is our life, continuing until we can no longer find the energy to keep up our end of the engagement. Between our beginnings and our ends, the chief source of continuity is the outlook we bring with us as unique individuals. In my case, that outlook is the subject of my introspective research into how I construct a meaningful world around myself, and engage that world in such a way to make myself happen as I do. It always surprises me how little attention some of us give to the leading role we play in enacting our own lives—*as if* life were a summer stock drama that makes us happen instead of being the result of the ongoing engagement with our surroundings that is our primary business as unique individuals. No one has the power to make us happen as we desire except ourselves.

Through introspection, I find my personal power stems from my uniqueness, and our collective power stems from our diversity in each one of us suiting him- or herself to a particular situation by means of a personal loop of engagement with that situation. Freedom, that is, flows within my inner horizon as a gift to myself, and is nothing I can receive from any external power or reality. Others may hamper me, but they cannot give me freedom. If I am to be free, I have to make myself free inside-out. Which I can do only by getting to know my capabilities through introspection because the recipe for freedom exists in my mind, not in world documents or institutions.

In promoting introspection as a way of getting to know one's own mind, I am not suggesting yet another means of mind control by which I expect you to come up with conclusions similar to those I have set down in these pages. I can only expect your findings to differ from mine in echoing the fact of our diversity. Which is all to the good in that your situations are different from the ones I meet in myself, and to suitably adapt to those situations we need to marshal our own mental forces. The best protection against hostile corporate takeovers of our minds and concerns is to make sure we are free in our own minds to conduct our loops of engagement according to the personal interests, feelings, and values we discover through commitment to an open-ended course of personal introspection.

What I recommend is that readers make a short list of incidents drawn from their personal experience that share three qualities of saliency in being *alluring, memorable,* and yet *mysterious.* Which in my case comes down to the inexplicable yet emotionally-charged mistakes I have made in living my life. Try it: Admit your mental mistakes so you can learn from them. Above all, don't deny them, or you'll learn nothing. They're yours; own up to them. Make something of them as I have done here so you can make something of yourself. I suggest you regard such incidents in your own mind from different perspectives such as those I have applied to incidents from my own life—or in light of whatever perspectives reflect your personal understanding of the workings of your own mind—to see how you interpret sensory patterns on actual occasions, how you understand your mental handiwork, how you feel about the results, and so on around the stages in your personal loop of engagement with specific situations in your own life. Whatever system you use, the goal is to acknowledge as many facets of your mind as possible in developing insights into the processes behind your making yourself happen on specific occasions as you do.

I think it important to pay particular attention to your mental state every day upon first awakening, and to the remnants of receding dreams. This will expand your appreciation for the hidden depths of

your mind, which are just as much yours as your open-eyed awareness. With experience in introspection behind you, turn your gaze
outward to see how others are getting on in a culture featuring an
economy fostering dominance of the many by the few, and see if that
culture represents your interests in growing into the person you hope
to become. Look carefully at the level of detail you account for in
discerning your personal reality to see if you can dig any deeper to
make sure you've hit rock-bottom certainty that you have the full
story. If, on circumstantial grounds, you think m-o-o-n spells banana,
check it out to see if you are right. By then, you will be well on your
way to making yourself happen in the world on the basis of a fuller
understanding of the processes by which you facilitate that work for
yourself. I don't offer any guarantee, but I will make the prediction
that based on increased self-knowledge, you will be enjoying new-
found mental powers and having—literally and metaphorically—the
time of your life. O

APPENDIX

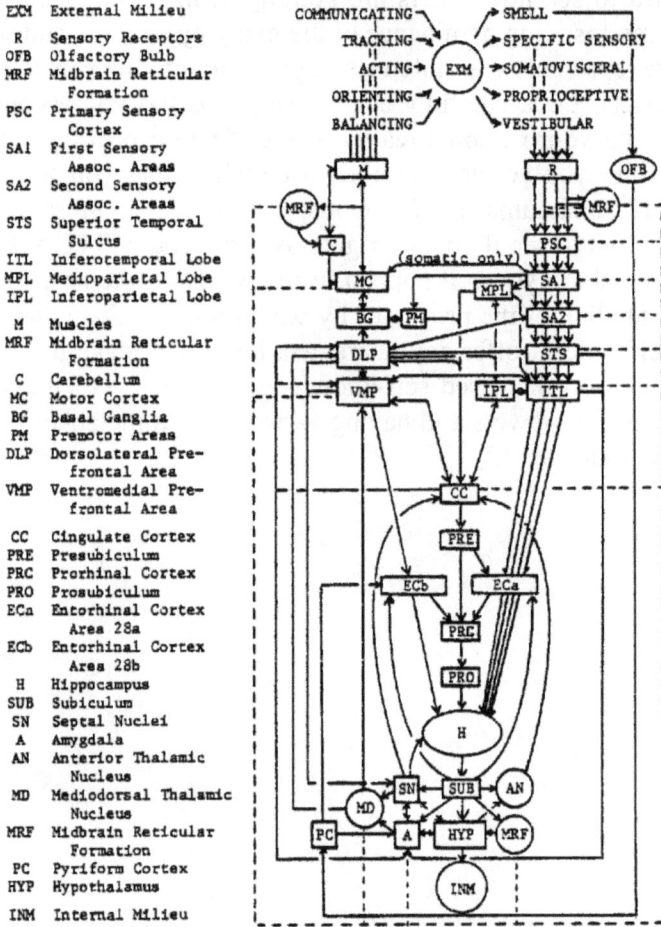

EXM	External Milieu
R	Sensory Receptors
OFB	Olfactory Bulb
MRF	Midbrain Reticular Formation
PSC	Primary Sensory Cortex
SA1	First Sensory Assoc. Areas
SA2	Second Sensory Assoc. Areas
STS	Superior Temporal Sulcus
ITL	Inferotemporal Lobe
MPL	Medioparietal Lobe
IPL	Inferoparietal Lobe
M	Muscles
MRF	Midbrain Reticular Formation
C	Cerebellum
MC	Motor Cortex
BG	Basal Ganglia
PM	Premotor Areas
DLP	Dorsolateral Prefrontal Area
VMP	Ventromedial Prefrontal Area
CC	Cingulate Cortex
PRE	Presubiculum
PRC	Prorhinal Cortex
PRO	Prosubiculum
ECa	Entorhinal Cortex Area 28a
ECb	Entorhinal Cortex Area 28b
H	Hippocampus
SUB	Subiculum
SN	Septal Nuclei
A	Amygdala
AN	Anterior Thalamic Nucleus
MD	Mediodorsal Thalamic Nucleus
MRF	Midbrain Reticular Formation
PC	Pyriform Cortex
HYP	Hypothalamus
INM	Internal Milieu

Figure 5. The routing of sensory pathways within the brain.

Schematic diagram of motor (left) and sensory (right) pathways in the neural substrate of the mind (i.e., the brain). The External Milieu (EXM) represents the external, physical substrate of the mind. Mind itself arises from connections in the lower portion of the diagram, the loop of engagement resulting from a clockwise flow of neural energy through the complex seat of consciousness. Note the several upper pathways linking sensory and motor areas of the brain directly, bypassing consciousness (INM). (Perrin, S.G., *Metaphor to Mythology: Experience as a Resonant Synthesis of Meaning and Being*, University Microfilms International, 1983, page 635).

272

FURTHER READING

I belong to no school of introspectors and follow no exemplar in my empirical research. But introspection is a large field represented by a great many individual practitioners. Beyond those who have conducted formal self-analyses such as Sigmund Freud and Carl Jung, or participated in psychoanalysis mediated by others, everyone who makes herself happen in the world as guided by her personal affect and values is a practicing introspector. Artists exercise their unique loops of engagement in creating their bodies of work. Emily Dickinson worked inside-out in that way, as did Marcel Proust, E. E. Cummings, Hieronymus Bosch, Johann Sebastian Bach, Hector Berlioz, and just about every other creative person I know of. They might not have recognized themselves as introspectors, but within their respective mediums of expression, they all succeeded in externalizing significant facets of their interior selves.

As products of their authors' loops of engagement, autobiographies, novels, plays, and poems are outward and visible signs of a creative mix of inner turmoil, emotion, insight, and harmony. Even Buddhism is a product of looping engagements governed by training and meditation. You know all this. If art or any human endeavor speaks to us, it is because people recognize their inner selves in its striving, deeds, and creativity. But there is a crucial difference between others and yourself: with others, you have *their* deeds, words, and behavior; with yourself, you have access to the actual process of making sense of *your* life experience. Borrowing from Gandhi, the challenge is to become the change you seek—yes, in the world—but first in yourself. That is, through self-knowledge and extensive practice, to make yourself fit for the life you want to lead.

In my own introspective research, I have been moved more by incidents such as those I include in Chapter 1 than by understandings achieved in other minds. I have proceeded inside-out almost the whole way. Which is an arduous method, yet it is my chosen way because I have ready access to no other situated mind than my own.

Over the years, I have found sympathetic engagement with works by the following authors, among many others:

Henry David Thoreau—*Walden, or, Life in the Woods* (1854).

Emily Dickinson—*The Complete Poems of Emily Dickinson* (1960; poems written 1850–1886).

William James—*The Principles of Psychology* (1890); *The Varieties of Religious Experience* (1902).

Hans Vaihinger—*The Philosophy of 'as if': A System of the Theoretical, Practical and Religious Fictions of Mankind* (1924).

Marcel Proust—Remembrance of Things Past (1934).

E. E. Cummings—*i: six nonlectures* (1951).

Michael Polanyi—*Personal Knowledge: Towards a Post-Critical Philosophy* (1958).

Maurice Merleau-Ponty—*Phenomenology of Perception* (1962).

Joseph Campbell—*The Masks of God,* encompassing four volumes: 1) *Primitive Mythology* (1959), 2) *Oriental Mythology* (1962), 3) *Occidental Mythology* (1964), 4) *Creative Mythology* (1968).

Joseph LeDoux—*The Emotional Brain: The Mysterious Underpinnings of Emotional Life* (1996); *Synaptic Self: How Our Brains Become Who We Are* (2002).

Gerald M. Edelman—*Bright Air, Brilliant Fire: On the Matter of the Mind* (1994); *Wider than the Sky: The Phenomenal Gift of Consciousness* (2004); with Giulio Tononi, *A Universe of Consciousness: How Matter Becomes Imagination* (2000).

We all know full well what consciousness is—life impinging on our awareness, and ourselves doing the best we can to hold our own. But to actually describe the process of being mentally and emotionally aware is a daunting challenge at best. If nothing else, such books as I have listed make clear what we are up against in trying to understand, account for, or even describe the nature of our own minds. ○

GLOSSARY

Abstract and Concrete—These are mental qualities that define a continuum of awareness from the sensory, detailed, clearly seen, and specific to the conceptual, schematic, known about, and general. These qualities distinguish two aspects of mind, the sensory and the conceptual, allowing in turn either direct acquaintance in personal experience, or a more distant *familiarity with* or *knowledge about.* The English verb *to know* covers the full spectrum between knowing through personal acquaintance and knowing about by reputation.

Accommodation—Enlarging understanding in the mind to allow for (accommodate) new learning incommensurate with the old order of knowing. Expanding the mind. (*See* Assimilation.)

Action—Appropriate muscular activity (behavior) as the end point toward which consciousness aims. A large part of unconscious mental activity is directed toward achieving smoothly coordinated bodily behaviors representing deliberate intent.

Affect—Feeling and emotion taken together, as opposed to thinking or cognition. Allied to aesthetic appreciation.

Appetites—We value that which satisfies our drives, motives, and yearnings. It is often hard to tell whether a value or an appetite is acquired or innate. Different people vary in the relative strengths of the pleasures they seek and discomforts avoid. (*See* Values.)

Assimilation—Fitting new learning to the existing order of one's knowledge and understanding. (*See* Accommodation.)

Attention—The capability of consciousness to place one aspect or another of a situation under focal observation.

Awareness—Mindfulness. The mental capacity to pay attention to a scene or particular facet of consciousness.

Behavior—Overt physical gestures (including speech acts), postures, and deeds by which we engage other persons and the world.

Being—That which *is* or *exists* in conscious awareness, and may or may not exist apart from human experience. Being is not a property of objects; it is bestowed by consciousness through recognition. That which we are not aware of does not exist for us until we learn otherwise. Gods exist in the mind along with rainbows, atoms, virtues, and other conceptual ideas.

Bioenergetic Reality—Our sense of reality is based on an exchange of energy between the biological systems which we are with their surroundings which we are not. That exchange has the quality of being both biological and energetic, hence is referred to as being *bioenergetic.* The loops of engagement I propose here are bioenergetic systems primarily responsible for our participatory, bioenergetic sense of reality. When we sleep, that reality goes into remission; when we die, it comes to an end. These thoughts

275

came to me while considering the different media in which our internal and external realities exist. The currency of external reality includes radiant energy and molecular matter; that of internal reality is the flow of ions across cell membranes and of molecules across synapses from one nerve cell to another. The latter is the medium giving rise to our minds; the former is the medium of life itself. In my view, consciousness is kindled by discrepancies revealed by comparing incoming sensory signals against outgoing motor signals in the brain, the disparity between them providing the signal of which we become aware. For humans, inner reality is prime, and outer reality is derived through mental construction.

Categorization—The sorting of sensory phenomena as instances of conceptual categories derived from earlier experiences of a similar nature, or from such categories as defined and/or described by others. The process of deciding what sort of thing a phenomenon *is*. Synonyms include recognition, identification, interpretation, and assimilation. *Kategoria* in Greek refers to assertions or predications, so categorization includes acts of predication, which are basic to syntax and to speech itself. The Latin equivalent of *kategoria* is *praedicamentum,* meaning predicament, based on *praedicare,* to proclaim or predicate; that which is proclaimed about the subject of an utterance. Categorization, then, is fundamental to language.

Category Error—Sorting a phenomenon into an inappropriate conceptual category. Also called miscategorization, misidentification, misinterpretation. All of which imply standards or conventions for assigning identities. Mistaken identification.

Coherence—A judgment that all subsystems of the mind are working together in a concerted, coordinated, or harmonious manner. This is particularly relevant to the loop of engagement which comprises so many dimensions of awareness. (*See* Integrity.)

Concrete—(*See* Abstract.)

Conflict—(From Latin *confligere,* to come to blows.) Disagreements in perspective, attitude, understanding, assumptions, or values between different minds, or within a single mind.

Consciousness—(*See* Bioenergetic Reality; Loop of Engagement.) Venue of human experience. Here, the sum of all facets and dimensions of a person's inner awareness. Commonly used in reference to the capability of being aware. Consciousness exists in different modalities including dreaming, daydreaming, thinking, feeling, imagining, anticipating, remembering, and so on. In practical terms, consciousness maintains our participation in the bioenergetic reality we cooperatively maintain with our surroundings via our loops of engagements' interactions with a world we cannot know in-or-of itself.

Construction—That which is construed or interpreted on the basis of personal experience. (*See* Construe.)

Construe—To construct or interpret for oneself. Suggested by such phrases as: What I make of it; How I see it; It seems to me, It strikes me.

Decision—A judgment by the mind's evaluative faculty leading to clarity about how to proceed regarding particular issues offering a variety of alternatives within a given situation.

Discernment, Level of Discernment—The fineness of detail accounted for in categorizing a phenomenon as an instance of a type or class of conceptual experience. Phenomena feature specific sensory qualities or details; categories group similar phenomena sharing a specifiable set of common features. A duck can be classed as a thing, a being, a living being, a bird, a winged biped, or perhaps a juvenile male eider.

Drives—(*See* Appetites, Values.)

Education—(From Latin *educare,* to draw out or lead forth; the opposite of to lay on or impose.) The issue is: What proportion of a child's education is meant to empower her self-determination, and what proportion is set by the needs, wishes, or beliefs of her family or community? That is, where do personal freedom, temperament, and inclination fit into the curriculum?

Emergent Property—A quality or property that arises from or becomes evident in a system of which it is not a basic constituent. Life is an emergent property of matter and energy taken together under specifiable conditions. Consciousness is an emergent property of energy interacting with the embodied brain, again under specific conditions. Neuroscientists are trying to discover what such conditions are or might be.

Emotion—Neurotransmitters and hormones exert a strong affective influence on the workings of the mind, drawing attention to and heightening particular aspects of mental awareness, placing emphasis on or recommending certain courses of action. Examples include fear, anger, happiness, sadness, joy, excitement, wonder, loathing, and despair.

Empiricism; Empirical Method—Understanding gained through personal sensory observation or practical experience, as distinct from theory. Here, the method of introspection. Trial and error.

Energy—(Derived from the Indo-European root *werg-*, meaning to work or to do.) Used here in reference to the conversion of nervous energy into force or motion through behavior, and the conversion of radiant and sound energy to nervous energy, enabling sensory phenomena to appear in awareness.

Environment, Surroundings—The setting, milieu, or situation that a person can physically interact with. These days that territory reaches as far as a cellphone can carry your voice.

Evolution—Changes in the genomes of those best fitted to their environmental niches as expressed through characteristics of their physical descendants.

Experience—Implies both remembrance and strong emotion. That which happens in a lifetime of consciousness. Mental life as an ongoing process made possible by our loops of engagement. The vehicle of empirical trial, error, and observation; the object of introspection. The outstanding emergent property of the human brain.

Feeling—As I use the term, the polarity or valence with which a mental event is received by the mind, incurring an attitude of affirmation or suspicion, like or dislike, acceptance or rejection. Determinant of mind and behavior.

Gesture—A deliberate bodily movement meant to affect or respond to events in one's situation or external environment.

Goals—We make ourselves happen in the world by setting goals that challenge the current version of who we are, inviting us to work at becoming the person we want to be. Based on prior experience, we pull our minds forward through our own efforts, inventing the future at the same time we reinvent ourselves as its inhabitants. Goals emerge from tensions between our values and current situations which fail to meet the expectations we hold for ourselves, inciting us to bring about new situations in which we picture ourselves doing better. Working toward goals stirs up hope and endurance. Goals enable purposive behavior.

Habit—A routine repeated so many times its performance becomes automatic or unconscious. Riding a bicycle, say, or playing Ping-Pong become so ingrained that the skills they entail can be picked up after years of disuse. Also drug dependency as an alternative to constructive behavior.

Integrity—Taken literally, the word means untouched in the sense of being sound, whole, intact, and reliable. Applied to the mind, it suggests all facets working together in harmony without conflict or confusion. The opposite state would be a mind at odds with itself. In practical situations, integrity supports judgment that the way ahead is clear. (*See* Coherence.)

Intentionality—The seemingly objective quality of consciousness in always being *of* one thing or another. Intentionality applies to phenomena as they are categorized by the mind. That is, to novel or unique sensory phenomena as sorted into preexisting conceptual classes, and is not a property of phenomena in themselves. Conceptualized phenomena bear the label of the category, not that of the sensory presentation. This book is largely about the difficulty of sorting phenomena into appropriate conceptual categories, and the learning that results from confronting that fact.

Interoception—The origin of sensory phenomena can be internal as well as external. Refers to sensory stimulation arising in the body's interior, such as abdominal pain, migraine headaches, sciatica, toothaches, breathlessness, among many others.

Interpretation—(*See* Categorization.) I prefer to use interpretation because it emphasizes the subjective nature of the process by which identity is ascribed to phenomena. A phenomenon is a fundamental presentation of sensory stimulation; a category is a mid-level interpretation of a phenomenon; understanding is a high-order, abstract interpretation of a field of categorized phenomena.

Introspection—(From Latin *introspicere,* to look within.) The directing of attention inward toward salient features of personal consciousness. Awareness of awareness itself as a facet of mind. Often coupled to assumptions about a causal reality being responsible for mental representations. Questioning such assumptions, and recognizing the crucial role of the human brain and sensory system in maintaining inner awareness, phenomenologists begin with phenomena as original presentations, and work outward from there. That is the approach I take here, that the true beginning of consciousness is in sensory phenomena, which the mind sorts into categories derived from experience with similar phenomena in the past, constructing an understanding of a world beyond the sensory horizon, a world created by the ongoing operation of a loop of engagement with a world that can be known only indirectly, but not as it is in-and-of itself.

Judgment—The mind brings its evaluative faculty to bear on whatever options it has for deciding how best to proceed. "All things considered, this is what I recommend doing,"—that is the mind's judgment speaking. The full breadth of viable options is suggested by that "All things considered" clause. Good judgment reflects wide-ranging consideration; poor judgment reflects hasty or only partial consideration. Judgments are based on preferences attached to different options for action, in turn reflecting personal values applied to particular situations. A precursor to action.

Knowledge—Apart from human consciousness and experience, an inert fiction. That which is known is always known personally by someone unique.

Loop of Engagement—Within a current situation, ambient energy impinges on our sensory organs, leading to formation of phenomena, which are categorized and interpreted within a larger understanding, prompting further nerve activation that is translated into bodily actions announcing our participation in that outward situation. I view the mind as being suspended between two hidden substrates, one external, one internal—the physical world and our physically embodied brain. Lacking direct access to either one, the mind does its best to mediate appropriately between the two in bringing them into accord with each other. I propose that consciousness itself arises from a comparison between physical effort and sensory oversight (analogous to binocular vision arising from the relative displacement of images formed by our two eyes), its job being to reduce the error signal resulting from such a comparison. Various aspects of the loop by which our minds engage the physical environment include attention, sensory awareness, categorization, understanding, values, feeling, emotion, a sense of our situation as understood, judgments, decisions, goals, projects and relationships, planning—all culminating in actions gauged to be appropriate to a particular situation. This loop can be viewed as a serial expansion of the idea of working memory over time in accounting for the flow of both sensory attention and resulting motor performance.

Mapping—A term I adopted from its use by Gerald M. Edelman in reference to reciprocal traffic between different, similarly organized areas of the brain. Edelman's term for such two-way neural traffic is *reentry*. If one area maps color and another shape, then reentry would allow emergence of purple circles and green squares through reciprocal comparison.

Meaning—The fit of a categorized phenomenon within a larger field of understanding at a given level of discernment. The field can be spotty if full of gaps, or coherent if extensive over a wide range of experience.

Memory—The residuum of prior experience coded into the network of neural connections, made retrievable by activation of relevant portions of that network. Working memory holds attention on particular matters for a few

seconds within streaming consciousness, while episodic memories consol-
idated by strong emotions can persist for a lifetime, as can semantic
memories arising from repeated activation.

Metaphor—A novel theory of meaning at a singular node of experience as
seen from the theorist's perspective within a particular situation. Metaphor
reminds us that we live in a fluctuant world of appearances rather than a
literal world of *is*. A way of regarding something in terms of something
else—that is, of seeing one thing *as* another.

Mind—The human faculty of awareness over time as a general capability, or
the content of that faculty at a particular moment. Mental life as a whole.
Sometimes contrasted with matter, but more properly seen as an emergent
property of organic matter arrayed as the most complex physical system in
the known universe—the human brain. (*See* Loop of Engagement.)

Miscategorization—Committing a category error. Unconventional or novel
labeling of a phenomenon. (*See* Category Error.)

Motivation—(*See* Appetites, Values.)

Neuron—Basic unit of the nervous system, a single nerve cell consisting of a
cell body, dendrites conducting electric potentials toward the cell body,
and a single axon conducting potentials away from the cell body to multiple synapses with subsequent neurons. Collectively, forming complex neural networks. The human brain contains some 100 billion neurons.

Neuroscience—The concerted discipline of studying the mind by studying
molecular goings-on in the brain, by whatever means are available.

Neurotransmitter—Chemical molecules transferred from one neuron to another across the synapse or junction gap between them, enabling an electric
action potential to move forward in the brain.

Perception—The process by which sensory phenomena are formed. Sometimes including categorization and understanding in the mind.

Perspective—A given mind's situated outlook on experience. The mental
landscape as viewed during a particular instance of consciousness.

Phenomenology—The science of phenomena as providing the basic data on
which all knowing is based. In this case, phenomena are internal to the
mind, not external *as if* in the world.

Phenomenon (pl. Phenomena)—That which appears in the mind via one
sensory modality, or combination of modalities. That *of* which we are
mindful, aware, or conscious. Neither objects nor representations, phenomena are what the mind makes of nervous stimulation set off by energy or
molecules affecting its sensory organs (whether external or internal).

Planning—The mind is nothing if not a person's planning capability for making oneself happen in the world. Based on prior experience, the mind
largely concerns itself with what to do next in a given situation to achieve a
desired result.

Power—Effort directed by: 1) a person toward making herself happen in the
world, 2) supportive others, or 3) those set on controlling people for the
purpose of achieving a personal advantage. In that sense, interpersonal
dominance and submission are major concerns when elevated to a social or

cultural level regarding, for example, class distinctions, religious or political beliefs, relative wealth, legal standing, citizenship, or personal freedoms.

Preconscious—Refers to something once conscious, but subsequently forgotten, perhaps to be recalled through mental effort. I give the example in Chapter 1 of a song I once knew, but can no longer remember yet still have a vague yearning to hear. I also think of the thought kernels I am aware of when I needlessly talk to myself because I already know what I am going to say before I part my lips—these, too, serve as a kind of preformed consciousness. On such occasions I feel, with the poet, that I am peering into a deep well, and below the surface, glimpse something faintly gleaming there, indistinct, yet at least something. (Recall of Frost's poem, "For Once, Then, Something,"—which I haven't thought of in forty years—is an example of preconsciousness kindled by writing this entry.)

Project—(From the Latin verb *proicere,* to throw forward.) A program of personal awareness, concentration, and action directed toward achieving a particular goal. Projects are one way of making ourselves happen in the world according to ongoing dedication to preconceived plans. One type of project is devoted to building and maintaining personal relationships. Projects channel spontaneous energy into a sustained effort to bring about a cumulative effect over time.

Projection—Defensive ascription or attribution of one's own mental characteristics to others. Passing the psychic buck. Inappropriately mapping one thing onto another.

Proprioception—Mental awareness of one's physical position, motion, balance, and orientation in space.

Qualities of Mind—Attributes of consciousness revealed through introspection. Often distinct qualities given by the senses, such as color, motion, direction, texture, size, shape, smoothness, relatedness, pitch, loudness, tone color, sweet, sour, coherence (going together), integrity (wholeness), among many others. Neuroscientists speak of such sensible properties as *qualia* (singular, *quale*).

Reality—Our personal understanding on the highest level of generality of the true nature of things. As I present it, reality is a construction of a situated loop of engagement that is dependent on attention and memory to create awareness consistent with one's deep-rooted identity. (*See* Bioenergetic Reality.)

Recognition—(*See* Categorization.)

Reentry—(*See* Mapping.)

Reflex—An automatic or preprogrammed course of fast and efficient action that bypasses awareness until it is completed.

Relationships—Awareness of spatial or temporal proximity and relatedness between qualities of sensory phenomena. Also, awareness of connections between different people such as family members, friends, colleagues, members of the same or opposite sex, enemies, etc.

Routine—A sequence of actions performed in the same way time and again so it seems to be remembered by the muscles themselves without prompting by long-term memory.

Self—The seat of personal history, values, and feelings in the mind as informed by episodic or autobiographical memory. Familiarity is a quality associated with the self, a sense of being one's own person on her home turf.

Self-Awareness—The awareness is not our reflection in the store window so much as the internal quality of mind that makes us sensitive to how we present and conduct ourselves. Self-awareness is situational in nature, as is the whole of consciousness. Its ever-present quality leads to the illusion of ourselves as little homunculi in the screening room, watching ourselves being ourselves. This is a truly amazing quality of mind—that we can be so self-aware. It allows for self-reflection, introspection, and self-knowledge, always under the influence of our situated perspective upon ourselves. I view these internal mappings back and forth within our minds as reflecting the complex reciprocal connections within the neural networks enabling our minds. Self-awareness is the basis of ethics, moral behavior, guilt, pride, and related human attributes. In my view, self-awareness is fundamental; opposed to any so-called reality we must construct for ourselves.

Self-Consciousness—(*See* Self-Awareness.)

Self-Reflection—Synonym for introspection; contemplating, thinking about, or reflecting on the flow of events in one's mind.

Self-Understanding—(*See* Self-Awareness.)

Sense—(From Latin *sensus,* the mental faculty of feeling, thought, or awareness.) I employ sense in five ways in reference to: 1) sensory faculties (sense of smell), 2) sensory impressions (sense we are not alone), 3) meaning (it makes sense to me), 4) the seeming objectivity or intentionality of consciousness (awareness *of*), and 5) a particular perspective or point of view (in an aesthetic sense, in a physiological sense).

Sensory Pattern/Figure—(*See* Phenomenon.)

Situations—As we are able to construe them, the (local) circumstances with which we interact at any given time. The immediate settings of our minds, awareness, actions, and life. The local universe available and relevant to personal awareness. That which our loops of engagement interact with.

Speech—Energy-efficient shorthand for bolder actions in the world. Speech is code for our mental life short of commitment to a program of action. Speech emerges at an advanced stage of our loops of engagement within particular situations as we experience them, backed by our passions and rhythms of blood and breath. I identify preconscious kernels or nuggets of awareness in myself that provide the foundation for meaningful utterances relevant to particular occasions.

Subjective Awareness—All awareness is not only intentional in being *of* a particular phenomenon or object of attention, but is perspectival in being *from* a particular point of view. The observer is always mentally *situated* as he looks about, while the circumstances at the moment determine his outlook and what he is aware of. We often forget that what we become aware *of* is largely a product of what we are looking *for,* that is, of expectations based on our findings on similar occasions in the past. In that sense, looking about us is influenced by prior experience as preserved in memory. Without doubt, we are situated in the lives we have led, each one unique.

Substrate—An underlying layer or structure upon which something else rests or develops. The embodied brain provides the substrate of consciousness; matter and energy are the twin substrates of the physical world. The mind mediates between the two without having immediate access to either.

Thought—Here I present thought as mental activity emerging within particular situations under tensions affecting the loop of engagement with the external world at the time. We think of thought as being verbal in nature, but that is only thought on the verge of speech. Through introspection, I identify nonverbal kernels of thought in which content is fully developed but not yet shaped into words. Sitting at the keyboard of my computer, however, turning out a glossary, I keep reading and rehearsing words to discover if they express what I mean to say. At base, thought is an inner dialogue between a person and the situation he visualizes himself to be in.

Time and Space—Gauges of temporal and spatial change, adopted as standards to which other changes can be compared, and so measured. Time is experiential in nature, an effect produced by sitting still and fixedly observing phenomena change on their own, the mind interpreting such passive changes as changes over time. Night turning to day is one such change, as is the sweeping second hand on a clock, or the rusting away of a junk car deep in the woods. On the other hand, a sense of space is had by moving about, jumping over puddles, sweeping aside branches, having to subtract one's own movements from phenomena in order to capture a sense of the space through which we pass. Such active changes, adjusted for our participation, is interpreted as space. I experience getting up from my computer and walking to the kitchen as a spatial change, as I do shoveling snow from my walkway, and playing Spider Solitaire on my computer, swinging my eyes back and forth across the screen.

Transduction—The conversion of energy from one form to another, such as radiant energy to electrical energy in a solar panel, from radiant energy to neuroelectrical energy in the retina of the eye, or from sound energy to neuroelectrical energy in the ear.

Transference—Regarding one person as a surrogate for a significant other by generalizing a particular attitude to a different subject.

Unconscious—Mental activity not available to conscious scrutiny. Such activity is often evident at the start when an issue is framed, and later when results of unconscious processing are disclosed to the mind posing the concern. This often takes place at night when one retires with something on her mind, and awakens next day to a spontaneous resolution. The framing and the result are available to introspection, but the actual working out of the solution is not. Learning to trust such mysterious goings-on is one of the rewards of introspection.

283

Understanding—A high-order mental process encompassing an interrelated field of categorized phenomena at various levels of discernment. Where phenomena and categorization apply to specific instances, understanding suggests a more comprehensive background of experiences regarding a field of concern considered as a whole in mental awareness. A general term, understanding is based on a coherent arrangement of specific sensory phenomena and the categories they have been assimilated to within a larger range of human endeavor and experience.

Valence—(*See* Feeling.) The positive or negative impetus resulting from comparison of mental input and output, perception and action. The polarized signal driving consciousness and the loop of engagement.

Values—Inherent appetites or drives that provide a backdrop for everything appearing on the stage of the mind, clarifying it, making it relevant to our personal perspective. Food, drink, shelter, safety, health, rest, friends, lovers—our wellbeing and survival depend on such values in furthering the unique biological experiment which each one of us is.

Working Memory—As a span of time, the few seconds over which specific details of the loop of engagement can be retained through deliberate concentration.

O

INDEX

Glossary pages in bold.

• A •

Meaning (*continued*)
empiricist's dilemma, 93
engagement and, 165
fashion and, 83
feeling and, 102
forgotten, 81
humor and, 81
interpreted, 46, 112
intuited, 40
level of discernment, 166, 208
metaphorical, 28
mistaken, 76, 77
"m-o-o-n banana," 85-90
naming and, 82
phenomenal, 32, 34, 35
play and, 82
process of, 85
reaching for, 88
semiotic, 158, 194
situated, 44, 137, 154
subjective, 78, 80
Thoreau, 93
travel and, 84
understanding, 70
verbal, 62, 72, 153, 155-157, 160, 162, 165, 229
Media, 118, 127, 263, 276
Memory, **279,** 182, 207, 249
affective, 96, 97, 101-103, 109, 115, 117, 152, 199, 203, 270
assumptions and, 23
attention and, 87
autobiographical, 8, 59, 97, 117, 137, 213, 229, 250
calibrated, 58
categorical, 52, 58, 77, 86, 156, 224
childhood, 8
conceptual, 20, 25, 41, 77, 86
conflict and, 252
dreams and, 115, 120, 224
empirical, 199, 200, 203
episodic, 59, 87

Memory (*continued*)
expectancy and, 87, 130
forgetfulness, 13, 14, 42, 130
project, 216
reality and, 228, 234
referential, 59
repetition and, 152
rote, 182, 239
semantic, 12, 22, 59
short-term, 162
values and, 180
verbal, 162, 167
working, 14, 128, 129
Merleau-Ponty, Maurice, 30, 235, 274
Metaphor (Seeing *as*), **280**
analogous, 52,
antiquated, 63, 258
as possibility, 128
bootstrap, 71, 188, 189
carabiner, 218
cartwheel aurora, 41, 232
categorical, 80, 84, 85, 255, 260
causal, 61
dreams as, 115
economic, 64
emphasis and, 50
experience of, 258
forgotten, 62, 158, 159
in obituaries, 53
militant, 260
mind and, 259-261
miscategorization, 17, 255, 256
moccasins, 146
moving target, 147
political, 261
power of, 257, 261
Quaker, 64
reality, 128, 256, 258, 267
seeing *as,* 17, 59, 60, 255, 280
situated, 71
spiritual, 257
tension in, 85
treadmill, 70, 71
truth, 257
ultra-orthodox, 264

Microscopic life 172
Mind (selected), **280**
adaptable, 140
affective, 20, 72, 95, 98, 106, 108, 110
agility of, 146
-altering drugs, 106
as wilderness, 94
associative, 41
building a world around, 90
calibrated, 74, 116, 118
categorization, 20, 21, 23, 41, 43, 50, 58, 73, 155, 162
certainty, 238, 239
coherent, 173
comparative, 119
complementary, 156
conflict, 237, 243, 254
consciousness and, 8
control, 54
cooperative, 262
diet and, 106
doubt and, 8
empirical, 194, 259
engaged, 4, 18, 22, 23, 30, 111, 112, 129, 132, 162, 163, 165, 166, 268
fallible, 24, 154, 156, 256
fluid, 104
generalizing, 68
goals, 105
gullible, 182, 185
imitative, 22
interpretation and, 20, 23
introspective, 21, 24, 53, 76, 90, 109, 119, 124, 138, 151, 184, 241, 264, 270, 273
kernels of thought, 72
Machiavellian, 122
maps, 69, 120
metaphor and, 17, 71, 256, 257, 259
of my own, 45, 46
possibility and, 11
power of, 255, 261, 263
preconscious, 44

O

www.ingramcontent.com/pod-product-compliance
Lightning Source LLC
Chambersburg PA
CBHW031459270326
41930CB00006B/166